W9-BYV-970

Rivergods

Rivergods

EXPLORING THE WORLD'S GREAT WILD RIVERS

RICHARD BANGS *and* CHRISTIAN KALLEN

A YOLLA BOLLY PRESS BOOK PUBLISHED BY

SIERRA CLUB BOOKS

SAN FRANCISCO

FIRST EDITION
Photographs copyright © 1985 by the photographers credited. Entire contents copyright 1985 in all countries of the International Copyright Union. All rights reserved. No part of this work may be reproduced or transmitted in any form by any means, electronic or mechanical, including photocopying and recording, or by any information retrieval system, without permission in writing from the publisher. Printed by Dai Nippon Printing Company, Ltd., Tokyo, Japan.

A YOLLA BOLLY PRESS BOOK
Rivergods was produced in association with the publisher at The Yolla Bolly Press, Covelo, California. Editorial and design staff: James Robertson, Carolyn Robertson, Juliana Yoder, and Barbara Youngblood. All maps by EarthSurface Graphics/David Fuller.

The Sierra Club, founded in 1892 by John Muir, has devoted itself to the study and protection of the earth's scenic and ecological resources—mountains, wetlands, woodlands, wild shores and rivers, deserts and plains. Its publications are part of the nonprofit fifty chapters coast to coast, in Canada, Hawaii, and Alaska. For information about how you may participate in the club's programs to enjoy and preserve wilderness and the quality of life, please address inquiries to Sierra Club, 730 Polk Street, San Francisco, California 94109.

LIBRARY OF CONGRESS CATALOGING IN
PUBLICATION DATA
Bangs, Richard, 1950-
   Rivergods : exploring the world's great rivers.

   "A Yolla Bolly Press Book."
   Includes index.
   1. Rivers.   2. Stream ecology.   3. River life.
I. Kallen, Christian.   II. Title.
GB1203.2.B36   1985   910′.02′1693   85-2147
ISBN 0-87-156845-4

PHOTO CREDITS
Page i, Jim Slade; page ii, Richard Bangs; page iv, William Boehm; page vii, Skip Horner; page viii, Skip Horner; page xii, Don Briggs; page 1, Michael Nichols/Magnum. All other photographs credited at point of use.

To Lewis Greenwald, the original spirit of Sobek

ACKNOWLEDGMENTS

WE WOULD LIKE to express our thanks to a long line of explorers, adventurers, passengers, and friends who have made *Rivergods* a reality. An exhaustive list would be impossible; a partial roster, however, must begin as follows: Curt Smith, who devoted uncounted hours sorting through thousands of color transparencies to illustrate this book, and the photographers themselves, who generously supplied the images to illustrate the text; and Marti Morec, whose tireless and imaginative researches provided many helpful and fascinating facts and figures for the text and the marginalia.

In addition, we willingly thank the following: Friends of the River, the people most responsible for the fight to preserve the songs that rivers sing; Rick Laylin of Pan American World Airways, who has had the vision to find merit in outlandish-sounding proposals; Avon Inflatables, which have seen us through rapids that would have deflated lesser crafts; Minolta Cameras, whose support has led to many of the photographs within; James and Carolyn Robertson, whose enthusiasm and insight brought to life this handsome book; Ted Hatch, who was inadvertently responsible for launching this series of international expeditions; Tom Cromer, George Fuller, and John Kramer, willing members of the first Sobek Expedition in Ethiopia so many years ago; and the dozens of guides who have led and joined the expeditions that followed; the many sponsors of the various expeditions, in particular The North Face; Bill Graves of *National Geographic*, who supported some crazy ideas and may yet not regret them; the two other steady and hard-working partners in Sobek, John Yost and George Wendt; the crocodile god of the Nile, who has been good to us; and the people who love the experience of floating down a wild river, wherever it may be.

Any collaboration poses the question of who wrote what portions of the work, and who should shoulder the glory—or blame—for the finished product. Perhaps more than most works of joint authorship, *Rivergods* has drawn from the writing skills of both its principals. There is no ghost within these covers; both of us wield pens as well as oars. Because of this, we have chosen the third-person voice to tell these tales, and the reader may find one of the authors referred to as a character within his own account. Occasionally, the immediacy of a moment is so overpowering that we felt it best to describe it in the first person; these segments are presented in italics, with the writer's initials for identification. Though this may be a bit unconventional, we believe it makes for a livelier and more credible read than the swashbuckling first-person voice of other exploration accounts. We hope you agree and enjoy these tales of discovery on the wild rivers of the world.

R.B., C.K.

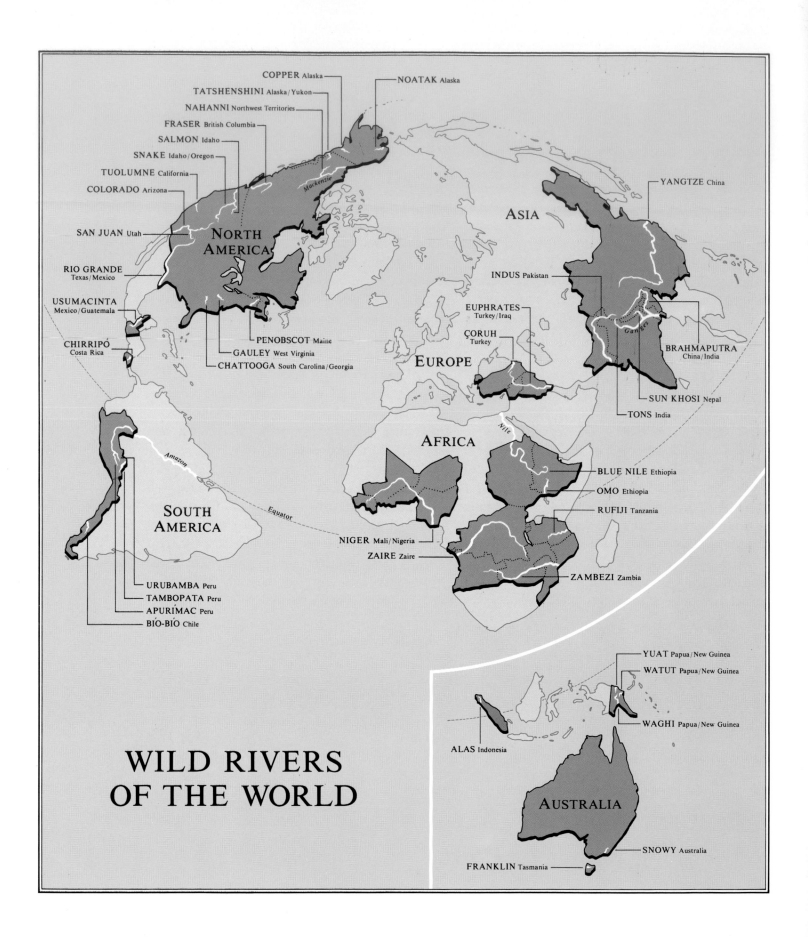

COPPER Alaska
NOATAK Alaska
TATSHENSHINI Alaska/Yukon
NAHANNI Northwest Territories
FRASER British Columbia
SALMON Idaho
SNAKE Idaho/Oregon
TUOLUMNE California
COLORADO Arizona
YANGTZE China

ASIA

NORTH AMERICA

SAN JUAN Utah

INDUS Pakistan

EUPHRATES Turkey/Iraq

ÇORUH Turkey

EUROPE

RIO GRANDE Texas/Mexico

BRAHMAPUTRA China/India

USUMACINTA Mexico/Guatemala

Ganges

CHIRRIPÓ Costa Rica

SUN KHOSI Nepal

PENOBSCOT Maine

TONS India

GAULEY West Virginia

CHATTOOGA South Carolina/Georgia

Nile

AFRICA

Amazon

BLUE NILE Ethiopia

OMO Ethiopia

SOUTH AMERICA

Equator

RUFIJI Tanzania

NIGER Mali/Nigeria

ZAIRE Zaire

URUBAMBA Peru

TAMBOPATA Peru

APURÍMAC Peru

ZAMBEZI Zambia

BÍO-BÍO Chile

WILD RIVERS
OF THE WORLD

YUAT Papua/New Guinea

WATUT Papua/New Guinea

WAGHI Papua/New Guinea

ALAS Indonesia

AUSTRALIA

SNOWY Australia

FRANKLIN Tasmania

TABLE OF CONTENTS

INTRODUCTION

EXPLORATION IN THE WORLD seems to have occurred in stages, or waves. The Spanish influx to the New World at the interface of the fifteenth and sixteenth centuries was one such wave; the American-Soviet penetrations into space in the 1960s was another. There are, of course, many smaller stages of expansion, such as the rapid conquest of the Himalayas' 8,000-meter peaks during the 1950s. During those tides of curiosity and achievement, it is as if humanity itself reaches out to unknown regions and floods them with the light of knowledge.

We hope, in some small way, to have been a surge in these tides—a brief rise in the surf, an unexpected swelling of the river. The years of the recent past, when Sobek Expeditions and other explorers have shed new light on remote river corridors, may be seen as the florescence of international river rafting. We have written of rivers we know, from our experiences in this distinctly modern age of exploration. *Rivergods* comprises ten tales of rivers that we have explored since the late 1960s.

One of the risks of discovery—of a river, wilderness, or continent—has always been that there will be an eventual alteration of those pristine qualities that first attracted the explorers. Probably the best example is the New World itself: only a few acres of the original plant communities of the Great Plains remain intact today, the Amazon Basin is being deforested at an alarming rate, and an appalling number of native animal and plant species has been eliminated or poise on the brink of extinction. We hope that our impact on the regions, as river runners, has been, if any, positive. If our efforts have led to the slightest increase in understanding the rôles rivers play in human history and natural process, then every flipped boat, wearisome portage, and icy swim were well worthwhile.

Surely, not all changes in today's understanding of rivers is owing to a handful of rafters pouring over topographic maps and careening through unscouted rapids. History, too, has been at work. A quarter

century ago the Zambezi flowed through Rhodesia, the Congo drained the Belgian Congo, and only about 1,000 people had been down through the Grand Canyon on a raft. Now the Zambezi borders Zambia and Zimbabwe; the Zaire drains (what else?) Zaire, and nearly a quarter of a million people have floated between the canyon walls of the Colorado.

The rivers included in this book are certainly not all the world's "great rivers"—not by far. There may be some mad gazetteer at work, calculator in hand, who will some day complete a tabulation of all the trickles, rushes, and cascades of water that have a name and give us the final count of the world's rivers. A million? More? It hardly matters. What does matter is that of all our planet's activities—geological movements, the reproduction and decay of biota, and even the disruptive propensities of certain species (elephants and humans come to mind)—no force is greater than the hydrologic cycle. Water evaporates, clouds, freezes and falls, melts and flows, and makes its way to the sea to evaporate again. The physical features of that process—glaciers, rivers, seas—are the most powerful shaping forces on earth.

So where does "greatness" enter into this? Every creek runs, sooner or later, to the sea; every mile-wide artery of a continent's watershed is fed by a thousand trickling streams. Over the years, Sobek has rafted over 100 rivers, more than 30 of them for the first time. We do not make our first descent on a river because "it's a great river," and certainly not for the simplistic reason "because it's there." We run it because it inspires us.

The rivers in this book were chosen because they have carried us upon their bosoms, and between their banks our lives have been formed, eroded, and enlarged with the same deliberation as a sandbar, gorge, or watershed. But there are other rivers in the world, and it would be unfair—to say nothing of impertinent—to list only a small percentage of the world's classic raftable rivers. So if we append a list of "lesser gods," adding twenty-five more names to this volume of our own explorations, we do so using the same criteria that have led us to run a number of them: gradient, volume, location, and a quality we might as well call glamour.

Gradient refers to the drop of a river's course over a given distance—usually measured in feet per mile. The Colorado through the Grand Canyon drops about 8 feet per mile, though at Lava Falls it spills over 30 feet in about 100 yards. The gradient on the Tuolumne is around 67 feet per mile in its stimulating first six miles; a few raftable rivers boast a gradient of over 100 feet per mile, though in such cases either the gradient is quite constant or the channel is broad enough to allow clear routes through the drops.

Volume, like gradient, is a variable that depends on the river's topology. A small narrow channel may be runnable with only 300 cubic feet per second flowing past any given point (the usual measure of volume); a flow of 10,000 cubic feet per second may be moderate on the Colorado, or flood stage on the Tuolumne. Scale must be called into the judgment for such rivers, and here our third quality, location, comes into play. Does the river flow through the industrial section of a city? Is it a nearby culture's traditional burial place? Has it cut a canyon a mile deep? The answers to such questions determine if these are reasons for running the river, or reasons to avoid it.

As for that fourth quality: What made Livingstone search the entire length of the Zambezi, looking for a gateway to "civilize" Africa? What drove James Bruce to the farthest headwaters of the Blue Nile? What has brought the pilgrims of Asia up the Indus for thousands of years to the trickles of its icy springs? *Glamour* may not be the right word, but not because it is too overreaching: it is only insufficient. In short we have explored and written about these rivers simply because they mean something to us.

In the past twenty-five years, river rafting has become a sport that almost anyone can join, and that nearly all can enjoy. For some, a river trip means water fights and wet summer fun; for others, it is mainly a testing of personal mettle. But for nearly all there is something more, something ineffable yet deeply satisfying, as we join with the ancient currents and flow, for a brief time, between the timeless banks. Whether these rivers are small, crystalline streams percolating through granite boulder gardens, or huge juggernauts of hydraulic insistence creating the very landscape they inhabit, every waterway that we have explored has brought us more than we expected. Rivers, as we quickly found out, are greater than their grandest canyons and biggest drops. They are habitats, as well, for plant and animal species that depend on the steady flow of water for their survival; and among these species is man.

On the river, we recognize the identity we share with the people who have come before us, whether the Anasazi in the Grand Canyon, who left behind a few stone structures and fewer rock paintings, or the likes of David Livingstone and John Wesley Powell, who challenged the waters of the unknown. On the river, we see in the faces of today's inhabitants our own faces. We discover our kinship with the Bodi along the Omo, who had never seen sunglasses or cameras before a 1973 river expedition, or with the Papuan natives, who like us must speak in a pidgin tongue to communicate their knowledge. On the river, we see ourselves as motes in God's bloodstream, venturing along the planet's arteries, observing and, perhaps inevitably, changing as we go. For while the rivers we offer in these pages still flow strongly and powerfully to the sea, for the most part undammed and undaunted by humankind's treacherous acquaintance, they are not eternal. In varying degrees, all are under siege, be it by diversion projects for irrigation, dams for hydroelectric power, or unthinking pollution. Yet don't look elsewhere for villains or turn aside in despair. We are all rivergods; and whether we act as creator or destroyer—or like Shiva, the cosmic dancer of the Indus, who is inextricably both—is up to us. It is a choice offered repeatedly wherever we go, every time we labor or travel, on every river trip we make.

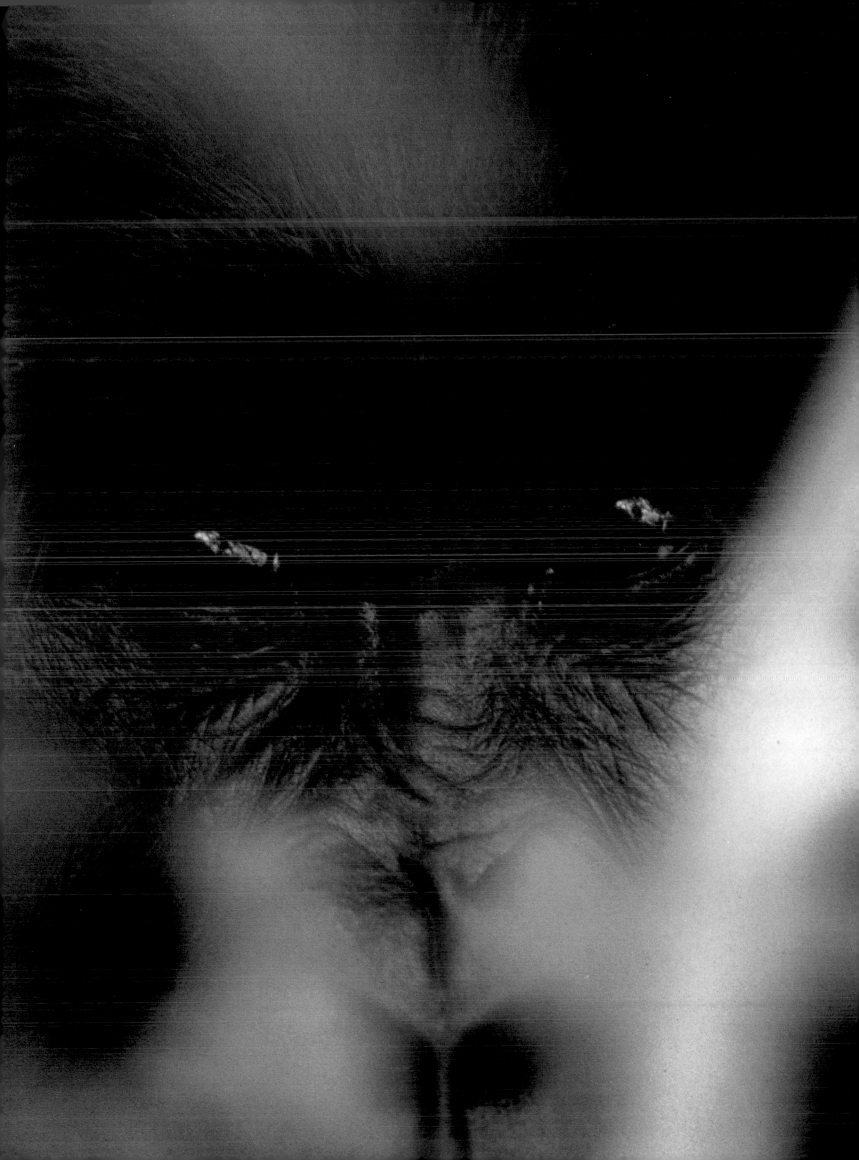

Omo

THE ETHIOPIAN PLATEAU rises 8,000 feet over the northeastern corner of its continent, in the region known as the Horn of Africa. It is an area that has long existed on the far shores of civilization's influence: Homeric poets regarded Ethiopia as the edge of the habitable world, and legends say the gods retreated there for relaxation. Positioned at the headwaters of the great River Nile, which embraces Egypt within its annual flood cycles, Ethiopia stands between the cultures of the circum-Mediterranean region and the lingering tribal societies of the African interior. Isolated by geography from the tides of the centuries, Ethiopia has always been a land of mystery and the unknown, wherein could still be found, even as recently as the 1970s, tribal people bypassed by empires. And rivers uncharted, and unrun.

Just as mountaineers scour the world in search of unclimbed peaks to mark their "first ascents," so river runners look to hidden, remote, or difficult waterways for their "first descents." In the United States all the great first descents were made years ago: Bus Hatch down the Middle Fork of the Salmon, Amos Burg and John Mullens through Hells Canyon on the Snake, John Wesley Powell down the Colorado. So when rafting became popular during the late 1960s as an ecologically reasonable yet exciting sport, the rising generation of river guides on Powell's long-tamed Colorado yearned for the sense of original discovery, the thrill of not knowing what was beyond the next bend. Some of us turned, in our search for new horizons, to Africa.

A continent prominent in any account of the age of exploration, Africa held the promise of unrun rivers in every quarter. Political situations prevented access to many areas, and of those that were accessible few regions were as appealing as Ethiopia, not only because of its mountainous terrain and tribal cultures,

but because of its pivotal place in river history. James Bruce's reputed discovery of the source of the Blue Nile—then considered the major tributary of the world's longest river—is one of the glory tales that schoolboys dream about; and a 1968 descent down the Blue Nile by a British expedition further fueled the fires of ambition and adventure.

The history of the 1968 Blue Nile Expedition— officially, The Great Abbai Expedition, after the native name for the river—is characteristic of the European obsession with discovery, with far reaches, and with firsts. A monumental undertaking, led by thick-set, pith-helmeted Captain John Blashford-Snell, the expedition boasted seventy team members, an astronomical budget, tons of equipment, sidearms, and military rifles—and no whitewater experience to speak of. They called their endeavor The Last Great First, in open evocation of the glory days of the British Empire. It was a pompous and nearly disastrous expedition: they suffered attacks by native bandits, they destroyed boats and equipment in capsizes, and they failed to navigate several particularly troublesome stretches of the river. One man was drowned.

Yet somehow it was also an inspiration; and to the young river guides of the Grand Canyon, it pointed the way. Or, rather, it pointed the wrong way: instead of a bloated army of explorers with superfinancing, elaborate publicity, an excess of ambition, and little river experience, the expedition we had in mind would be quite the opposite. Once the crew was assembled and the plans, permits, and logistics were worked out, the result was a far cry from the Blashford-Snell example: a lot of whitewater experience, a small crew, and almost no money.

In the fall of 1972 circumstances finally coalesced to allow a rafting expedition: a diplomatic contact assured governmental approval from Addis Ababa,

PREVIOUS PAGE The Omo leaves the highlands behind in its reach across Ethiopia toward Lake Turkana (Richard Bangs).

OPPOSITE, TOP Where broad and slow moving, the Omo passes hidden villages of herdsmen and gardeners (Stan Boor). BOTTOM Silt-laden waters of the Omo appear chocolate-brown after the rainy season (Bruce Helin).

5

OPPOSITE, TOP Native boy armed with a fishing spear (Stan Boor). BOTTOM A Bacha tribesman poles his dugout canoe across the Omo's quiet waters (C.S. Ghiglieri).

On November 4, 1770, Scottish adventurer James Bruce reached Lake Tana at the root of the Blue Nile River, after spending six years among the savage chieftains in Ethiopia. He thought he had reached the "source of the Nile"—most coveted prize of the Age of Discovery. He was mistaken: not only was he not the first European to reach Lake Tana (a Portuguese missionary beat him by 150 years), but it is the White Nile that is the longer stem of the great river, not the Blue Nile.

Ethiopia's capital, and the Grand Canyon season was over until the following spring. Why not now?

Our beginnings were in the Library of Congress, where every drop of information on Ethiopia was squeezed from the shelves over a period of two months. Our thirst for information unslaked, a flood of correspondence began; and finally came a round of meetings throughout the United States and in England with those few who had scratched the surface of that mysterious part of the world we planned to penetrate.

Our efforts aside, solid relevant information was scarce, and we had to scrutinize every morsel we could find to reach valid but "between-the-lines" conclusions. It didn't take much research to figure out that these rivers, locked in canyons sometimes greater and more precipitous than the Grand Canyon, were isolated environmental sanctuaries, far from any vestige of civilization. As the project came into focus, we saw that we were into much more than we had originally anticipated. If we capsized and lost a boat or vital equipment on an Ethiopian river, we couldn't hike out to the nearest house and phone for help. If someone were badly injured, we couldn't signal a passing plane. We would be entering real wilderness, with hundreds of miles separating us from the familiarity and security of civilization.

The research revealed a number of rivers whose courses made them naturals for historic first descents. But one stood out: the Omo, rising from the same highlands that give birth to the Blue Nile, flowing in a twisting course south, and expiring in Lake Turkana. What lay between those regions? Nobody was sure.

The maps showed the river rising in the Ethiopian plateau and flowing southward in a reckless course,

cutting a gorge nearly a mile deep. From the confluence of the Gibe River—a short tributary that had an easily reached bridge near the town of Jimma and, therefore, would be the most likely put-in—the Omo still had almost 400 miles to flow before it spent its currents in Lake Turkana. Aside from the Soddo Bridge, 140 miles downstream, the only possible take-out before Turkana was at a small outpost and airport near the confluence with the Mui River, 330 miles downstream from Jimma.

Until the mid-1960s Lake Turkana had been known even in Kenya, within whose borders it lies, as Lake Rudolf, the result of that quaint nineteenth-century European custom of naming far-off natural features after monarchs and their offspring. The lake itself is no prize, however; it was described by Alistair Graham as "green and greasy to the touch . . . a 180-mile-long trough, 6 to 30 miles wide, of slippery green water, brackish enough to make one vomit and vindictive enough to make one hate." The lake is brackish because it has no opening to the sea and only one perennial source—the Omo.

At one time in the long ago, the Omo left the Ethiopian plateau for eventual confluence with the Nile itself, but a series of earth movements associated with the East African Rift System—of which Olduvai Gorge is the most famous feature—interrupted its course and created the inland drainage. Because of its greater flow at Khartoum, the Blue Nile was frequently explored into Ethiopia during the eighteenth and nineteenth centuries in the romantic search for the "source of the Nile," while rivers such as the Omo were left in mystery. Curiously, although well-documented hominid remains (including *Australopithicus afarensis*, *A. boisei*, and early represen-

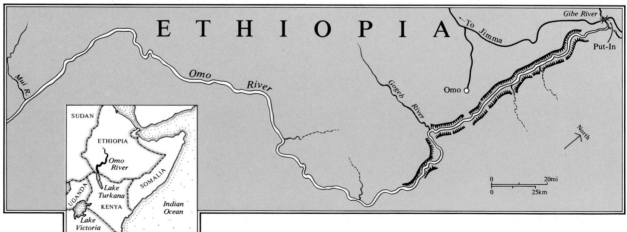

tatives of *Homo erectus*) have been found along the lower Omo, near Lake Turkana and elsewhere in the region by the Leaky family and others, the tribes that still live along the Omo are all but unknown. To journey down the Omo was, as much as any river exploration in 1973 could be, a voyage into the heart of darkness.

■ ■ ■

Diving into the project with blind enthusiasm, we —a small group of friends including George and Diane Fuller, Lew Greenwald, Tom Cromer, and Rich Bangs—soon began to question our enterprise. The list of dangers seemed endless, and it grew with each new bit of advice. "You have to be very careful of the Sudanese buffalo," a longtime African hunter counseled. "They charge unprovoked." "The buffalo are bad, but the people are the ones to worry about," an ex-embassy employee advised. "Life is cheap there." "Yes, the natives can be unfriendly, but it's the little creatures that can do the most harm in Africa. The insects will be the ones to protect yourself against," said a Smithsonian researcher. And almost always came a final warning: "But there's nothing worse than the crocodiles."

Flipping in rapids in the United States was something everyone could deal with: going for a swim, intentionally or otherwise, is part of the sport. With the possibility of a hungry croc pooled out at the end of the rapid, however, whitewater became of only secondary concern.

The most deadly existing reptile, the Nile crocodile has always been considered to be among mankind's worst enemies. Legends of twenty- to thirty-foot monsters in the turbid waters of Africa persist, though the largest crocodile on record was just over nineteen feet in length, and few reach even fifteen. Still, fifteen feet is over a ton of hungry lizard, and the beast has a known fondness for human flesh. According to native belief in the Lake Turkana region, crocs attack only people who are morally bad or uncertain of their place in creation. "To a man who has no doubts about himself, an attack from a scaly, evil crocodile *must* be bad magic," as Alistair Graham succinctly phrases the Turkana attitude in his classic *Eyelids of Morning: The Mingled Destinies of Crocodiles and Men.* His characterization of crocodiles, after a season of research at Lake Turkana on their

feeding habits, behavior, and size, was summed up in his term "the devil's mafia."

We soon discovered that there are as many different theories about how to handle the giant reptiles as there are rivers in Ethiopia. The major schools of thought, though, that were related to us repeatedly were: 1) be as noisy as possible when passing through a crocodile pool in order to scare them off, and 2) be as silent as possible so as not to attract their attention. One expert even warned us not to laugh in a certain manner, because it resembles the sound of an infant croc in trouble, and the noise would immediately alert all the larger crocodiles within hearing distance to rush to the rescue. Unfortunately one of our party laughed exactly that way, so it looked as though we might have quite a somber trip.

Clearly some kind of protection was called for. Handguns didn't promise enough force; rifles, bazookas, and howitzers were unfashionable in that era. A children's book on crocodiles in the Library of Congress suggested an alternative. In some areas of the world, including the Nile Valley, people have responded to crocophobia by deifying the devils. Most notable of the several crocodile gods in African myth is Sobek (or Sebek in some transliterations), one of the dozens of Egyptian animal gods. Along with the falcon Horus, the vulture and the cobra representing the kingdoms of the Upper and Lower Nile, and even the portly Hesamut, the hippo goddess, Sobek gives an animal's visage to the face of the unknown and the dangerous. The Omo was, by all accounts, a river ruled over by the crocodile god; besides, the name had a nice ring to it, so our first expedition adopted the name *Sobek* as its own.

The Sobek Expedition began its journey at the Jimma Bridge on the Gibe tributary, as planned, on April 26, 1973. Two boats put in to the river, with a total crew of seven. Less than an hour downstream, the first crocodile was sighted. It was about three feet long and scampered into the river, frightened by the monstrous presence of a bloated riverboat nearly six times its length. Simultaneously we crowded together in the center of the boats and tried not to laugh in that certain way.

Despite the fears and uncertainties that we felt at the outset, the first day on the river went well. We drifted just three miles downstream to set up camp at

OPPOSITE Bodi tribesmen of the lower Omo Valley display tribal signatures in hair style (top right, George Fuller; all others, Stan Boor).

Long ago, when God was creating mankind, He did so by molding the shape of a man out of clay and putting it in the oven to cook. The first time He did this, He left it in the oven too long, and the clay figure came out too dark. This, God threw toward the south. The second time he didn't leave it in the oven long enough, and the clay figure came out too pale. This, God threw toward the north. The third time He timed it just right and pulled out of the oven a perfect and evenly cooked human, whom He named Adam and set down in Ethiopia.
Ethiopian folk tale

9

OPPOSITE, TOP In the Ethiopian highlands buildings constructed of baked clay characterize housing for villagers (Richard Bangs). BOTTOM Bodi women along the Omo River dress for the weather in the tropical lowlands (C.S. Ghiglieri).

the Gibe's confluence with the Omo. Here we hiked a short distance back up the Omo; the clear water was the size of a small trout stream, with several pools and a slight gradient, perhaps runnable at a higher water level than that which we found. Beautifully pelted black-and-white colobus monkeys, duiker antelope, and the tracks of a single hippo were seen, and the bark of a baboon was heard at dusk. High barren hills rolled into the star-filled night: it was the end of the dry season in northeast Africa.

The Omo began to prove itself the next day as several moderate rapids were run. Along the way, waterbuck and colobus loitered along the banks, and a twelve-foot python was seen slithering into the water. Flocks of yellow-and-black weaver birds, who build complicated and efficient shelters of bark strips that make a robin's nest look like a shantytown, flickered amidst the underbrush. Snowy egrets flew away as the boats approached, to circle back upstream out of danger; high in the dry branches of a sycamore tree, the noble silhouette of a black-and-white fish eagle pivoted to watch the passing boats. Then, as vervet monkeys screamed and scurried at the top of the rising banks, shafts of columnar basalt erupted out of the river's edge, and a small canyon not unlike that of the lower Grand Canyon began to take shape.

The rapids began to grow more challenging over the next few days, and as the scenery became more magnificent, the analogies to familiar places became more frequent. Sheer rock walls rose 3,000 feet, scenes reminiscent of Yosemite or Zion national parks; a mile up a tributary, a 250-foot waterfall looked like Deer Creek Falls off the Colorado. And rapids of surprising strength gave us familiar, even comforting, rushes of adrenaline and splash.

On Sunday morning, during a weekly ritual, everyone consumed a cholorquine tablet to combat the malaria endemic to tropical Africa. One of the reasons the Omo River valley has resisted infiltration by the ancient civilizations of Ethiopia or the more recent ones of Europe is the number and severity of diseases that flourish there. George Fuller, one of the expedition members, who studied the epidemiology of diseases at Ethiopia's Institute of Pathobiology, listed the afflictions to which the people and animals of the valley were prone.

There was *kala-azar*, a protozoal disease carried by sandflies, which had helped to halt a British incursion in 1941. There was *onchocerciasis* or "river blindness," caused by a parasitic worm. There was *Echinococcus granulosis*, a tapeworm that can cause huge cysts in the liver or lungs or, more rarely, in the bones or brain. There were two types of malaria, including the notorious and often fatal "black-water fever." And there were the irritating and dangerous bites of the tsetse flies, which carry a sleeping sickness that affects mainly cattle—the primary reason few herding tribes come to the Omo for water, even during the dry season. Indeed, the Italian troops who briefly attempted to set up rule over Ethiopia in the late nineteenth century gave a name, still found on some maps, to the lower Omo Valley: The Plain of Death.

Though many of the side creeks and flumes proffered cooling slides and soaks, their differences from Deer Creek, Havasu, and other Colorado tributaries were never far from awareness. Standing water, in particular, had to be carefully examined along its edges for what is perhaps the most insidious of African creatures: the snail.

It was not snails, per se, that caused the throat to constrict in fear or the small fleet to flee the quiet, cooling pools. It was that snails are the vector for an intestinal ailment that makes our domestic giardia and amoebic dysentery seem relatively benign: schistosomiasis. Gastrointestinal cramps, diarrhea, blood in the stools, loss of nutritional value from food, and eventual tissue damage are the results of encounters with the parasitic flatworm *Schistosoma mansoni*. The ailment is commonly called bilharzia, after the physician who categorized the symptoms; and "schisto" by those familiar with the disease on a personal basis. Today it is easily cured, but it is so rare in the Western world that recognition of it is often quite tardy.

The schistosomes have evolved a curious interdependence between two very different species, snails and humans. Their life cycle begins in human refuse, as their eggs are washed into water to hatch into miracidia. These microscopic larvae soon find their way through the skin of water snails to set up residence in the liver of the unfortunate creatures. After a couple of months, the miracidia develop into cer-

caria, the fork-tailed intermediate stage, which set about looking for a warm-blooded host by first erupting out of the snail, killing it as they do so.

In the waters of Ethiopia, the cercaria find their hosts in primates: sometimes baboons, vervet monkeys, or, most commonly, humans. They burrow through the skin by digesting it as they enter, causing a symptom no more irritating than "swimmer's itch." Once inside the human host, however, the cercaria are washed through the bloodstream to the gut, where they set up a love nest in the blood vessels that drain the intestine.

"Love nest" may not seem a suitable term, scientifically speaking; but, as Fuller describes it, it may be the only accurate one: "The adult worms live what seems like a life of hedonistic overindulgence. They spend their lives making love, bathed in the copious supply of food (human blood) that flows through the vessels draining the intestines or bladder of their infected hosts. Certainly, once they've reached this adult stage, they lead a utopian existence, that is, unless their host dies. The long, slender female worm remains entwined in the folds of the broader, stouter male, who surrounds her like a protective sheath. They remain secure, nestled together, bathing in food and warmth, copulating for life (which can be as long as thirty years), propagating their species." The daily result of this perpetual orgy of generation is some 1,200 eggs, which work their way through the gut wall—creating the symptoms mentioned earlier—and leave the host via the bowels.

Even though these marauders of the bloodstream were one of the more distressing threats on the river, their attacks would not be manifest for several weeks. Our concerns were more sensibly directed toward the other, more immediate, dangers of rafting through this African wilderness: "flat dogs" and "river horses." Crocodiles and hippos were daily dangers, which persisted in displaying very little respect for the rafts or the historic importance of a first descent. We tabulated some 260 crocodiles and over 1,000 hippos; and despite all the theorizing about how to deal with these wild beasts, there were few reliable precedents to follow, and little indication of what to expect.

The crocodiles ranged in size from three feet to nearly fifteen, though most were in the moderate four- to six-foot range. As a rule, they were shy and

The spotted hyena, one of three species of hyenas, ranges throughout southern and eastern Africa, north to Ethiopia.

would quickly dive underwater, where crocs can hold their breath for up to an hour. Bolder ones would resurface for a second look, and the bravest—usually, of course, the biggest, with the beadiest eyes and the yellowest teeth—would charge the rafts with the speed of a motorboat. More than once they struck the rafts with their bone-hard snouts, as if to see how tasty these huge morsels might be; then they sank, to reappear a few yards away. Their judgment of the taste of hypalon-coated nylon remained hidden behind thick scaly visages.

To deter them, we adopted the modern method tested by the British 1968 Blue Nile Expedition—frantic shouts and thrown rocks. Not only was this satisfying in some primal man-against-beast way, but it usually worked.

Our only real mishap with crocodiles occurred once we let our guard down. We were fifteen days' downstream and well seasoned, accustomed to sharing the river with the leviathans. Since most of the crocs would dive as soon as we'd snarl at them, and we wanted to get some photo documentation, we decided to withold our shouts until the very last seconds so we could get some special movie footage. George Fuller was busy filming the sought-after charge when he became aware that the approaching croc suddenly filled the entire viewfinder of his camera. He came back to reality as the croc struck the raft and locked his Mesozoic jaws around the bow of the inflatable raft. With excellent presence of mind, George leapt to the oars and began rowing downstream as fast as possible to prevent the croc from climbing on board. George's wife, Diane, with just the right spirit, leapt to the front of the boat and started beating the bewildered saurian on the head with the bailing bucket. After ten long minutes, during which George must have rowed about fourteen miles —setting, perhaps, a new world speed-rowing record— the crocodile finally let go and disappeared into the river's depths, no doubt still hungry and shedding real crocodile tears. (RB)

The hippos, meanwhile, were by far the more numerous and in some ways the more dangerous threat. Their danger lay in their unpredictability: in the murky waters they might resurface directly under a raft, elevating it by several feet before realizing their mistake; or they might choose to run a rapid right next to a boat, playing a weird, nerve-racking

14

version of hide-and-seek through the muddy brown turmoil. And almost every night their snuffling and feeding filled the dark with the fear that they might find the camp's mess appealing or, worse, that they might inadvertently trample a sleeping explorer under their huge feet.

Hippopotamus amphibius is the earth's third largest land animal, behind the elephant and the Indian rhinoceros. Individuals of the species grow to fifteen feet in length in the rivers of Africa, from the Nile to the Zambezi, as long as all but the very largest crocodiles. Their stout legs support a broad, barrel-shaped body that can weigh between four and five tons. The huge creatures can be comically clumsy on land—though they can outrun a human for a short but perhaps telling distance—yet they are surprisingly graceful in their preferred element, water. Protruding nostrils, ears, and eyes make it easy for hippos to float submerged, yet sentient and breathing. They are fast swimmers, and can even walk along the bottom of rivers with a slow, bounding gait reminiscent of astronauts on the moon.

They are also territorial, especially during the long nursing season, which seems to be almost year-round. During the breeding season, the males sometimes engage in disputes fatal to one party or another, making huge wounds in each other's thick hides with their deadly tusks. And it is perhaps not surprising that the bloated shape of a riverboat, inflatable tubes encircling a wide flat floor, is sometimes regarded very reasonably as a significant interloper in hippo territory. Since that first Omo river trip, the rafts have actually been punctured by the ivory tusks of these animals eight times: four times when panicked, out-of-breath hippos were trapped under the rubber floor of one of the rafts and bit their way to air; and as many again when angry cows stalked the boats and gave them an oral reprimand for drifting too close to their calves.

As we passed into the lower reaches of the Omo, the steep canyons and rolling hills of the upper half were left behind, to be replaced by a broad horizontal plain through which the river lazily meandered. Only along the course of the river did a thick bushbelt remain, sometimes closing in around the rafters and preventing views of the territory, sometimes opening up to show the grasslands, the distant bulk of Mount Smith to the east, and the wildlife. Here warthogs, dik-diks, and waterbuck were seen frequently, and suddenly the daily count of hippos dropped to almost zero. On one day some 375 of the beasts were encountered in one twenty-mile stretch. Two days later, none was seen. This was a telling statistic: where hippos are numerous, people are few. And vice versa, for the very simple reason that people eat hippos. The expedition had reached the inhabited portion of the Omo Valley, where the Bodi and Mursi tribes were to be found.

Indeed, as we passed into the broadening valley, small cultivated fields were seen, and a few cautious natives gathered in the wide shallows near the river. These places apparently served as fords for the migratory people, who, during this season—early May—were on their way to the eastern highlands, away from the river, in anticipation of the coming rains. At the sighting of a small village of beehive-shaped thatched huts on the nineteenth day, Lew and George pulled the two boats to shore for a visit.

It may have been the first time the natives, members of the Bodi tribe, had seen white people; it was certainly an unusual event, in any case. Most of the men were already gone, herding the clutches of cattle the Bodi prize into the drier hills to the east; a few women and children remained behind, to complete the harvest of the simple crops of corn and sorghum. Communicating with broad smiles and sign language, the natives managed to trade for some empty cans and bottles, though they clearly coveted the red bandannas sported by the boatmen. Then we took our leave, uncertain of the limits of hospitality of a people who lived just a few cultural contacts away from the Stone Age.

The presence of the natives indicated the proximity of the Mui River, the anticipated end of our trip. According to the information we gathered before the trip, the Mui was lined by a dirt track and marked by an abandoned hut, with the airport not far away. But in the slow-moving waters of the lower Omo, the river braided into a thousand islets and side currents, and it was all but impossible to tell which rivulet coming in from the side was a diversion around an island and which might be a tributary. Furthermore, abandoned huts were no longer uncommon in these reaches of the river because of the

The canoe is dead! The canoe is dead! A hippopotamus has killed the canoe! We at once paddled back, and soon met various articles floating down the stream, amongst them my cooking pot, which having the lid on, was full of air, and the waterproof bag containing my blankets; and I realized that I had met with one of those accidents to which one is liable on African rivers.
Frederick C. Selous, 1893

15

OPPOSITE A Dassanetch woman from the Omo delta region builds a temporary domelike structure to protect against the desert heat (George Fuller).

BOTTOM RIGHT Displaying her dyed rush fibers at a village market, a highland woman hides from the sun (John Kramer).

greater numbers of people. It was one structure's tin roof, a feature impossible without the presence of a road, that brought us up short one afternoon several days before we had anticipated reaching the Mui.

Investigation was not easy; it wasn't simply a matter of tying up at the boat ramp, trotting up the road, and dialing the auto club. In fact, it took several hours simply to find something that looked like a road, and it had obviously not been used in years. Two of us took off alone to see if we could find the promised settlement at Mui, with its airport.

After a full day and a half of wandering through meadows thick with wild grass taller than a man's head, through thicker forest that ripped and snagged at skin and clothing, the clear-flowing stream of a tributary was finally found. But was it the Mui? Even after following it for several miles, cautiously skirting the huge Sudanese buffalo drinking from its banks, it was still impossible for us to be certain.

We deliberate for some minutes about where the station might be, then with a last flicker of hope, we trudge up the largest hill in the area. My dreams of the night before come back to me as we climb. They were really just nightmares of our trip—which had been a huge success up to this point—as it turns into a complete disaster. We don't find the Mui, head downstream with inadequate food and ammunition for hunting, and face an expensive and embarrassing helicopter rescue, or death.

At the top of the hill we slowly scan the horizon and see nothing but beautiful vastness and distance. Even in our dilemma the great beauty of the scene strikes us.

Then, just as I'm ready to abandon all hope and suggest we give up and head back to the boats, Lew shouts, "I see a hut!" Sure enough, off in a cluster of trees in the center of the grass field is a tiny tin-roofed building. Our legs are killing us, but we scramble down the hill and wade through the grass toward our goal. Could it be just a hunter's cabin? It's isolated, all by itself in a broad grass field, so we can't think of any reason for its existence if it's connected with the Mui. But at least it, too, has a tin roof.

After forty-five minutes, we reach the cluster of trees, but at first we can't find the hut. Could it have been just a mirage? Then simultaneously I see the hut and Lew finds the track. Great Powell's ghost! We speed up our feeble pace for the last few yards, and I

duck inside the mud-walled, two-section building. Inside I find a vacant room, empty, with one exception—a small airline luggage tag on the floor that reads "Destination: Mui." We must be at the airport! (RB)

It was two more days before word reached our contact in Addis Ababa and a plane was flown in to collect the ragged, tired expedition. So after twenty-one days on the river, floating through 330 miles of true African wilderness, contacting little-known native people, avoiding death by whitewater, hippos, and crocodiles, the first Omo expedition was adjudged a success.

But something was missing. The wildlife was extraordinary; the river itself was a surging pulse through a landscape as varied and beautiful as any ever seen; the sense of discovery was there, too, on the first descent down a wild river through the dark heart of Africa. But the encounter with the natives of the Omo was brief, too brief: a tantalizing glimpse of the social life of these tribespeople eking out an existence on the fringes of the known world.

What was known then about the people who lived along the Omo was precious little. These people were Nilotic, a broad term that denotes habitation along the Nile and its tributaries. There are, to be sure, other common characteristics among the Nilotes: the language group is the same (though numerous different languages, as different as French from Rumanian, belong to this eastern Sudanic group); and the economy of cattle raising, seasonal agricultural, and occasional hunting is fairly common. But the Bodi are surely different from the Mursi and the Dime, for each was still engaged in occasional warfare with other tribes.

The rainy season moved in; the rivers of Ethiopia swelled with the moisture falling in the highlands; the native people led their cattle into the drier, more hospitable regions away from the summer floods; and some of us who ran the Omo went back to Arizona for another season in the Grand Canyon. But the desire to run the Omo was not satisfied by a single expedition, and the newborn Sobek Expeditions advertised for passengers for another trip down the Omo—to be one of the first commercial rafting trips in Africa. Five Americans joined the trip as paying passengers; several Grand Canyon boatmen enthusiastically came along on the second trip. A

16

total of sixteen explorers in four boats set out from the Jimma Bridge on November 12, 1973 to duplicate the route taken six months earlier.

The water at put-in was about five times higher than it had been in April because of the heavy precipitation in the highlands that summer. Some of the rapids were washed out by the higher volume, while others were rendered more challenging by the bigger waves and faster current. Side creeks appeared where none had been before, and the hippos and crocs were as plentiful as ever. Downstream was another story: the water flow diminished radically to a level *lower* than that of the previous trip because less water was coming in from the tributaries. But, right on cue, the hippos suddenly stopped appearing as we once again penetrated the land of native people.

It was an opportune time to visit the people of the Omo basin. The seasonal rains had peaked in August, and the flow of the Omo had decreased since then; by the last weeks of November, the river was easily forded, and cultivation of the riverside fields could begin. Of the two known tribes along the river, the Bodi—the same people whose women we encountered on the first descent—were the more predominately agricultural and, therefore, the more likely to be met. Their territory was upstream from the Mui River; the Mursi were their neighbors to the south.

In both tribes the men concerned themselves primarily with husbandry, herding their cattle in a year-long search for safe water and forage. The man/animal, woman/plant division is residual from the hunter-gatherer stage of social development, which is now practiced by no more than a couple of thousand humans worldwide. As with hunter-gatherer societies, it is the women who supply most of the food, though the cattle-derived proteins of meat and milk are of high ceremonial as well as nutritional value. The men, although they eschew the womanly work of cultivation, do find time to go fishing in the season between harvests—in the months from November to January, the season of this second river trip.

Despite similar habits and habitats, or because of them, the Bodi and Mursi are not always on friendly terms. While some degree of cooperation is necessary, all-out wars between Bodi and Mursi occur with periodic regularity. Late in the 1950s extended hostilities occurred, though none were recorded during the time anthropologist David Turton did his fieldwork among the Mursi (1969 to 1970). But in 1971 brief skirmishes between the two tribes did take place. Unlike many tribal war situations, where a "coup" is counted by merely touching an enemy with a staff (as among the Plains Indians), encounters between these people frequently resulted in death, and the victor was hailed by his tribal mates and decorated in scarification ceremonies.

It is perhaps just as well that the Bodi and Mursi reopened their hostilities, according to one study: the Bodi had been making systematic raids against the Dime to the east for some years, and the Dime tribe was in very real danger of total collapse as it was driven away from its lowland homes into the higher country. The Bodi-Mursi conflict, minor though it was in comparison, helped distract the Bodi from their genocidal course.

Such wars most frequently occur over cattle—not cattle theft, though that, of course, can be a cause; but, rather, because of the relationship of a man to his favorite cattle, his *morare*. If a man's *morare* is sick, he may sacrifice another animal in the hope that his own will get better; or he may raid a neighboring group and kill someone. It seems as if no enemy is more highly valued than another—no one is "safe": the victims may be an old woman, a seven-year-old, a young couple making love. Although the brief encounter with the Bodi women in May had been friendly and fascinating, the Bodi in general do not enjoy great relationships with their neighbors.

Much of this information, however, has been collected and published only since the Omo river trips of 1973. At the time the Bodi and Mursi were virtually unstudied—the Bodi in particular were a mystery, and Turton's studies of the Mursi had only just been submitted as his thesis at the University of London.

Just before noon on the eighteenth day on the river, one of those experiences that adventurers dream of began to unfold. Cheryl Jensen, one of the expedition members, later recounted the events in an article in *Mountain Gazette*.

Our first glimpse was a dramatic one: we rounded a bend in the river and saw before us a group of naked hunters gathered around a freshly speared hippo.

OPPOSITE, TOP The end of the journey approaches, and the river slows to meet Lake Turkana at the border between Ethiopia and Kenya (Stan Boor). BOTTOM The flood-washed channel of a tributary leads into tropical montane forest (Richard Bangs).

19

They were just starting to butcher it, and we pulled into shore nearby to watch. At first they were aloof and distrustful, but once they realized we didn't mean to steal their meat, they became friendly and curious. We laughed and talked with them (in sign language) for most of the afternoon as they went about the work of cutting off large chunks of meat and hauling them off into the forest. After a while, the chief of the group had one of the younger men build a fire and roast strips of the meat, which he then offered graciously to us. We ate and enjoyed our first fresh meat in weeks, hardly noticing its toughness. By the time the bladder of the dead hippo was cut open and left reeking on the ground, the smell and the heat had made all of us nauseated, so we answered the parting waves of the hunters and headed downriver again.

The next day another group of natives approached the rafters as they rested after lunch, and one spoke a few words of Amharic. He and George Fuller carried on a halting conversation, and Fuller had the scientific pleasure of translating some words of his previously unrecorded language. He found that the men were indeed Bodi, but that the people of the day before were Bacha, hunting people who lived in small clutches along the Omo all year around. No one on the trip had ever heard of the Bacha before. Had we, a ragtag bunch of American river rafters, happened upon an unknown tribe?

It turned out the Bacha were known, but barely. They are true hunter-gatherers and among the most primitive people in the Omo Valley and all of Africa. Perhaps the most striking fact to come to light about the Bacha is their unique relationship with the far more numerous Mursi. The Mursi feel that living without cattle, being forced to "live like a monkey" in the Omo forest, eating fish "like a wading bird," and never leaving the Omo's banks, are the very depths of social degradation—and all are characteristics of the Bacha lifestyle. The Bacha speak Mursi, but the Mursi don't deign to learn Bacha; the Bacha can visit a Mursi cattle settlement but cannot sleep inside a cattle compound and can't even linger too long in the village. Naturally there's a ban on marriage between the two tribes.

There is some reciprocity, however; the Mursi get honey and meat from the Bacha, who are excellent hunters; while the Bacha are sometimes given milk by the Mursi. Most important, the Mursi will often sponsor a Bacha girl's marriage by supplying the bride-price—an economic symbol of considerable value.

Despite the Mursi's arrogant attitude toward the Bacha, their debt to the more primitive, loosely structured bands of the riverbank is enormous. Some anthropologists think that the Mursi are recent immigrants to the Omo Valley, coming from the South at the end of the nineteenth century; upon arrival, they subjugated the native Bacha while learning cultivation from them. Perhaps the Mursi are protecting themselves from the insult of having to learn the basics of subsistence in the Omo Valley from people who seem to them little better than monkeys.

Our initial contact with the Mursi came just a few miles downstream. The Mui River take-out was within the core area of the tribe, and it was only because our first descent was in the spring that we didn't have contact with them at that time. The first meeting with the Mursi was almost as striking as the hippo barbecue with the Bacha had been, for the Mursi are among Africa's most vividly decorated—though some might call it mutilated—people.

The men shave their heads, shaping and braiding their hair into patterns. The painful rituals of scarification were evident on their stomachs, shoulders, arms, and faces, each man as decoratively distinct from another as his range of pain allowed. But what the men do to themselves is nothing compared to the excesses that custom demands of the women. Their lower lips are sliced when they reach puberty, and ever-larger disks of clay are inserted to stretch the lip out to outrageous lengths. Lips dangling past the chin are not uncommon in mature women, though when a lip disk is present, the clay plate is thrust out in a bold and strangely beautiful statement. Ear lobes, too, are subjected to the same modifications, clay plugs or brass hoops are set in the ever-more-distended flesh.

Such ritualized mutilation is found the world over, especially in the tropics: where tribal clothing is not practical, people often resort to decorating their skin as a way of affirming their place in society. Lip plates have been interpreted as an effort to make the women too ugly to be desirable for slavery, but beauty is in the eye of the beholder: the people themselves see lip plates as a symbol of a woman's ability to bear children. However, as Cheryl Jensen theorized, "One thing is certain about these people with their strange mouth decorations—they never do any kissing."

Over the past dozen years from two to six parties have floated the Omo every year, except during one year in the mid-seventies when Ethiopia's political turmoil made tourism difficult. The passengers on those trips have experienced a memorable and unique window into wildlife and lifestyles that are all but lost to the modern world. For the people who live along the Omo, commercial floats down their familiar waters have provided the single most significant contact with the Western world. There has been, unavoidably, some impact on the Bodi, Bacha, and Mursi; but it has been slight. European-style shirts are occasionally sported by some of the more well traveled Bodi and Mursi, and their patterns of trade

—and goods thought worthy of trading for—have become more astute.

Wildlife counts taken by professionals in 1976 and again in 1982 revealed very little difference in the numbers of creatures or of species sighted. And the Bacha and the Bodi are still shyly delighted when the adventurous strangers come floating down the river. Even the Mui take-out is still almost impossible to find, unless you know exactly where it is. Now, however, once you pull in to tie up the boats and wait for the shuttle truck to come coughing down the rough track, word spreads rapidly across the meadows and forests. Within a couple of hours the Mursi appear to watch the show of derigging, to barter for Western goods, to mug for the cameras. And to hear tales of far-off lands called California and America—and Ethiopia.

Batoka greeting.

21

Zambezi

SINGLE-SPAN STEEL BRIDGE links the two African nations of Zambia and Zimbabwe across a sixty-yard-wide basalt gorge. The view upstream is of Victoria Falls, plummeting down in a mile-wide curtain, erupting in foam and riot at its base. Downriver, through sinuous gorges, is a tableau luminous and arresting, rarely photographed by the tourists, who are distracted by the sublimity of the falls. The bright serpentine-green ribbon of the Zambezi River stretches and tenses between the seven hairpin turns that mark its course from the falls, creating one of the great river corridors of the world. This is the domain of Nyaminyami, the rivergod of the Tonga people, described in their folklore as a huge snake coiled to strike, with the hungry head of a crocodile.

The fourth largest river in Africa, the Zambezi stakes its claim to greatness at Victoria Falls. From its headwaters at an insignificant spring near the borders of Zambia, Angola, and Zaire, it slowly gains in size and scale until, 720 miles downstream, it is a broad, slow-moving river, surrounding forested islands up to several square miles in size. It seems to have reached senescence there, still 900 miles from its outlet in the Indian Ocean; then it leaps magnificently into an immense rift in its basaltic riverbed and regains the vitality and grandeur that have made its name evocative of the Age of Exploration for over a century.

Throughout 1855 Scottish missionary David Livingstone had been engaged in the first extensive European exploration of the African interior to the north of Capetown. He traveled down the Zambezi by canoe, with hopes of finding the African equivalent of the "northwest passage"—that elusive goal of explorers of the New World, a water route through a continent for the sake of commerce. The river had been flowing serene, wide, and languid amidst an archipelago of beautiful islands teeming with wildlife.

On November 16 Livingstone reported distant spray, moving like columns of smoke from a grass fire, though it was still evidently some distance away, and it was not until the next afternoon that Livingstone landed on an island perched in the midst of the spray storm.

Crawling to the edge of the island, he peered into a huge mist-filled rent in the earth's surface. The appropriateness of the local Kololo dialect name for the falls at that moment must have been manifest: *Mosi-oa-Tunya*, Smoke That Thunders. Dr. Livingstone, ever the good champion of civilization and Christianity, renamed the cascade for his queen. We know it today as Victoria Falls.

Now, 130 years later, the sight is still beyond belief. The waters of the Zambezi plunge into the chasm and explode at the bottom, breaking with a roar into a driving mist. The deluge carries down a strong draft, which eddies through the canyon and captures the spindrift, driving it up in tremendous columns several hundred feet high, shot through with iridescence. It was sufficient to inspire Livingstone's most lyrical image in his several accounts of his explorations: "The snow-white sheet seemed like myriads of small comets rushing on in one direction, each of which left behind its nucleus rays of foam. . . . [The falls] had never been seen before by European eyes, but scenes so lovely must have been gazed upon by angels in their flight."

Livingstone abandoned his descent of the Zambezi at the falls, continuing instead overland to the east coast of Africa in his search for the waterway that would support commerce, colonization, and the conversion of natives he believed was necessary for the good of the continent (and the British Empire). The sheer enormity of Victoria Falls and the impossible turmoil of the river as it twisted through the gorges downstream made passage up or down the Zambezi

PREVIOUS PAGE Spilling over a mile-wide lip, the Zambezi at Victoria Falls plunges into a narrow serpentine gorge with a furious roar: *Mosi-oa-Tunya*, or Smoke That Thunders (Jim Slade).

OPPOSITE The gorge at the falls, from top to bottom (clockwise from top: Richard Bangs, John Kramer, Gary Lemmer).

25

OPPOSITE, TOP The historic first launch in 1981. BOTTOM Into the maw of the rapids at the base of Victoria Falls (all Michael Nichols/Magnum except bottom left, Bart Henderson).

impossible. Running its steep, chiseled gorges seemed forever out of reach.

It was Valentine's Day 1981 when I first saw the river, and it was love at first sight. Along with a party of travel agents and tour operators, I had been shuttled between game parks and hotel lobbies for several days, all leading up to this: Victoria Falls. While the other occupants of the Land-Rover pressed for a glimpse of the great falls upstream, I looked the other way, out of habit. Some 350 feet below the bridge we were driving over, a mighty river coiled and cursed through a dark basalt gorge. I could see two rapids interrupting this otherwise peaceful stretch, between the hairpin turns that divide the Third Canyon from its cousins. They were pieces of effervescence, feather white, inviting. They looked like they could be run. (RB)

The very idea of rafting the Zambezi, picking up where Livingstone left off, was only just becoming possible. For over a decade the river had been the staging area for the majority-rule struggle in Rhodesia that led eventually to the creation of the state of Zimbabwe. In 1966, a year after Rhodesia's unilateral declaration of independence from the British Empire—a move designed to prevent the turnover of power in Rhodesia to majority rule—black nationalist freedom fighters crossed the Zambezi into Rhodesia from Zambia (which had gained its own independence in 1964). The Zimbabwe African National Union (ZANU) was formed to bring down, through armed struggle, the Rhodesian white minority government of Ian Smith. The river and its many side canyons and tributaries, offering a network of passageways and retreats for raids, quickly became a refuge for guerrillas.

The border between Zambia and Rhodesia—the Zambezi—was closed in December 1973, and land mines and other anti-personnel devices were placed up and down the river by Rhodesian security forces. As the war heated up and white Rhodesians began to make incursions into the area across the river to raid enemy camps, ZANU also started placing land mines along both sides of the river.

In April 1979 the Commonwealth heads of nations met in Lusaka, Zambia, and British Prime Minister Margaret Thatcher told the world that her government was "wholly committed to genuine majority rule in Rhodesia." The death knell had sounded for the white government of Ian Smith. Early in 1980, when the new nation of Zimbabwe emerged by treaty and election from fourteen years of conflict, the border once again opened. An effort was launched to deactivate the mines in the more accessible tourist areas, such as around Victoria Falls and Lake Kariba. But no effort had been made to clear the mines within the Zambezi gorges. None had seemed necessary; who would go down into those gorges?

The expedition we proposed in 1981—to raft the Zambezi River, a modern exploration in the tradition of the great river expeditions of the past—sought to take advantage of a unique opportunity, a rare crack in history that would permit an experience unavailable in the past and, quite possibly, in the future. Before the late 1960s, the specially designed inflatable rafts needed to negotiate the rapids in the Zambezi gorges just didn't exist. Throughout the 1970s, when international rafting began to come into its own, it had been impossible to voyage through these gorges because of the war. And a few years hence, if the most ambitious plans of the nations of Africa are fullfilled, a second major dam on the Zambezi will be built midway through the Batoka Gorge (that portion of the Zambezi below its confluence with the Songwe River, some six miles below the falls); nearly all of the free-flowing Zambezi below Victoria Falls will then be backed up by a giant reservoir.

The Zambezi had already been dammed once: at Kariba, downstream from the Batoka Gorge and its rapids, a huge earthen plug built in the Zambezi blocked the river and created one of the largest manmade lakes on earth. The Kariba Dam was at the time the largest building project in Africa since the Great Pyramids, a wall of restraint 420 feet high and 1,200 feet wide (as long as Hoover Dam on the Colorado River in Nevada, though some 300 feet lower). The lake that resulted drowned some 2,000 square miles of land, including much of the homeland of the Tonga.

The Tonga are, like many of the tribes of southern Africa, cultural and genetic descendants of the aboriginal Bantu culture endemic to southern Africa. They worship Nyaminyami, the god of the mighty river that was the focus of their ancient life-style of small villages and farms. His lair, they believe, was

26

OPPOSITE A market in Lusaka, Zambia, brings together the people and products of the region (Skip Horner). BOTTOM Fishermen along the lower Zambezi River display their smoked catch (Skip Horner).

below the dark water of Kariba Gorge, and they knew he wouldn't stand for a wall across his river.

Construction on the Kariba Dam was proceeding according to schedule when early in March 1957 the Zambezi unleashed a flood of unprecedented ferocity, tearing villages off the face of the earth on its way to the temporary cofferdam erected to allow construction of the larger wall. The surge hit the dam and submerged it, causing thousands of dollars in damage. But in ten months' time a second, higher, cofferdam was built.

The next year, incredibly, the Zambezi above Victoria Falls reached a crest 15 feet *higher* than the level of the record 1957 flood. It suddenly seemed that the Tonga beliefs might not be mere superstition. Nyaminyami had already sent down a spectacular flood, as if to proclaim to one and all that the god of the river still lived. It had failed to dislodge the dam builders; now a second and larger flood hurtled toward Kariba. On February 16, 1958, the cofferdam succumbed to the torrent and burst; yet the water still continued to rise. On March 3 the construction crew's essential suspension bridge was shattered and borne away as the flood finally peaked at more than 100 feet above its low-water level. Nyaminyami had struck a savage blow. But the juggernaut of progress was in motion; construction was resumed and accelerated, and before the rivergod could muster his energies again, the dam wall was closed in December of 1959. Nyaminyami was tamed—for the time being.

■ ■ ■

Twenty years later Dr. Kenneth Kaunda, the leader of Zambia since its independence, agreed to our plans for a rafting expedition down the Zambezi, through the twisting gorges below Victoria Falls.

More than nine months of preparation went into what would become a nine-day expedition. Reconnaissance included helicopter and fixed-wing flights over the river, intense examination of a series of stereoscopic aerial photographs of the gorge, and a cautious hike along the dangerous mined rim of the first seven gorges, in the company of government "sappers," who are trained to spot and disarm the still-active land mines.

The only possible access for a river put-in was a rugged trail on the Zambian side down to the Boiling Pot, an immense whirlpool at the end of the First Gorge just 200 yards from the base of the falls. Takeout would be at the head of Lake Kariba, sixty miles downstream, at a small Zimbabwe fishing camp. Because sanction and cooperation were needed from both sides of a border so recently the scene of violence, the undertaking took on special significance. President Kaunda agreed to formally launch our expedition, somewhat to the frustration of Zimbabwean government officials who also wanted to sponsor the trip. As if to add the final blessing—sanctification by the international media—an ABC film crew joined to document the endeavor.

With all these responsibilities and risks in mind, the 1981 Great Zambezi Expedition approached the matter of Nyaminyami and his river with reverence, painting the name of the rivergod on the prow of the boats. The gesture harkened back to the very first Sobek trips in Ethiopia eight years earlier. There, fearsome tales of the crocodiles on the Omo and Awash rivers had led to our invocation of Sobek—ancient Egyptian crocodile god—and the name had become indelibly linked with international rafting.

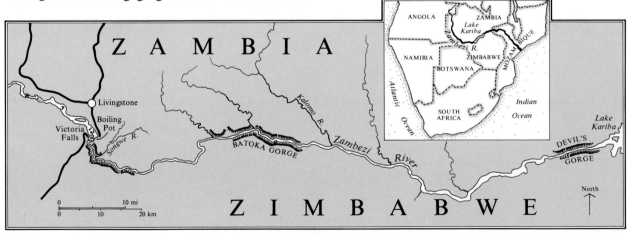

OPPOSITE An afternoon smoke-bath dispels mosquitoes (Michael Nichols/Magnum). BOTTOM Paintings in caves along the Zambezi betray human presence hundreds of thousands of years ago (Lynn Gaffikin).

By Monday, October 26, the expedition team had collected in Livingstone, Zambia. Eight of Sobek's most experienced guides arrived first, to be followed by the ABC film crew and actor LeVar Burton (who portrayed the young Kunta Kinte in the television epic *Roots*), who was to be the principal figure of the television documentary. The team was rounded out with representatives from Zambia and Zimbabwe and several prominent American businessmen. The Great Zambezi Expedition was changing from a century-old dream to a reality.

I squeezed hands with a group of local boys who had scrambled down the steep slope to see us off. Slipping on a pair of studded cotton gloves, I settled in the seat of a five-meter-long inflatable raft. My passengers: photographer Michael Nichols and Joanne Taylor, both as somber as the dark canyon walls. Setting the bowline free, I let the boat drift upstream in the eddy to its confrontation with the rapid known as the Boiling Pot.

Then I dug the oar blades deep, powering out of the eddy and into the main current. The first stroke seemed solid, and I was confidently preparing for the next when the boat canted up a wave. The right oar sliced ineffectually through air. I grappled with the ill-spent oar and saw, through the heaving water, a black wall looming. With a panicked push on the other oar, I turned the bow toward the wall, which was hurling water from its face.

Three meters from the wall I dropped the oars and held on. A blast of water pushed the boat up on its side, where it hung for a tense second. Through the wash of white I saw Michael, camera pressed against his eye, still shooting; then I thought I heard Joanne scream. The boat plunged over, upside-down, into the rolling mess.

I had capsized in the first rapid, ten minutes after launching our expedition. (RB)

It was the first of no fewer than five capsizes on the Great Zambezi Expedition. Any first descent is subject to flips, swims, and the unexpected, but it was clear that Nyaminyami had not given up his regency. Rapids that looked straightforward suddenly lashed out with furious reversals, while those that seemed like impossible maelstroms, run only on a dare, proved straightforward. Having a television crew along to film the mishaps, as well as the successes,

added to the larger-than-life tone of this encounter with one of the great rivers of the world.

There was another aspect to this first descent, however, that made it particularly poignant. A mile downstream from the fourth rapid we made camp for the first night at a peaceful eddy called The Silent Pool. Here, between three 400-foot-high waterfalls created by a Zambian hydroelectric diversion scheme from the river above Victoria Falls, a Zimbabwean military helicopter landed on the bank. It was an Alouette, used not so many years earlier by white Rhodesians for "search-and-destroy" missions within this very gorge. It was being loaned to us by the Zimbabwean government in case we needed logistical support for emergencies. Michael Arogyaswamy, the Indian-born supervisor of the power station, summed it up: "This must be the first time a helicopter from the other side has landed in Zambia with good intentions in ten years. This proves that the Zambezi is now a river of peace."

■ ■ ■

During the expedition, the Zambezi was flowing at around 15,000 cubic feet per second—a fraction of its rain-season flush, but a powerful current nonetheless. Generally rivers of this scale are best run by oared rafts, with a single guide maneuvering the boat through the large waves and strong hydraulics created by the high waterflows, while passengers hold on to whatever safety lines are available. But included in this expedition was a paddleboat—the same size and design as the other rafts, but captained by a veteran guide, Dave Shore, and crewed by a mixed group of first-timers and experienced boatmen, all of whom used small canoe-style paddles to help power and control the raft. Among the first-timers was LeVar Burton; among the more experienced was sixty-six-year-old Grant Rogers, one of the founders of commercial river rafting in the United States, who had already run many of the world's toughest rapids. The paddleboat had made some excellent runs on the first day of shooting, though Shore and his crew elected to portage one particularly nasty rapid, Number Four.

Based on aerial observation, Number Five had been appraised as "unrunnable" during our pretrip planning, and a portage was anticipated. The current forced its way between a steep drop over a rock on the right side and a huge pour-over in the middle of

Motifs from Stone Age cave drawings along Zambezi River gorge.

the river, where gushing water barely covered another enormous boulder. But a scout early that second morning revealed a clear run down the right side, if only the first monstrous pour-over could be avoided. The first boat through was rowed by John Kramer, one of Sobek's most reliable oarsmen; he narrowly missed the pour-over and emerged in fine shape. He was followed by the two kayakers, who had come along as safety in case of swimmers, since kayaks in experienced hands are extremely maneuverable. The two oarboats that followed also made it through, and paddle captain Dave Shore decided to test his crew's mettle on this rapid.

He lined up for the crosscurrent traverse to position his boat at the top of the rapid; then to those on the bank—and to viewers of the television special that resulted—seemed to call an inexplicable "Stop paddling" at a crucial moment. Almost at once he cried out for the crew to dig harder, but it wasn't enough—the raft collapsed into the hole behind the pour-over. One tube was sucked under, while the other rose like a whale. Out washed two swimmers—LeVar Burton and Grant Rogers.

The paddleboat caromed down the right bank, Burton and Rogers following like lost ducklings. The cameras followed them down as LeVar passed beneath the boat into the main current, where kayaker Neusom Holmes picked him up, without a scratch and only a trifle winded. But Grant was swept against a barely submerged boulder, then rolled over a yard-high waterfall. He began to recirculate in the backwash below the falls, popping free just as help neared him. Then the current carried him back toward the middle of the Zambezi.

John Yost and Rich Bangs jumped into an oarboat, cast off, and began the chase, catching him almost at once. Grimacing and barely conscious, Rogers was hauled into the safety of the boat, groaning as he clutched his side—while the ABC cameras kept rolling. The army helicopter accompanying the expedition whined into action, and within an hour Rogers was undergoing treatment at Wankie Colliery Hospital in Zimbabwe, eighty miles to the southeast.

Four broken ribs and a collapsed lung were no laughing matter, and we were abruptly conscious of our intrusion into a realm long off limits for diverse reasons—politics, floods, and rivergods. Rogers made a complete recovery and a year later was again rafting whitewater rivers; but for both rafters and cameramen continuing through the deep basalt gorge that afternoon, surrounded by hidden land mines, missing a much-loved member of our group, looking forward to an unknown number of dangers ahead as we rowed ever closer to the crocodile feeding grounds of the lower Zambezi, the security of familiar rivers and friends seemed a long way off.

■ ■ ■

Rapids like Number Five have been created on the Zambezi by one of two conditions: a boulder-strewn channel, caused by slippage from the steep canyon walls, or the radical S-turns the river takes as it careens through its basalt gorge. Both are factors of the peculiar geology of the Zambezi. Dennis Huckabay, an American geographer teaching at the University of Zambia, had leapt at the chance to join the expedition on its historic passage through the gorges of the Zambezi; in the first two days he had spent many hours in close study of the canyon walls, while the rafters examined the hydraulics and risks. Perhaps to take the tension out of the evening's camp, he sought to explain the singular phenomenon of Victoria Falls and its serpentlike gorge.

Unlike most major falls of the world—such as Niagara, in which a stratum of hard rock is underlain or crossed downriver by a layer of much softer shale, which erodes faster and creates a declivity—the sides of Victoria Falls are hard basalt from top to bottom. These basalts belong to a great sheet of lava that was erupted long before the Zambezi ever flowed, probably around 150 million years ago in the Jurassic period. As the molten lava cooled, vertical fissures formed, which then filled with sedimentary material from the ancient course of the Zambezi, before the creation of the falls. For much of the course of the river, the fissures run parallel to the current; but in the region of the falls the river suddenly swings southward, bisecting the angle of the basalt fissures, allowing rapid erosion through the softer sedimentary deposits and creating abrupt falls.

The falls we call Victoria is not the first cascade to roar over the lip of the Zambezi's basalt channel. The seven gorges downstream zigzag like chevrons, and each at one time was a major falls that eroded its way upstream, cutting across the lines of soft-filled fis-

OPPOSITE, TOP A small plane flying over the Zimbabwe savanna frightens a herd of zebras (Michael Nichols/ Magnum). BOTTOM Sudanese water buffalo find security in size and numbers (Roland Dare).

33

OPPOSITE River horses and flat dogs. TOP A bloat of hippos floats cool yet wary in African waters (Skip Horner). BOTTOM The Nile crocodile, *Sobek* to the ancient Egyptians (Skip Horner).

sures. Millennia ago the Zambezi rolled over the hard lip of its first falls; soon the river, prying and searching, found a weak place in the lip. It may then have dislodged a block of rock or eaten away at a crack, and that done, hydraulic force pursued its advantage. Even a small lowering of the lip allowed more water to concentrate its erosive potential, soon toppling more blocks and bringing a greater concentration of erosion. Eventually the whole river's volume flowed through this nick, leaving the rest of the fall line as a gorge. Then, not quickly but inevitably, the river eroded back into another sediment-filled fissure until, as it twisted back to correct its direction, it reached another hard basalt fall line and again formed a cascade.

The present falls, the eighth in the prehistoric series, is eroding in this same manner, with the western-most section of the falls, the Devil's Cataract, wearing down significantly faster than the rest; it is already some 120 feet lower than other parts of the falls. In some unknown number of years Victoria Falls as we know it will no longer exist; but soon—geologically "soon," which is measured in epochs—another one will shower just upstream.

■ ■ ■

The rest of the second day progressed smoothly. A scimitar-beaked, cinnamon-shouldered bird wheeled above the rafts—the African fish eagle, national bird of Zambia. The sea-green river swept past a pair of limestone alcoves, with lush hanging gardens dripping over the yawning entrances. It was the proverbial calm before the storm: after a couple of minor rapids, the body of the river funneled to a narrow chute, then plunged into a hole that seemed to have no bottom. A shambles of white followed until the river reared to a wave that must have been as high as the hole was deep. It was simply the largest rapid most of the party had ever seen. Portaging was the only possible way around the rapid, Number Nine; it is still a rapid no one has attempted to run.

The process was long and laborious. All gear had to be untied, taken out of the rafts, and carried over the rocky bank to where navigating the river again became practical. Then a crew of four or more had to be assembled to carry the rafts, which although considerably lightened, at over 100 pounds, sixteen feet long, and eight feet wide, are still cumbersome and

Crocodile vs. Alligator
The fourth tooth of the lower jaw of a crocodile is visible when the mouth is shut. The alligator's fourth tooth fits into a groove on the upper jaw when the mouth is closed. The alligator's head is broader and shorter, and his snout more obtuse, than the crocodile's. Crocodiles are found in Florida, Africa, Asia, India, and Australia; alligators are found in China and the southeastern United States.

awkward. Finally all gear had to be tied again into the rafts, to prevent loss in case of a flip or a rough ride, before the rafts were boarded once more and set loose into the current. Under the best of circumstances, with a crew accustomed to the back-and-forth rhythm of the portage, such an operation can take about an hour. More extraordinary circumstances can lead to portages of several hours or a full day; under the worst possible circumstances, large and potentially dangerous rapids are run simply because the portage is too difficult or, for that matter, impossible. Our portage of Number Nine was, thankfully, short and to the point: in less than an hour we were back on the river.

Camp that night was at the end of the Seventh Gorge, only six miles downstream from the falls, where the Songwe River joins with the Zambezi. Alongside a sweeping sandbar and tarnlike lagoon, terraced reefs and irregular bosses of rock marked the tributary mouth. The basalt there was deeply pitted with well-like potholes, ground smooth by whirling, torrent-driven stones. A footpath led up to the canyon rim, one of the few places of access on the sixty-mile route. Downstream from that point, below the most ancient of the eight "Victoria Falls" that have marched back upriver over millennia, lay the Batoka Gorge. The miles ahead were so inaccessible that the fear of land mines was no longer a consideration: not even the most dedicated guerrilla was willing to climb down into the wild steepness of the Batoka Gorge.

The plateau above and to the north of the gorge was named the Batoka Highlands by Livingstone after the tribe that lived there. Yet as was so often the case in the Age of Exploration, the European forces and missionaries interrupted an ongoing history, filled with its battles and power struggles. The natives that Livingstone encountered in the area were only recent emigrants themselves, yet another wave of migratory tribes that coveted, and fought for, the lands surrounding the Zambezi. The archaeological record of the region, in fact, is one of the world's oldest, stretching back to the earliest cultural tradition of which we have evidence—the so-called Oldowan Industry, named for the Olduvai Gorge in Kenya.

In the sedimentary deposits along the Zambezi,

34

ancient stone choppers are found. These were made by flaking chalcedony stone from one or two sides to create irregular edges used for cutting or chopping. They are the characteristic hand tools of the Oldowan Industry, the earliest known human artifacts. Such tools, along with hammering stones, and the small flakes used between the finger and thumb, also indicative of the Oldowan Industry, are clear evidence that the Zambezi region is one of the oldest inhabited areas in Africa. Perhaps not the oldest—human fossil remains are few and inconclusive—but the evidence is strong for the continued habitation of the region over the past million years or more.

Other excavations have uncovered a steady series of increasingly more evolved hand tools, leading to the Later Stone Age traditions that were still being practiced by the natives of the area as recently as a thousand year ago. Then, the first Early Iron Age cultivators and herders began the transformation of the region, introducing more advanced tribalism, agriculture, husbandry, and the other signposts of the Bantu culture groups. Far from pointing to the "savagery" of the area's inhabitants, however, this unbroken history of artifact and tradition is evidence of the harmony in which the people lived. The land was rich with food sources, including wild game such as elephants, hippos, elands, sables, kudus, pigs, and smaller mammals. Yet competition for these resources must have been minimal, or this stage of cultural evolution could not have lasted as long as it did. Perhaps it was a "golden age" for the humankind in the area, one which recent border wars and tribal conflicts have forever changed.

■ ■ ■

Our first day in the Batoka Gorge was surprisingly easy. The morning presented a series of thoroughly runnable, thoroughly delightful rapids, not unlike the best of the Colorado: huge standing waves providing classic roller-coaster rides. Only as the expedition approached the last rapid of the day did Nyaminyami once again strike.

The water poured over two gargantuan boulders, fallen in some previous era from the canyon walls. The current was forced into the twenty meters between the rocks, but it would be easy to wash over the submerged boulders unless the entrance to the fast-moving rapid was exact. The hydraulic effect of the current flowing over a submerged obstacle creates a "hole"—an actual reversal of the downstream flow of the river as the force of the water's abrupt drop literally turns it back on itself in an irregular spinning motion (known to those who have been caught in such a hole as the "Maytag Effect").

It was a risky run, but nowhere near impossible, as the first two rafters proved. The third boat through was piloted by John Yost—running alone, since the Zambian wildlife and national parks representative accompanying the group elected to walk around the rapid. Yost missed the entry mark by a yard, and it was enough for the current to sweep him into the second hole sideways. The boat climbed the watery rampart, balanced briefly on its flank, then flopped over almost on top of him. Neusom Holmes, one of the two kayakers, rescued him almost at once; the only injury he received was a nasty bump on the head. Coincidentally, when the raft was righted, the only damage it showed was to its spare oar, inexplicably snapped in two. Yost claimed the two casualties, bumped head and snapped oar, were directly related.

At camp that evening Holmes was the last to pull in, having been playing with his kayak in some riffles upstream. His face was waxen as he climbed up the bank to the campside. "I think I was just chased by a croc," he announced. "It had a head three feet long." He gazed uncomfortably at the river, his eyes darting. We joined him on the bank, searching the turbid waters of the Zambezi. "I must have lost him in that small rapid," he said at last.

The news was heartsickening, since none of us had expected crocodiles yet—the river was too fast, the gorge too abrupt. Crocodiles generally favor slack stretches with gently sloping banks. A consensus was quickly reached that it was probably just a floating log. Nonetheless, everyone bathed in groups that night while one member swept the river with a flashlight for the telltale ruby beads of a crocodile's eyes.

The old Edgar Rice Burroughs image of the crocodile as a man-eating terror of African rivers is, strangely, true. Crocs easily reach fifteen feet in length and half a ton in weight; it takes a lot of protein to support a lizard's system when it's that size. In 1968, for instance, a crocodile was shot in the Okavango Swamp (in nearby Botswana, just south and west of Zambia) whose stomach included the remains of a zebra, a donkey, two goats, and the still-clothed body of a woman who had been missing for seventeen days. Some legendary crocodiles are said to have been responsible for up to 400 human deaths. Even modern-day figures of African populations estimate that crocs make a meal of humans once a week in Zambia.

But crocodiles serve their function, and in the Zambezi it's the control of barbel and venu fish, which favor the bream and mormorous that people like to cast for. The Zambezi crocodile population has declined drastically of late, especially along the more accessible stretches of the river below the Batoka Gorge, along the banks of Lake Kariba, and above Victoria Falls in the quiet waters of the upper Zambezi. Their hides—usually sold to fashion-conscious French clothiers—fetch up to $100 each these days, perhaps more. But $100 did not seem like a fair market value, at least to us, for the creature that had eyed Neusom Holmes's kayak.

The next day was Sunday, and we greeted sunrise with the weekly antimalaria tablet. By this point on the expedition virtually everyone had some degree of diarrhea or stomach cramps, but no fever. The dry, warm climate of the Zambezi region is not the sort of locale favored by malarial mosquitoes, which are among the most persistent of Africa's threats. Over much of the tropical world today, a twenty-five-milligram tablet of Daraprim Pyrimethamine suppresses the mosquito-borne disease, though resistant strains are becoming a problem. In Livingstone's time, however, the etiology of malaria was unknown, and he used grim doses of quinine, calomel, and jalap to fight the fever while brushing aside the mosquitoes as a nuisance. Malaria killed his wife, and, after Livingstone had spent nearly three decades in the African bush, it finally felled him near Lake Bangweulu in Zambia on May 1, 1873. It was just two years after journalist Henry Stanley tracked down the famous explorer on assignment for the New York *Herald*. Stanley found the missionary gaunt and weak, the victim of persistent malaria attacks. Although he was only fifty-eight years old at the time, he was already older than most of the natives with whom he lived much of his life, and who had no scientific or effective traditional remedies for either mosquitoes or malarial fever.

The Batoka Gorge, now 200 meters deep, tapered back a little, revealing more sky and irregular rows of the native mopane trees on the rim. It was the last day on the river for actor LeVar Burton. A willing crew member on the paddleraft despite his harrowing swim, he had been clearly fascinated by the clean lines and quick response of the kayaks throughout the journey. Before the helicopters came in, he asked Neusom for a lesson. Within an hour, he was cutting through the chop of a small rapid with facility, even finesse.

The helicopter landed on the bank, and LeVar and his producer, John Wilcox, bid us farewell. Three members of the ABC film crew were left to continue the coverage of the expedition, which still had to float another thirty miles to Lake Kariba. Before he climbed aboard the helicopter, Wilcox had a few final reassuring words for the remaining rafters. "Good luck downstream. Don't worry, though. There're no crocs on this river. Old wives' tale."

Fifty meters downstream, in the riffle just beyond the one LeVar kayaked, Yost's boat was attacked. A ridged snout lunged from beneath and, sinking two long rows of teeth into the raft, exploded one of the inflated tubes. A veteran of two hippo attacks on rafts he was rowing on the Omo in Ethiopia, Yost reacted instinctively and defensively: he lifted an oar out of its oarlock and began slapping the croc over the head with the blade. Amazingly, the croc made a second lunge, then dived and disappeared. Yost frantically rowed the half-deflated raft to shore, and the rest of the boats, rafts, and kayaks made a hasty landing on the nearest beach. If the crocodile had gone for a kayak, low in the water, small and pregnable, it seemed unlikely the paddler could have survived.

Photographer Nick Nichols, a passenger in the victimized boat, estimated the croc at two or three meters; Yost guessed four. This was only the second croc bite in Sobek history, the first being on the Omo eight years earlier. Over the years river runners in Africa had come to expect certain behavior from crocodiles. They usually displayed their displeasure with charges, the reptiles' turreted eyes and nostrils riding just out of the water. This usually allowed enough time to hurl a rock or simply to shout at the skittish creatures, who then normally sank to the

David Livingstone (1813-1873), Scottish missionary and explorer, was the son of an itinerant tea vendor. Largely self-educated, he was accepted into the London Missionary Society at the age of twenty-seven, and a year later was in Capetown. He spent much of the rest of his life in Africa as an explorer and medical missionary, believing that he was divinely appointed to spread Christianity among the heathen. His famous meeting with Henry Stanley, who was sent by the New York *Herald* to find the missing missionary, took place at Ujiji, near Lake Tanganyika in 1871. Though Livingstone was weak and destitute, he refused to leave Africa with Stanley and pressed on with his explorations. He was found dead, in an attitude of prayer, in a small village on Lake Bangweulu early on the morning of May 1, 1873. His embalmed and eviscerated remains were carried by a procession of Africans to the coast, and were taken from there by boat to England and interred in Westminster Abbey.

bottom and hid. Never, however, had a croc attack come unseen from directly beneath a raft. The conclusion was drawn that on the murky rivers of Ethiopia and Tanzania crocodiles approach with eyes surfaced to discern an intended victim. Here the river was clear, and the croc could probably see the boat overhead from the riverbed. Assuming it was a dead hippo, he had shot up for an easy meal.

The tear was too jagged and too big for repair, so the raft was lifted out by one of the Zimbabwean helicopters still escorting the expedition. The two kayaks were also helicoptered out, since neither Neusom Holmes nor Doug Tompkins, the other kayaker, was eager to continue paddling. And though the three members of the ABC team were supposed to continue, they, too, elected to make a hasty exit. Our expedition was reduced to a party of rafters, without media equipment, film stars, or television sensibilities to surround each moment with tangential concerns.

We floated on downstream, quiet and intensely alert, eyes searching the water and shores for crocodiles. Soon we reached Moemba Falls, which aerial reconnaissance had marked as a certain portage. Named for a chief of a nearby tribe, it was a spectacle that Livingstone had viewed from the canyon rim in 1860. He had diverged from his route along the northern plateau on the native report of a waterfall in the gorge, the description of which "seemed to promise something grand." But with the memory of Victoria Falls fresh in mind, he was disappointed. However, G.W. Lamplugh on his 1905 survey actually made it down to the river's edge, and there he formed a different impression: "Insignificant in height, it is true, but when one stands on the brink and sees the whole volume of the great Zambezi converging into a single pass only fifty or sixty feet in width, shuddering, and then plunging for twenty feet in a massive curve that seems in its impact visibly to tear the grim basaltic rocks asunder, one learns better than from the feathery spray-fans of Victoria Falls what force there is in the river, and one wonders no longer at the profundity of the gorge."

Just a couple of miles below Moemba another spectacular waterfall split the river—only this was a completely uncharted falls. No recorded description of it was found, and no name known. It proved to be an even more difficult portage to reach the calm waters below the falls, including a struggle over sun-baked rocks to lower our five remaining rafts at a ninety-degree pitch over a short cliff. The unanticipated additional time we spent at this portage brought us into late afternoon. At least three unexplored miles lay ahead to the next campsite, where a helicopter had air-dropped our night's supplies.

All too soon a huge rapid roared in the waning light. We scouted hurriedly, and fortunately it looked runnable straight down the middle.. Neusom Holmes, now behind the oars, volunteered to row first. He rode cleanly over the first wave, then rode sideways up the second and flipped. He and his passengers disappeared in the dusk downstream, swimming for shore. Skip Horner, in the second boat, made it through, barely riding over the wave that had turned Holmes's boat upside-down; then Jim Slade capsized in the same place. Two flips in one rapid, and two more rafts to go, with barely enough light to read water.

It was almost black, and it was my turn. I desperately surveyed the rapid for a "cheat" run, but I couldn't even see 100 yards ahead. I had no idea how the others downstream had fared, whether the water, the rocks, or the crocs had done any damage. I could, however, barely make out the silhouette of Horner's boat tossing in the eddy below, and it gave me an idea. I quickly tightened all the ropes that held the gear in my boat and took out my waterproof diary and camera box. Then I stepped from the boat, kicked it out into the current and watched.

The abandoned boat descended into the maelstrom farther to the left than the others before me, pirouetted in the first wave and then rode up over the plume of the second wave, right side up. I stumbled down the side of the rapid, and found my boat pitching in an eddy, still right side up, with Neusom inside bailing. (RB)

The final boat, rowed by John Yost, made it through in almost pitch blackness without trouble, but it was the eerie penumbral run of the empty boat that gave the rapid its name—Ghostrider.

By the beams of our pocket flashlights we proceeded downstream toward the comfort of the coptered camp, but a narrowing gorge, a quickening current, and the rising noise of whitewater forced a bivouac on a rocky ledge for the night.

39

With the first light of the next day, our seventh on the river, we wearily surveyed the rapid we had elected to shun the night before. It had been a wise move: the river coiled into a thin slot, then rebounded in a white fury off a rock wall. The first four boats were slapped and twisted in the gauntlet, but all made it through. Then Jim Slade, fresh from his capsize the evening before, entered last and was battered by the currents directly into the wall. His raft bucked on its side, rode up the rock wall, and spilled first one passenger, then another, finally the entire crew—and at last flipped over.

It was the fifth flip, and it proved to be the last. The elusive campsite was soon reached and the tepid beer and soda broken out for a much-needed lengthy lunch and longer siesta.

The next two days led to a reversal of the first seven: fewer rapids and more wildlife. Crocodiles reverted to more normal crocodilian behavior and eyed us from afar, and a few bloats of hippos crashed loudly into the water as the boats approached. Over the years hippos have proven to be the greater danger to rafts on the rivers of Africa, responsible for eight attacks on Sobek rafts since the first trip down the Omo eight years earlier. Their reaction was probably the same as the crocodile's had been: that an intrusive hippo was invading their territory. Gray and swollen, the Avon rafts look more like hippopotamuses than any other creature in the menagerie of African rivers, and in some ways the confusion was almost forgivable.

Finally, in the early afternoon of November 5, the current of the Zambezi died in the waters of Lake Kariba. The journey was over.

I wish I could send a report to Livingstone, so he might have the final chapter on this river he spent so long exploring, so he might close the book.

The Zambezi curls through the final gate into this new lake, Kariba, sparkling like hammered gold. I begin to thank God we made it, then send my prayers of gratitude to Nyaminyami, rivergod of the Zambezi. (RB)

OPPOSITE, TOP "King of the jungle," perhaps, but a well-fed lion is no threat (William Boehm). BOTTOM The scaly visage of Lord Sobek (David Edwards).

Euphrates and Çoruh

SOME RIVERS SPRING from the mountains of myth, deep in the recesses of racial memory, at the very foundation of humanity. The Euphrates is such a river. From the mountainous eastern half of Turkey, it begins a 1,700-mile journey over the Turkish plateau, across a slice of Syria, and through the center of Iraq to the Persian Gulf. This is the land known to the ancients as Mesopotamia; the Euphrates was its lifeblood.

The waters of the Euphrates helped slake the thirst of a dozen empires and perhaps bathed Adam. The people who have cupped their hands in its currents are as varied as the landscapes along its course. Steeped in a history deeper and richer than its own floodwaters, the Euphrates is one of the great classical rivers—as is its sister stream, the Tigris. Both are born in Turkey and flow first toward one another, then shy away, undulating across Iraq and Iran for over a thousand miles in what could be seen as a great riverine dance. The two finally come together just a few miles from the Persian Gulf, at Basra, where they unite their flows at last.

Between the watersheds, on a broad floodplain rich in minerals and soil nutrients, traces of the first civilizations are to be found. Some scholars place the Garden of Eden on the lower Euphrates; archaeologists are still uncovering evidence of the early cultures that led to the civilizations that thrived in Mesopotamia (Greek for "between the rivers"). Babylonia, Chaldea, Assyria, and Sumer all flourished along the Euphrates well before the time of Christ. The river has been ruled by Persians, Greeks, Romans, Ottomans, Mongols, Kurds, British, and others.

The largest tributary of the Euphrates, the Marat Su, leaps to life in the perennial snows of Mount Ararat, Turkey's highest peak at 16,946 feet. This is the mountain, according to Genesis, on which Noah's Ark was grounded. For some 300 miles through Turkey's escarpment, the Euphrates drops like a steep, spiral staircase, kicking whitewater spray against sheer canyon walls and darting through narrow gorges. Midway, the bellicose flow is arrested by the 620-megawatt Keban Dam, a French project completed in 1974. Below the dam runs the longest, deepest canyon of the river: the Kemer Khan, Grand Canyon of the Euphrates.

The idea of rafting the Euphrates germinated in mid-1977 when, in the midst of a long portage on the Yuat River in Papua New Guinea, one weary guide turned to another and asked, "What next?" "How about the Euphrates?" came the reply. It started out as a joke; it became an obsession.

Knowing little about the Euphrates but feeling its pull across the centuries, we explored every avenue of information and support we could think of in pursuit of our plans to run the river. We found that, in spite of its long and illustrious history, little was known of the navigability of the upper Euphrates. There were maps, indeed; but securing a good one—suitable for gauging the drop of the river by the mile, estimating surrounding terrain to make an educated guess about the best part of the river to run, and finding road access for the put-in and take-out—was an altogether different problem. For the public, they don't exist. The Turkish Tourist Board in New York will happily rush out its selection in response to a phone call, but their best is an impressionistic rendition of the western half of the country; the entire eastern flank, including the Euphrates, is simply left off the map.

Even the 1:500,000 Tactical Pilotage Charts, never lauded for accuracy but available for most of the world, are listed as "classified" at the Library of Congress. And the State Department and CIA politely decline any assistance in providing maps of politically sensitive areas. The eastern half of Turkey is the NATO flank against the Russian border, and public knowledge of the area is not encouraged.

When public sources of information fail—as they frequently do in the organization of an exotic trip of any sort—a barrage of letters must be released to every remotely relevant government agency, club, organization, and individual. For Turkey, that meant hopeful correspondence was initiated with everyone from Suleyman Demirel, then Prime Minister, to the Tennis Club of Istanbul, to the hotels in the towns near the Euphrates, where English is as common as Swahili. The standard response: silence.

PREVIOUS PAGE Rice fields irrigated by the Çoruh River, in northern Turkey (Skip Horner).

OPPOSITE Children of Isper enjoy the ancient ruins of their Seljuk ancestors (Richard Bangs).

45

Alexander the Great (356-323 B.C.) extended Hellenic culture across Asia Minor to India in the single greatest military campaign in history, finding as he progressed many of the great temples of the Babylonians and Assyrians in ruins, destroyed by Zoroastrian fanatics.

One notable exception was the Ministry of Tourism and Information. Our letter of inquiry, outlining the proposal, posed a battery of questions about the sections of the Euphrates on the Armenian Plateau, the sweeping anticline that supports half of Anatolia (the eastern half of the country). The official reply from the Ministry of Tourism and Information minced no words: "Thank you for your recent letter. Unfortunately there is no place called Armenian Plateau on the Euphrates River, nor can we help you with your request. Thank you for your interest."

Our faux pas was in calling the area the Armenian Plateau. It was a name that had stood for centuries, but as part of an effort to erase memories of the Turkish massacre of almost two million Armenians from 1894 to 1981, the Turkish government refuses to acknowledge the existence of anything "Armenian." Officially the place is now called the Adiyaman Plateau, and referring to its traditional moniker is an affront of some magnitude.

The breakthrough came with a novel approach—writing all the American authors of guidebooks to Turkey. Both of them. Fodor didn't answer, but Tom Brosnahan, author of *Turkey on $5 and $10 a Day*, found the proposal exciting and sent back a notebook full of contacts and information, along with the warning that the Euphrates area was "wild" and the Kurds, who live along the lower stretches of the Euphrates canyon, are beyond government jurisdiction or control.

Brosnahan's contacts proved invaluable: they supplied detailed information on transport, accommodations, and equipment availability. They could not, however, facilitate the process of obtaining government sanction for the project, or even permission to travel to the banks of the Euphrates. The date of departure was nonetheless set, based on studies of the anticipated water volume for the river, which showed June as the optimal month. Airline tickets were secured, menus planned, contacts made. Then less than a month before our start, the frustration of a series of official no replies was capped by the arrival of a demonically long application form for each and every member of our expedition—with the promise that approval or disapproval would be sent in four months' time. The bold course beckoned. We would simply leave, permit or no, and the Turkish govern-

ment was sent a letter explaining that the party would continue on to Turkey regardless of word from Ankara.

Our second mistake had been in using the word *expedition*. Traditionally, in Turkey, expeditions are either military maneuvers or archaeological digs. Of the latter there are many. The country is a treasure trove of ruins and remains of early civilizations. The government is justifiably concerned about foreigners who turn Turkish soil: countless artifacts, irreplaceable and priceless, have been smuggled to private collections and black markets. And archaeological expeditions have occasionally whipped up other problems, such as when one dig in the East turned out to be a cover for an intelligence operation that was training listening devices toward Russia. So, it was not without warrant that *expedition* clicked and registered in some offices in Ankara, and the appropriately discouraging form was sent out.

With our commitment to proceed firm, preparations continued with high spirits and few hitches. At the worst the expedition—or, rather, "tour"—could settle for a hike through the Turkish backcountry, an extended tour of the Grand Bazaar, a swim across the Bosporous, belly dancing lessons . . . there would be some alternative adventure.

■ ■ ■

The team was originally to be five: John Yost, Tom Cromer, Jim Slade, trip doctor Micki McEwen, and Rich Bangs. But Slade and Yost were needed to work river trips in Papua New Guinea and would join us later, so only three of us touched down at Istanbul's Yesilkoy Airport in mid-May of 1978. In the crowded waiting area a thin, mustachioed man held up a hand-scribbled sign with a single word: Sobek. He was Armag Mustafa Nurettin Suleymanfil, or Nuri for short, an agent for Imbat (Soft Wind) Turizm, apparently the only company bold enough to respond to our call.

Flashing a coffee-stained smile, Nuri led the group in the direction of customs. Almost at once he was stopped by a young village woman who threw herself to the floor at his feet and began to wail. Before anyone could react, an armed soldier parted the crowd, grabbed the woman, and dragged her away to be swallowed by the press of people. Nuri didn't miss a drag on his cigarette during the fracas; he seemed unconcerned and even mildly annoyed with the inconvenience, while the team blanched. A melodramatic introduction to life in Turkey.

With sweat beading our foreheads, we stood in the agonizingly slow customs line. We didn't have enough money to pay duty fees for the gear; it had to pass through customs gratis or the expedition would be doomed. Nuri showed his stuff: spewing authoritative Turkish at the inspection officer, he hit all the right notes. The group was waved through.

The relief was brief, however. A check of the cleared gear showed just one missing item: our only raft. Almost any piece of equipment could be replaced or substituted in Turkey—except the $2,300 Avon Professional whitewater inflatable raft. Panicked, we tracked down the Pan Am representative, who calmly theorized that the raft was still on Flight One, which circled continually around the world. He promised to telex the various stops, from Delhi to Hong Kong to London, and have the boat back in only a few days—or so.

With that problem unresolved there was little to do but hail a taxi and see Istanbul. The drive from the airport spun past the Golden Horn, the famed harbor that jabs a crooked finger through the city, and along Kennedy Caddesi (street) by the Sea of Marmara, then past small fishing piers and outdoor cafes, along Roman city walls. Istanbul has one of the highest traffic fatality rates in the world, and the taxi drivers seem determined to keep their city Number One. As our cabby wielded his vehicle within millimeters of car metal and human flesh on every side, he glanced over his shoulder and practiced his English with an old Turkish proverb: "Every day is a holiday for a madman." It must have been his New Year's Day.

En route to the Anka Hotel, we passed a noisy procession led by a wobbly, wooden horse cart bearing a casket draped with green fabric and wreaths. An *imam* (priest) trailed behind, and just behind him the wailing woman from the airport dragged herself in obvious grief. Perhaps she had been so overcome that she threw herself down in front of the first sympathetic face at the airport; we never found out for certain. Clearly there were things about life in Turkey we might never find out.

Istanbul has been described as both the most beautiful and the ugliest city in the world, and it is.

Sweaty, clangorous, squalid, and cramped, it is also throbbing, exciting, and romantic. Minarets spike the skyline in all directions, from which can be heard five times a day the ululations of *muezzins* (holy men) as they call the devout to prayer. Though 90 percent Moslem, Turkey has been a secular state since 1923 when Kemal Ataturk, the national liberator of Asia Minor, initiated a series of reforms that included the banning of the fez (the Islamic hat that indicates devotion to Allah), enfranchisement for women, and discouragement of veil wearing. Like the Chinese leaders of the past three decades, Ataturk was attempting to toss off a yoke of traditional thought and usher his country into the twentieth century.

A recurrent theme of Turkish life is *yavas, yavas,* which, tightly translated, means "slowly, slowly." No matter how hard the expedition tried, matters would not move quickly. Telephone calls took hours to place; ministers were perpetually out to lunch, be it 10:00 a.m. or 4:00 p.m. Time was killed wandering the streets through skeins of moving people, dancing bears, shoeshine boys, macaroon stands, cucumber vendors with wooden pushcarts, porters weighted with 100 pounds of fruit, and assorted businessmen, barkers, and hustlers. We sampled *mezes* (hors d'oeuvres), plates of *dolmas* (stuffed vegetables), *boreks* (cheese puff pastries), *peynir* (cheese), *cheeps* (chips), *kofte* (meat croquettes), and *raki* (potent anise-flavored liqueur) with abandon. All of it was washed with *kahve,* the famous brew served in the tulip cup: Turkish coffee, thick, sweet, and strong, like Istanbul itself.

After several days, it was time to try another tack. Tom Cromer decided to make a bus-ride reconnaissance of the Euphrates's flow, while Nuri, Micki, and Rich took a flight to Ankara with hopes of securing final authorization for our adventure by making an in-person appeal. One of Tom Brosnahan's contacts was at the airport to meet the flight, Captain Whelan of CENTO (Central Treaty Organization, now defunct). A lacquer-faced, pipe-puffing, grinning man, Whelan was the perfect host. Under the curls of smoke from his meerschaum, he postulated on the ins and outs of doing anything remotely out of the ordinary in Turkey. Basically, he advised, the most effective method was to proceed with an air of purpose and the brisk tone of authority. To ask permis-

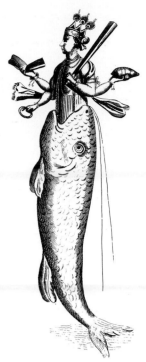

For the Assyrians of the Euphrates and Tigris rivers, the most powerful of gods was Ea, the huge fishgod who lived in the ocean and the rivers. The cyclical rising and falling of the river's flow, and the harnessing of the river for irrigation and civilization, were identified with the beneficent Ea. Other gods were less helpful: the Demon of the Southwest Wind, who brought the antagonistic breath of the desert across the land, was represented by a terrifying winged likeness.

O thou River who didst create all things,
When the great gods dug thee out,
They set prosperity upon thy banks,
Within thee Ea, the King of the Deep, created his dwelling. . . .
Thou judgest the cause of mankind!
O River, thou are mighty!
O River, thou are supreme!
O River, thou art righteous!
Early cuneiform inscription, c. 2100 B.C.

47

OPPOSITE Instant photographs are a quick invitation to friendship with curious youths (top, Richard Bangs; bottom, Skip Horner).

sion was to ask an official to be answerable, something few Turks would consider.

With those words in mind we made our way to the Ministry of Tourism. An assistant general director, Mehmet Korgan, a solemn man with staccato speech that included no English, held court. Nuri and he chattered along over tea; then Nuri turned to us and translated: the Ministry of the Interior had denied us permission even to travel in the East (though Tom was already there), citing student riots, political demonstrations, bandits, and angry Kurds receiving Soviet support as causes for aborting our rafting plans. The good news was that the lost raft had been found and was waiting at the airport. It seemed the inversion of being up the creek without a paddle.

Despite the setback, we still hoped to make our journey with or without official sanction. That night the mood picked up as one of Whelan's co-workers, Victor O. Dewey, joined the group at the Officer's Club over an American meal in the college-style cafeteria. Victor, a longtime veteran of Turkish ways, knew how to sidestep the rules. He had hiked solo through the frontier border area of Iran and Turkey, no small feat. He wanted to join the expedition, and by dessert he was a bona fide member.

■ ■ ■

That evening Tom called in to report on his bus-ride reconnaissance. The chief tributary of the Euphrates, the Marat Su, was not acceptable: its unexciting flow was through barren, unsightly terrain. However, the main Euphrates below Keban Dam looked fantastic, the size and configuration of the Colorado through the Grand Canyon. It was too challenging to handle without a crack crew, so he strongly urged the attempt be postponed until the arrival of Slade and Yost, who were not due for another ten days. Fine, but how to spend the interim?

After a moment's thought, Victor suggested trying a trip on the Çoruh River, in the far northeast corner of the country, as a warmup. The river tears through the Kara Deniz (or Black Sea mountains), then crosses into Russia where it finally flushes into the Black Sea. According to *Fodor's Guide to Turkey*, the Çoruh's scenery "is enough to bring the most blasé to a halt, with forests, peaks, and precipices unlike anything you've ever seen before. It would be idle to attempt to describe the beautiful Çoruh basin,

the gorges, the peaks. . . ." Laying out the maps and pouring over the contours, we determined that the gradient looked feasible, about the same as the Middle Fork of the Salmon in Idaho. The consensus was to give it a try.

So our party, enlarged to include Victor and Nuri, boarded the next flight to Erzurum, formerly Theodosiopolis, on a chilly plateau in the Northeast, not far from Mount Ararat. There the group reunited with *kardesh* (brother) Tom, a few pounds lighter for the brutal bus trip, and less a camera, stolen from his seat during a snooze.

Erzurum is packed with traditionally fez-topped, white-whiskered men and fully wrapped women walking noisy, narrow streets at the foot of snow-creamed mountains. A horse cart was hired to take the group to Erzurum University to find Alan Spencer Hindle, a professor of English who Victor thought might know something of the Euphrates and Çoruh rivers. The septuagenarian Hindle had been teaching in Turkey for sixteen years, was fluent in thirteen languages, yet was as deaf as a post. Delighted by our visit, he sputtered and spouted impressive classical literary quotes. However, he finally admitted he knew nothing of the rivers save what he had read in *Fodor's*. Bidding us goodby, he waved and spoke in his loud voice: "Good luck. And do not come to a classical end on a classical river."

The next morning, Saturday, June 3, the group hired a minibus to take us north to Bayburt, the projected put-in on the Çoruh. It was a long, hot ride over high passes with a single stop for tea and pudding at Cop Dagi, the 8,000-foot crest that marks the beginning of the country's greatest watershed. Dead Sea hawks and black-and-white kekliks soared above; streams weaved and funneled into rivers below. In another hour the group reached the Çoruh, a gaunt, cold flow, surrounded by the 10,000-foot snow-touched peaks of the Kara Deniz. This coastal march of mountains separates the dry steppes of the South from the rain forests of the wet northern side. Old Roman roadbeds and irrigation aqueducts wind along the water's edge; mallards, storks, herons, and egrets stalk the banks.

After a few paddling lessons for tyros Nuri and Vic Dewey in the quiet water of a back-eddy, our five-person team was ready to head downstream into the

48

unknown. It was a quiet launching; no fanfare, no whoops of delight. The current pulled the raft sideways as we fumbled to coordinate our initial strokes. After a few riffles, we attained a semblance of proficiency as our paddles dug deeper into the Çoruh. The river rolled softly past stark landscapes and uninterrupted vistas and brought us to a campsite on a poplar-covered peninsula. We celebrated our first camp in Turkey with Scotch and Courvoisier, as the night poured in over distant cliffs. It was a land thick with history, and in the shadows of night we imagined the Seljuk warriors who marauded this valley in the eleventh century, expanding an empire that at its height ruled the whole of Asia Minor.

This tribe of Turkmen invaded western Asia from the region known today as Kazakh, north of Iran and Afghanistan. They took their lead from a chief named Seljuq, who had led his nomadic people toward the south, where they embraced Islam and became a warrior force for hire. A century later Seljuq's grandson Toghril Beg took off for the west to conquer new territories. The result was an empire that, at his death in 1063, swept across the Middle East from the borders of India to the Mediterranean and included much of Persia, Mesopotamia, and Palestine. It was one of the first cohesive Islamic empires, and provided a stable base for the reestablishment of Persian cultural autonomy. Eventually it gave way to encroachments from the Crusades and the developing Byzantine Empire of the twelfth century and was reduced to the area of Anatolia, which is now eastern Turkey. The many remote fortresses of the Seljuks have been long abandoned, but modern Turkey is one remnant of their empire.

The next day more character crept into the canyon as the raft purled downstream. Willows, Russian olives, red poppies, lupines, yellow daisies, and tamarisk colored the banks. Flocks of ankaz, red-breasted geese, that migrate from the Arctic, wheeled overhead. The water was fast, minced with small rapids; the weather, wet and cold. Villages passed by that didn't appear on the map, and a silent concern was at last expressed. Since the river spills into Russia, without a timely take-out the expedition might do the same, possibly with disastrous results. It was, after all, not far from here that Gary Powers flew his infamous U-2 mission across the Turkish border and was shot down. Vic Dewey claimed he knew of several officers who had strayed across the border, never to return; and he himself had prepared for that error by carrying two passports—one military (his true one) and a civilian document (a fake).

The river flowed past cattle, water buffalo, sheep, and gaily dressed Black Sea children with almond eyes who stood amid lush gardens. Finally we floated past a village we could find on the map, Milehi. We camped shortly thereafter, beneath an eroded clay promontory lined with conifers. The beach was covered with bear tracks. The Çoruh spins its course through Turkey's most gnarled, rough-hewn mountains, the most thinly populated region of the country, with just thirteen people per square mile: a true wilderness, where wildlife still roams free.

The common American image of Turkey includes camels, sand dunes, vast expanses of desert—the makeup of much of the Middle East. And indeed Turkey possesses such country. But it also holds part of the belt of young mountain ranges that runs from

OPPOSITE, CLOCKWISE FROM TOP
A time-worn bridge across the Çoruh (Skip Horner).
A farmer's best friend in a Çoruh village (Skip Horner).
Commodious ferry crosses the Euphrates (Richard Bangs).

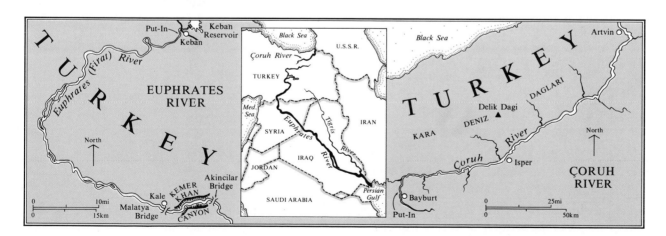

51

the Balkan Peninsula to Iran. The mean altitude of the eastern half of the country is over 6,500 feet, one of the highest of any country in the world. Lofty mountains are interspersed with depressions, surrounded by steep slopes and high plateaus. In the whole of Turkey just 9 percent of its land is level or gently sloping. The country acquired its rugged relief in relatively recent geological times and is still a very active region of the earth's crust, as evidenced by the devastating earthquake that hit Erzurum in 1983.

The next morning mizzled with icy rain, and the ponchoed crew paddled downstream with the movements of rusted soldiers, singing songs to keep spirits afloat. Then an extraordinary sight presented itself: a huge, buff-colored castle, pointing to the clouds, perched on a crag overlooking a gray-brown village. It was a fairy-tale vision, so entrancing that nobody noticed the quick acceleration of the current.

"My God, look!" Tom screamed. Immediately downstream the river went berserk, kicking brown water skyward in chaotic spasms. Frantically we dug our paddles deep, pointing the bow for shore, and made a brink-of-disaster landing at the feet of a cluster of wide-eyed Turkish boys. Behind them loomed the village of Isper.

In the muddy streets beneath the ancient Seljuk fortification was a living tableau torn from the Crusades: veiled women padding past crowded, smoke-clouded coffee houses, where the men feverishly pitched *tavla* (backgammon) dice between swigs of tea. A village elder greeted us; we were the first outsiders to visit Isper in over ten years, and certainly the first ever to arrive by water.

Nuri, who had been coaxed into wearing shorts while on the river, was embarrassed to walk through town in such a patently un-Turkish style. His fellow nationals would never understand, so deeply were they entrenched in a tradition of modesty. Yet his trousers were packed away, unreachable without a major effort. So Nurettin Suleymanfil became Norman Sullivan for the duration of the visit to Isper. As the townsfolk, none of whom spoke English, rambled on in Turkish about the odd arrival of the rafters, Nuri shot back the same uncomprehending looks as the Americans. Finally, one Isperian offered a few halting words in German, which Nuri also spoke; and the communication barrier was broken,

though the ruse continued. Accommodations were taken at the finest hotel in town, a ramble of ten-foot-by-fourteen-foot suites heavily perfumed with uric acid mixed with centuries of unidentifiable fragrances, all for $1.30 per double. Once checked in, we decided to explore the twelfth-century castle.

Burrowed from granite and fortified with limestone walls, the castle was a well-planned fortress, protected from the north by a river too wild to cross, from the south by the town itself. Lookouts could easily detect intruders from the east and west.

As the group poked in the crumbled chambers and turrets a mob of children milled around, swallowing the visitors in curiosity. As handshakes and smiles were exchanged in the rubble, a *muezzin* climbed up the highest castle tower, which flew the red crescent Turkish flag, and called the *Adhan* (prayer): "God is great, I bear witness that there is no god but Allah. I bear witness that Muhammed is His Prophet to prayer. Come to salvation. God is great! There is no god but Allah."

This monotheistic ritual has been performed before dawn, at noon, in midafternoon, at sunset, and at night for 1,400 years. Prayer is the second of the Five Pillars of the Islamic faith. Believers are obliged to practice five formal prayers each day, turning toward Mecca, reciting and genuflecting in the prescribed manner. And here, in the frontier at Isper, all are true believers.

After the prayer call a veiled woman appeared and motioned in invitation toward her home. She led us proudly to a backroom, where two very young girls—teenagers at best, wan from lack of sun—sat weaving a nine-foot-by-twelve-foot silk rug. Fingers flew as they tied endless knots, using homemade vegetable-dyed yarn, following a pattern on scale cards. It takes two years to finish such a rug, which fetches about $300 per yard, a fraction of what the final broker in Istanbul charges the tourist with the American Express card. Perhaps the veiled woman thought we would want to buy the rug, but fine weavings and river rafting don't mix, so we dreamed that night of the beautiful and expensive tapestries being created so near, in these rugged wilds of northern Turkey.

■ ■ ■

Tuesday, June 6, turned out to be a day for Isperians to remember. Shops and schools closed so that the

52

populace could come watch the Americans attempt to navigate what they called The Crazy River, one that had yet to yield survivors. In an atmosphere resembling that of a public hanging, a village patriarch, white with the wisdom of years, attempted to talk the rafting team out of the endeavor. Over 500 villagers crowded the old bridge, and as many or more pressed along the banks for a view.

Then, after an hour of securing gear and triple-tying the duffel, a soldier pushed the lone raft with its five passengers into the current, and into the gut of the rapid. We crashed into a series of mountainous waves, as the raft listed one way, heaved another, broached, churned, and emerged, with a thunder roll of applause, below the bridge in an eddy.

The celebration was brief: the river downstream kicked into overdrive, spitting rapids like machine-gun fire. A crude dirt road ran along the river's high bank, and on it a parade of vehicles—bicycles, vans, trucks, mules—followed the inflatable's progress. Then, as we careened around one corner, a group of ragged Turks began beckoning hysterically. The raft pulled in, and Tom followed the Turks downstream to investigate. There, just fifty yards below the raft's hasty mooring, the river erupted into a geyser, flying skyward then plummeting down a fifteen-foot waterfall. The boulder just above this mess, so the Turks explained, was known as Bride's Rock, named for a young girl who threw herself into the river in an attempt to reach her true love who was stranded on the other side of the then bridgeless Çoruh.

The rapid was unnavigable by any craft. So the raft was lifted out of the river for a portage, a task usually the bane of all boatmen. But here the chore of carrying hundreds of pounds of gear over uneven rocks became light work. Thirty men and boys, wrapped in ragged jodhpurs, hastened to help, hoisting the raft and its accessories to the road and onto a van, completing in fifteen minutes what otherwise would have been an hour's portage.

Downstream the rapids continued, increasing in frequency and magnitude. The canyon grew greener as aromatic cedars began to fill its side gorges. At one point we beached for a lunch beneath a weathered school building, where the schoolmaster, Mehmet Gultekin, urged us to join his table. Though he had never met creatures called Americans before, he was

eager to share his *ekmek* (bread) and tea. We reciprocated with Cheese Whiz and peanut butter, which Mehmet politely sampled, though he had difficulty disguising his displeasure. He spoke no English and looked to Nuri for comprehension, but Nuri was still Norman Sullivan and returned only milky stares.

Farther downstream magnificent vistas appeared as the Çoruh swerved into the shadow of Delik Dagi (Hope Mountain), at 12,175 feet the highest peak in the Kara Deniz chain. Incessant rapids frazzled and fatigued the crew, and camps were called early, often near farms, vineyards, or orchards. At one camp two wrinkled, seam-faced men with high-pitched, grandmotherly voices shuffled from the trees and squatted by the cook fire. One of them, gray-bearded and tattered, looking older than his sixty years, told Nuri that he had never traveled beyond his little farm, except once, to visit Artvin, a town downriver near the Russian border.

"Would you like to come with us downriver?" Micki couldn't resist offering.

"Oh no," the old man replied. "Even though I am very old, I would not trust my life to the Çoruh. It is The Crazy River."

The raft passed rice paddies and groves of maples, oaks, and acacias; the gorge constricted and exhibited its finest stratifications, from anticlines standing on end to angulated unconformities. The earth had done some fancy dancing in northern Turkey and left its footsteps along the Çoruh. Every inch of level ground was cultivated so that we were never more than a few deft strokes from peaches, cherries, peas, and other fresh fruits and vegetables. Gliding past, we would yell the traditional greeting, *Merhaba!* ("Welcome!"), to the astonished farmers, planters, and tillers who had never seen such a sight.

Measuring the water flow by tossing a log into the current and timing its course over a paced distance, Vic read the river speed at seven miles per hour. The Colorado averages four, and the difference was evident in the rapids. Once, after spinning past the village of Tekkale—where another ancient Seljuk castle was incongruously decorated with a television antenna—the raft skidded out of control above a cataract hiking spray high into the air. Where the usual routine was to pull over to shore to scout such disturbances, this time scouting was impossible be-

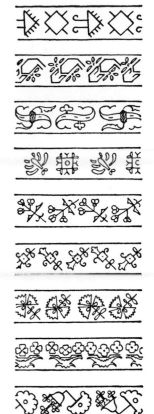

Islamic religion holds that God's creations—especially humans and animals—cannot be duplicated by man. Therefore, one of the principal characteristics of Islamic art is the arabesque, the intertwined geometric and floral figures found in the tapestries and carpets of northern Turkey.

PREVIOUS PAGES Landscape of the Çoruh, south of the Black Sea (Stan Boor).

OPPOSITE, TOP Forgotten monastery of the Byzantine Empire along the Euphrates in Kemer Khan (Richard Bangs). BOTTOM Women wearing the Islamic veil of modesty shake out a locally made rug (Richard Bangs).

cause the raft was sucked down the tongue into the maw of the rapid.

The boat wheeled sideways into a surging wave, pitching Vic over the prow like a pellet from a slingshot and kicking Tom out of the stern into the boiling water. Long seconds of white chaos ensued before the boat and its swimmers drifted into the soft water below. As Vic looked back into the stream that had nearly digested him, a gleaming, pink surface bobbed past. It was a body, human, naked, bloated in death. Like a rolling catfish carcass, it floated silently around the corner. An accident? Burial? Murder? A fisherman? Soldier? Criminal? Or one of the old men who had visited camp earlier, sucked unwillingly into The Crazy River? We glanced at each other nervously and tightened our grip on the line as we hauled the raft to shore.

More rapids, more portages, and more bad weather lay in store on the fifth day on the river as the sky cracked and sent down the Çoruh's equivalent in volume. Tom fell prey to some bug in the river and spent much of the day leaning over the gunwale, begging for euthanasia. Midway through the day, as the raft flushed through a gauntlet of huge compression waves, it climbed to a near capsize, and vaulted Nuri over the edge of his Turkish cool into catalepsy. At the brink of the next rapid, as the crew scouted a route from shore, Nuri still trembled.

"Let's do it." Vic slapped Nuri's back.

"It's too fast . . . we can't." Nuri, in monotone, countered.

"Come on, we've run bigger."

"No. I can't . . . I'm scared."

A powerful admission for a proud Turk. But his words echoed the common sentiment. Everyone was frightened; Nuri's courage in verbalizing what everyone else disguised was all we needed. A canvass was made, and with mixed emotions the decision was made to pull out. Nuri waved down a passing dump truck, and minutes later the crew was trundling on to Artvin, near the Soviet border. The Çoruh flowed on into vivid memory; but the Euphrates lay ahead.

■ ■ ■

Jim Slade and John Yost waited for us in Ankara, and we traded river stories from opposite ends of the world. Then the enlarged crew caught a minibus to the Keban Dam, which backed the largest reservoir in the Middle East. From its base the dam appears haloed by the cloud of mist created by the emerald water that gushes down a 4,200-foot-long concrete spillway at 36,000 cubic feet per second. When the water strikes the curled lip of the artificial sluice, it shoots hundreds of feet into the air in a tremendous waterworks arc, then crashes down in a deafening tumult. After a year of planning and preparation, we stood at last on the banks of the classical river, overwhelmed by the man-made creation that arrests the flow which once ruled men and their civilizations. Just a few bends downstream lay the Kemer Khan, the canyon we had come to run.

Since there was still no official sanction to raft the Euphrates, or even to stand on its banks, this would be another outlaw ride. Gendarmes patrolled the dam, so a discreet put-in just downstream and around a bend was selected, and the rigging of our single raft was undertaken in double time. As the last ropes were being tightened, a jeep rumbled up to the site. A soldier stepped out and strode over to the raft, his face stern with duty. For fifteen minutes Nuri engaged in an animated exchange with the visitor; the air was charged with tension, and everyone feared the worst. Was our great Euphrates descent, a historic first on the river where history began, over before it began?

Then hands stretched, grasped in agreement, and the soldier smiled. Nuri proudly turned to the group, triumph written on his face. "How'd you do it?" was the question on everyone's lips.

"I merely told him ours was a holy mission."

Just past noon the group launched onto the great, green, cold expanse the Turks call the Firat Su, one of the two main forks of the upper Euphrates. The yellow canyon was illustrated with folding whorls and faults; it was hushed save for the wingbeats of raptors, cranes, and storks. It felt like floating through an empty coliseum, layered and deep, reverberative, haunted by the ghosts of conquerors, of soldiers and courtesans, of the peasants and slaves of a dozen empires.

In another way it seemed anticlimactic to be floating down a canyon not so different in look and feel from that of the Colorado, the Blue Nile, or the Snake: another river, another gorge. The course for the first dozen miles was butter smooth: no rapids, no

obstructions. Mesopotamia was quiet. Slade broke out a deck of cards from his ammo box, and a few hands of an ancient game were played on the front thwart—bridge, supposedly named after the Galata Bridge in Istanbul.

At dusk the party pulled into a cobbled beach at a gooseneck bend. As the gear was being unloaded, Tom pointed upstream to an odd sight: two rafts drifting downstream toward camp. This was a curious vision, as we felt certain ours was the only whitewater inflatable within a thousand miles. Yet as the vessels gradually waved into focus, as though emerging from a desert mirage, it became clear that they were indeed inflatables, albeit of a different sort. They were jerry-rigged rafts of tractor-tire inner tubes lashed to planks, piloted by baggy-pantsed farmers. Using poles for propulsion, they slid past camp into the twilight without a sound.

An incongruous noise stirred the group to consciousness the following morning: the grating, chugging sound of a stuck tractor. This particular tractor, a Massey-Ferguson 148, was mired in the middle of the Euphrates—in a streambed barely knee deep. The day before this had been a full-bodied river, running at perhaps 40,000 cubic feet per second. Overnight the mighty Euphrates, river of antiquity, had been reduced to a rivulet, a tiny trickle bubbling fifty feet from where the raft had been moored. The Keban Dam floodgates had been shut down.

There was nothing to do but wait. Occasionally, when water and power demands are slack, the gates of the Glen Canyon Dam above the Grand Canyon will be shut to build up the reservoir; on those occasions, which are relatively rare, boaters downstream have found themselves high and dry without a river to run. Sometimes the wait would be just a few hours; other times, days. So, assuming the worst, the Euphrates crew took the day off. Half the crew decided to relax in camp, reading Homer or Edith Hamilton; the others decided to explore on foot.

Stepping up a bald hillside, we confronted a dried-mud Kurdish village with bleached, flat-topped dwellings, looking much like those of the Pueblo Indians of the American Southwest, even framed by crags, desert mesas, and in the far distance, snow-capped mountains. As Micki led the way into the small village, the heavily veiled women scattered like antelope. In the confusion a dirt-smeared man stepped from a corner onto the parched path running through town and gestured for us to follow. He led us through a black portal into his home: a dark, furnitureless hovel buzzing with flies and children. His name was Aptullah Kanat; his wife was called Imihan. Their five children bustled about, serving up flat bread, salty black olives, and white goat cheese to the visitors, and Imihan rushed to cover Micki's bare legs with a tablecloth.

The village was called Bilal usagi Koyu and appears on no map, though it has probably existed for centuries. Its people are Kurds, seminomadic pastoralists who still exist in modern Turkey as a nation within a nation. The women are pantalooned and veiled, the men ragtagged and tarbooshed, and sometimes slung with the Russian-built AK-47 rifle. If it weren't for the last detail and the occasional tractor, this could have been a visit to a village a thousand years in the past.

Two days were spent waiting in the dry heat for the river to rise. When at last it did, the expedition moved quickly downstream. Within four hours twenty miles were covered, and camp was called at the Kurdish village of Kale, at the entrance to the Kemer Khan Canyon.

There the Malatya Bridge spans the Euphrates, marking one of Turkey's most strategic spots as it allows passage to the eastern frontier and the border with the Soviet Union. Gendarmes swarm over the bridge, ready to thwart any threats, such as river expeditions hoping to pass beneath. We decided to attempt a predawn passage, and after a restless night's sleep pushed into the whispering waters in the grainy half-light of night's end. Quietly, with small, slow paddle strokes, we drifted mum beneath the bridge, eyes cocked upward to the steel girders.

"I think we made it," Slade whispered; then suddenly a uniformed figure strutted to bridge center and began yelling, waving wildly. We erupted into a paddling frenzy, and the raft rocketed around a bend as the frantic calls of an aroused police force faded behind the closing canyon walls.

Now we were in the Kemer Khan, the Grand Canyon of the Euphrates. Through this tortuous passage the river cuts its most daunting course, scything around a lava mass erupted from the Ka-

58

racali Volcano and stabbing across the anticlines of the Tarus Mountains. Here, too, are the river's most imposing rapids. Lulled by days of flat water, we were taken by surprise when the raft was tossed and slapped by a pair of rolling rapids.

Beyond the steep ochre canyon, snow-spotted mountains pricked at the horizon. It is an area rich in ruins, including evidence of man's earliest hominid ancestors. Not far away, near the village of Pasalar, the most complete record of man's ancestors outside of Africa has been unearthed, some 130 specimens of 12- to 13-million-year-old primates.

The people who live there now have a different story to tell. At the occasional tributary mouth Kurdish women were fetching water in long-necked clay jugs. The river was whirling into the heart of Kurdistan, the officially unrecognized region ruled by a militant faction hoping to break from both Turkey and Iran and establish an autonomous state. Their violent reputation notwithstanding, the worst outbreak we encountered was a clutch of children who tossed pebbles at the passing raft. Their gun-toting fathers never threw more than a few *Salaam Aleikums* ("Peace be with you") and *Merhabas* our way.

Late on the sixth day the raft slid into a limestone gorge pocked with shallow caves. High on the west bank, fitting into a limestone alcove, sat a remarkable sight: a masterfully constructed, abandoned Byzantine monastery, proud but paling. There, hidden on the banks of the Euphrates, stood a 1,500-year-old wonder with no written history. Honeycombed with dank passageways, festooned with swallows' nests, graced with Roman arched doors, and filled with bats, the place whispered softly of intrigues, romances, and activities long past. At the entrance to a high-domed chapel, Persian characters spelled an unknown message; in a small inner chamber a Maltese cross graced an altar. History seemed to seep from the masonry like vapor. The find seemed as though it must be significant, but it was like striking oil while stranded on a desert isle; nothing could be done with the discovery, at least at that place and time.

A bit farther downstream the limestone walls gave way to harder basalt, then to even harder schist. The raft rounded a bend to find not rapids, but tractors high above the river, moving in a slow rumble along the south wall. A diversion tunnel had been drilled through the rock near river level in the north wall. Workers were everywhere, busy at a sad task: the beginning of the Kemer Khan Dam, a project that would flood the entire stretch we had just floated. Ours was probably the first group to ever float that exquisite stretch of river, and it might well be the last. Within the decade the canyon, millions of years in the making, with its secrets and unwritten histories, would be buried beneath a reservoir: like Glen Canyon, another "place no one knew" lost to civilization, in the very region that gave birth to such.

A day later the river broke from the canyon, curled off the Adiyaman Plateau, and began its long, sluggish trek though the Syrian Trench to the sea. Spinning around a low-banked corner, a glint of steel shot over the stream before us: the Akincilar Bridge spanned the ancient flow, leading to the ancient Roman town of Malatya, then on to Ankara and Istanbul. This was the take-out for our expedition, which had just passed through time and the river flowing . . . but only for another click of a second in the clock of its long existence. The Euphrates—whose waters irrigated the first fields and anointed the first kings—was just another river to be arrested and choked, a slave of the people it once fed and slaked, bathed and buried.

Indus

CHAPTER FOUR INDUS *River of the Lion's Roar*

AT THE FOOT of Mount Kailas, a symmetrical mountain of quartz and ice in the high plateau of western Tibet, lies a lake holy to both Buddhist and Hindus. Lake Manasarowar, the Tibetans believe, is the source of the four main rivers of Asia, which flow to the four directions of the traditional universe. Kailas, the Precious Ice Mountain, is at the core of this universe and, to the Hindus, is the earthly paradise of Siva, the Destroyer. Some claim that the ancients dwell in a castle on the bed of the Manasarowar or that Siva, his consort, and attendants swim on the lake in the form of swans.

To reach this holy land, Hindu and Buddhist pilgrims come from all directions, bearing the ashes of their relatives, which they will scatter on the lake, or bringing jars in which to take home some holy water. They follow a traditional route around Kailas and Manasarowar, from east to west, stopping to pray at the many temples, monasteries, cairns, and shrines along the gutted path. Monks and pilgrims, many from sea-level communities and oppressed by the altitude, prostrate themselves in prayer, scratch a mark at arm's length on the ground, rise and advance to the mark, then lie down in prayer once more. It is twenty-five miles around the mountain, twice that around the lake. To make the complete circuit of Mount Kailas 108 times ensures eternal bliss, and to bathe in Lake Manasarowar earns forgiveness for all sins, future and past.

This place is the holiest in all Tibet; from it is derived the Tibetan mandala of *dharmadhatu*, the wheel of wisdom. Although modern geographers know that the four major rivers of Asia that originate in the high Tibetan plateau do not, in fact, have a common source in Lake Manasarowar, the belief that they do persists as a symbolic image of the unity of creation. In its many representations in the ancient art of Tibetan Buddhism, Kailas and its lake are at the center of the mandala, with the four rivers running to the four points of the compass from the mouths of sacred animals, symbolic of the thrones of the Buddha, different aspects of consciousness, different colors, and different directions—a whole constellation of associations at the root of the belief system. The Brahmaputra flows out of the mouth of the Horse, representative of Earth, or the wisdom of equality; the Ganges emerges from the Peacock's mouth, signifying Fire, or the discriminating consciousness; the Sutlej springs from the gaping mouth of the Elephant, the traditional symbol of Water, with its mirrorlike awareness; and the Indus roars from the jaws of the Lion, the beast of Ether, the source of wisdom itself. This is the story of the Lion River.

As it leaves Tibet and the rarefied realm where belief overpowers geographical fact, the Indus slices like the blade of a sickle between the Himalayas and the Karakoram, passing into India in the region known as Little Tibet, Ladakh. There it is joined by tributaries from the top of the world, gathering force as it drops 12,000 feet in 350 miles, crossing the northern provinces of India into Pakistan and joining with the Gilgit from the north. The redoubled flow twists through deep canyons to the base of Nanga Parbat, the world's eighth highest peak; then the Lion finally breaks free of its mountain domain and winds and wanders across the plains of Pakistan, across the Sindh desert, finally depositing its load of silt and glacial dust into the Arabian Sea from its broad delta near Karachi.

Cutting through Tibet, India, and Pakistan, slaking the thirst of three major religions—Buddhist, Hindu, and Islam—the Lion River has also tempted the explorer's hunger with its promised feast of firsts. More than thirty mountaineers have died on the slopes of Nanga Parbat, the 26,660-foot peak that marks the Indus's midpoint. The peak has been draped like a coffin with the sobriquet The Killer Mountain. And the currents of the Indus itself have carried at least one river runner to the farthest shore.

Early in July 1956 a strange crew converged on the banks of the Indus some thirty miles north of Skardu

PREVIOUS PAGE A narrow bridge spans the upper reaches of the Indus in its mountain canyons (Jim Slade).

OPPOSITE A watchful eye from an Islamic building in Rawalpindi, Pakistan (Richard Bangs).

63

OPPOSITE, TOP Village men of Gol watch Americans, foreground, prepare for a river trip (Jack Morison). BOTTOM Artistic urges explode on a truck used for river-trip transport (Jack Morison).

in the contested Baltistan region, claimed by both Pakistan and India since partition in 1947. One was Lowell Thomas, the journalist and broadcaster; he was with several of his skiing buddies—two actors and television director Otto Lang. Their reason for being there was a new film technology called Cinerama, which they hoped to boost with a full-length drama, showcasing its best qualities. A short Cinerama production, a roller-coaster ride, had already created quite a stir among audiences who viewed its huge, wrap-around screen and the lifelike resolution made possible by its three-lens camera system. Thomas's planned film, *Search for Paradise*, was to be about two newly retired air force pilots who search the top of the world for a personal Shangri-La, only to return to the States when they discover at last that "there's no place like home." The thin plot was an excuse to film some of the most extraordinary scenery on the planet, including a rousing finish with the first-ever raft trip down the Indus.

To run the two inflatable boats for the film, Thomas enlisted the father-son team of Bus and Don Hatch, experts in the whitewater rivers of the western United States. Bus, at fifty-six, was something of a pioneer in river running, having taken commercial passengers floating as far back as 1929, and having made a number of historic first descents in Utah, Colorado, and Idaho. His twenty-seven-year-old son was brought up in the family tradition, and it was said that he could row before he could walk. They were probably the best river rats around at the time; even so, nothing had prepared them for the power and the treachery of the Indus.

They brought with them two rafts: a twenty-seven-foot pontoon bridge of the type used on the Colorado, controlled by two Johnson outboard motors mounted on a rear transom, complemented by three sets of oars; and a small assault raft, sixteen feet long, manned by a single oarsman. Their first run was a trial, without cameras; Otto Lang, the Hatches, and a crew of four put on the Indus some thirty miles above Skardu and immediately were swept away by the powerful current. The Indus was running close to its peak, nearly 100,000 cubic feet per second; haystack waves towered as high as the pontoon raft was long. After covering thirty miles in four hours, including an enormous rapid squeezed deep between the walls of the gorge where a portage was impossible, the crew drifted into Skardu, the first to raft any portion of the Lion River.

The thrills notwithstanding, Lang and his crew unanimously decided that this stretch was too violent and unmanageable to risk the project's expensive equipment for extended shooting. The operation was moved to the Gilgit River, a major tributary that comes in from the north some 100 miles downstream of Skardu. A comparatively gentle run, with just a fraction of the volume of the Indus, the Gilgit also afforded views of Nanga Parbat wheeling in the background of some on-river shots.

For several days the crew negotiated the Gilgit without mishap, encountering heavy but runnable (and filmable) rapids. The only problems were from the monsoon weather's clouds, squalls, sandstorms, and flash floods. The Gilgit met with the Indus, and the filming drew to a close on July 20. On the final run before wrapping up the production, Jimmy Parker—

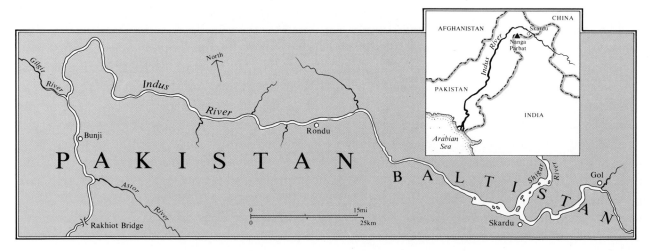

one of Lowell Thomas's friends, playing a pilot in the picture—decided to try the raft for the first time. There were only seven lifejackets on the expedition; Jimmy was the eighth person on the water that day.

They pushed off and almost at once came to the first rapid. Don Hatch led the way in the small assault boat, sliding down the tongue and riding into the standing waves of the turbulence below. As the pontoon followed, one of its outboard motors died. Bus couldn't get it started again and lost control as the huge raft slid sideways into a hidden hole. The craft was tossed up and over, capsizing ninety seconds after leaving shore.

Six swimmers struggled to shore through the mad glacial waters; Don Hatch rowed to an outcrop in the smaller raft, having barely taken in any water. The eighth man was missing. The soaked crew ran along the edge of the surging river yelling, searching, looking. A reward of 1,000 rupees was posted for any trace of the lost rafter. It was never collected. Jimmy Parker's body was lost forever in a region some have called paradise.

At the foot of Nanga Parbat, the Rakhiot Bridge crosses the Indus. Carved into one of its stone columns were the names of thirty-one climbers who had lost their lives trying to conquer The Killer Mountain. Now the traveler crossing the bridge finds not only the names of climbers, but that of Jimmy Parker, first rafting victim of the Indus.

■ ■ ■

I began working for Hatch River Expeditions as a river guide on the Colorado in 1969. I was nineteen. Bus Hatch had died a couple years earlier, and now Don and Ted, his two sons, ran the business. Sometimes late at night, with campfire shadows dancing on the canyon wall, talk would turn to Don's Indus expedition. None of the guides knew the full story, just tidbits dropped by Don at the office, the bar, or the put-in. He didn't talk much about it, but enough for the stuff of a legend. "I'd give my right oar to row the Indus," a guide once told me. And whenever I'd screw up in a rapid, break a frame, wash a passenger overboard, or simply scare myself with a close call, I'd think of the Indus. This is nothing, I'd say to myself. Don ran the Indus—ten times the size of the Colorado, three times the speed, and cold as winter.

Ten years later I found myself in Skardu with nine

companions, ready to retrace Lowell Thomas's expedition and to do what he had not done: connect the line between Skardu and the Gilgit confluence by rafting the Indus. (RB)

It was the second day of October 1979. Rich Bangs was joined in Skardu by a hand-picked crew from Sobek Expeditions, a group with the experience and enthusiasm necessary to tackle the Indus: Jim Slade, one of Sobek's top guides, veteran of a dozen first descents worldwide, including a run the previous year down the Zaskar River in Ladakh, a high-country tributary of the Indus; John Yost, Sobek's vice president, who had been with the company from the beginning; and John Kramer, another former Grand Canyon boatman who had graduated to the wild rivers of Ethiopia and Alaska. There were also two women aboard—Joy Ungricht, one of the top river guides in Utah and Arizona and an avid off-season skier; and Helen Clyatt, an M.D. whose practice was with the National Park Service in Yosemite.

The crew was rounded out by writer Mitchell Shields and photographer Nick Nichols, on assignment from the splashy new West German magazine, *GEO*; Jim Slade's brother Dave, a Boston lawyer; and Captain Sohail Iqbal of the Pakistan army, on assignment as chaperon in this politically delicate region. The Indians held that their border extended north to the Hindu Kush range; the Pakistanis felt this northwest frontier was theirs.

After the spectacular plane flight from Rawalpindi to Skardu, the crew was met by a landscape wild beyond their expectations. The Indus Valley at Skardu is fantastic, in the literal sense of the word. A great oval basin, 7,500 feet above sea level, some twenty miles long and eight miles wide, it is enclosed by mountain ridges and peaks that soar up to 17,000 feet. The air is thin and sharp, and the details of shapes and colors, even at long distances, show brilliantly clear. The valley is carpeted in fine pale sand, gray as tarnished silver, patched occasionally with ochre, lemon, and purple. In the middle distance, across the broad valley, the Indus snakes lazily between wind-ribbed dunes. Over millions of years the river has progressively cut its way into the rock, and the cliffs that now wall the valley are ledged and terraced at different heights by the old beds of the river. Farther back, the dry and bony mountains rise

OPPOSITE Askandria Fort above Skardu, an outpost over four hundred years old (John Kramer)

The four-faced, four-armed Brahma is one of the three most important gods of Hinduism, with Vishnu and Shiva. Known as the lotus-born and the first-born, he is described as the grandfather of gods and men. The four faces represent the Vedas, chief scriptures of the Hindus.

OPPOSITE, CLOCKWISE FROM TOP Taking goods to market (Ann Pierce). Men of Skardu pose while women remain all but unseen (John Kramer). A porter rests with his load of yak droppings—fuel for the fire (Jim Slade). Young merchants in a Pakistani marketplace (Jim Slade).

to their saw-toothed crests, intricately folded and overlapping. At the two ends of the basin, where they converge, it seems impossible that even a great and ancient river could force a passage through them.

It was a landscape that could have been created only by earth forces at their most powerful, and the entire welt of mountains that defines the North of India—the great Himalayas—is indeed the product of a phenomenal series of events. It dates back to Gondwanaland, the semimythical "first continent," whose outlines were long discernible only to the imaginative who perceived in Africa's west coast and South America's east a near fit. Imagination gave rise to investigation, and investigation showed odd parallels between the rock, the history of the land, even the life forms on these opposite shores.

With the modern theory of plate tectonics, this impossible theory has been confirmed: most of the land masses on earth were once joined in a solid hunk of matter, floating on a primordial sea. Over the eons Gondwanaland has been split and its pieces borne away along the convection currents of the molten mantle, separating into today's continents. The Himalayas have been created—are still being created, in fact, as the earth movements continue in our lifetime—by the collision of the Central Asian plate with the Indian plate, which was once tucked against the east coast of Africa. Along the front of collision, the crust has uplifted and folded and thrust and folded again into a mountain range over 1,500 miles long and, at its roof, 5 miles high.

An ancient camel trail runs from Skardu to Gol, where the Hatch party had begun its first descent; a police jeep escorted the Sobek group up the winding road to the put-in. Precipitous cliffs of somber rock, ancient metamorphic seabeds, and long-frozen lava towered over the milky flow of the river, and over the eight men and two women who had come to challenge it.

In the shadows we unloaded the two Avon rafts that would be home, hospital, diner, and means of conveyance for the next three weeks. I slipped down to the river's edge and dipped my hand in the dark water, as Don Hatch had done on his arrival. It stung with the cold, though the air temperature was in the eighties. Captain Sohail Iqbal, our liaison officer, had recounted that local lore told of a bare-headed man who

had once stretched his legs into the water after a long overland trek and had fallen asleep in the sun. When he awoke, he found that he was suffering from both heatstroke and frostbite simultaneously.

Since it was October, the water was at a medium-low level and dropping, whereas Hatch and crew had arrived at the river's peak flow in July. We estimated the flow to be about 20,000 cubic feet per second, not unlike the summer flow of the Colorado. Beneath a wall of pictographs, depicting ibex and Buddhist temples, we made camp. I drifted into sleep with the Indus softly calling at my feet. (RB)

Wednesday, October 3, dawned diamond clear. The boats were rigged, loaded, and launched with little fanfare beneath the curious, silent gaze of a score of the Islamic villagers—all men and boys. Almost at once the judgment of Don Hatch that the Indus was a river of deception rang true: Jim Slade steered the lead raft into what appeared to be a moderate rapid, but the raft and crew members were grabbed by a hidden hole and shaken like ice in a martini mixer before being released. The Lion River had growled its warning.

Slowly rowing through the big waves and threatening hydraulics of the rapids, the party made its way down the gorge toward the huge cataract above Skardu, at which point the Hatch party had been persuaded to move filming to a less dangerous tributary. With the lower water it didn't look like the monster Hatch had described, and Rich made the first run, sneaking down the left side, bumping between exposed boulders that would have been the dangerous heads of holes at higher water. Slade's run also was clean, and the group, reassured by success, set up camp just downstream.

That evening a villager came floating down the river, on a craft more easily portaged around the big drops of the canyon. His was fashioned from six inflated goatskins, tied together with legs upright and supported by a framework of sticks. Using a pole rather than oars, he carried a cargo of fruits and vegetables downstream to the market at Skardu. The goatskins leaked, but to reinflate a sagging portion of his craft, he merely blew down the upright legs. After we traded rides on the two far-distant generations of inflatables, he floated off into the sunset toward Skardu.

Hindu girl.

68

The next morning the party entered into the natural amphitheater of Skardu and passed the first major tributary along the route, the Shigar River, which drains the Chogo Lungma and Biafo Gyang glaciers to the north. The Shigar increased the flow of the Indus by a third, and the current sped past Skardu to the second night's camp at the Askandria Fort. Its origins are lost in history, but it is at least four centuries old; some say it is even older, dating from the time of Alexander the Great, whose easternmost thrust brought him to this region in the fourth century B.C. Standing on a narrow mesa 1,000 feet above the Indus, the fort overlooks the entire Skardu basin and has afforded an enviable security and inviolable sanctuary for its occupants—whether rajas, Sikhs, or Moslems, during the conflicts between India and Pakistan in just the past few decades.

The Askandria Fort has a long, narrow, spiral staircase leading to its entrance, which in the past was effectively protected by a wooden door covered with sharp metal spikes pointed at the approaching intruder. Now the fort was abandoned, so a handful of the rafters moved in for the night, taking photographs under the full moon and imagining a time when Skardu afforded protection against invasion from any direction. The enemies of the past were invisible that night, but the following day the untested waters of the Indus below Skardu would provide us with a different kind of conflict.

■ ■ ■

At daylight we left the sanctuary of Skardu's valley and rode the current downstream into the gorge. At first the rapids were runnable, though enormous in power and complex in design. Making technical cuts and turns in rapids was nothing new to our experienced crew, but rarely had the water level been near the 35,000 cubic feet per second we were now experiencing. By the start of the second day in the gorge, life got hard.

The rapids became littered with huge boulders, which the water twisted off, over, and around to create enormous hydraulics; some of these were dangerous holes, which could not be run without the very real possibility of disaster. Portaging was the only course; for the more experienced of the crew, it was an anticipated adjunct to the adventure. But for the newcomers to river running, it was a depressing tug

on the leash by reality's grim hand. Mitchell Shields wrote of the experience in his *GEO* article.

I found that day that the agony in a river trip is the portaging, being forced to bypass a rapid on foot. Fighting whitewater is one thing. It at least has the cachet of adventure. Climbing raggedly uneven hills saddled with food, tents, clothing, packs, sleeping bags, pots, pans, paddles, oars, lifejackets and dual sixteen-foot rubber rafts is something else entirely. I hated it.

The first portage was bearable. I could even endure the second, which came a quarter mile later. But the third, which started barely 500 yards after we'd put back into the water, left me tired and disgusted. The next day was even worse. Morning and evening ground down into the monotony of more portages. From shore to shore I saw nothing but slashing waves, nothing but impassable rapids. From ten miles a day, our pace had dropped to less than two—most of that on foot. Or on what feet we had left. John Yost and John Kramer had already suffered broken toes.

And the pattern continued. The river was dropping 100 feet per mile through this section, and as portage followed portage, morale dropped with the elevation. First the trip doctor, Helen Clyatt, found herself sapped of energy and unable to hold food; then photographer Nichols matched her symptoms. Jim Slade's mood was rapidly deteriorating, and he was the first to hint that if things didn't get better, and fast, he would rather walk out. Meanwhile the local residents of the isolated gorge, who would sometimes gather by the hundreds, watched passively the labors of portaging. They rarely made a sound or displayed a hint of emotion or judgment; and although a few of them helped with the portages, most simply stared.

Finally a labyrinthine rapid broke the river's course—it was a mess, defined by a series of rock columns and right-angle turns; but somehow it looked feasible, and everyone desperately wanted to avoid another portage. With Kramer at the oars and Bangs, Yost, and Shields riding the bow, armed with a paddle each to help with the tight turns, the first raft made its entrance.

They made the drop down the tongue exactly as planned, but at once something went wrong. The boat was captured by two recirculating crosscurrents, and it bounced in the turbulence like a Ping-Pong ball

OPPOSITE The three religions of the Indus. CLOCKWISE FROM TOP A Ladakhi Buddhist near the Zaskar River, one of the Indus's tributaries (Jim Slade). Hindu schoolboys near Skardu (Jim Slade). Islamic man (Jack Morison).

71

OPPOSITE, TOP Lamayuru Monastery in Ladakh, a region known as Little Tibet (Bob Whitney). BOTTOM Barefoot traders on the road in the Himalayas (Jim Slade).

in a pot of boiling water. The riders in the bow threw their weight from side to side and dug into the aerated water with their paddles, desperately trying to force the boat out of the hydraulic, while Kramer strained at the oars to no avail. The raft slowly filled up with water in the melee, so much so that Kramer, standing in the bilge, had water swirling around his chest. Finally the powerful current washed the boat up against a midriver boulder, and the crew leapt to the slippery top of the rock. Slade, on shore, slung a 100-foot rescue line out to the rock; and when it was attached to the bow of the raft, the crew on shore was able to pull the raft off the rock and toward the current. As it was freed, the crew leapt into the passing boat—out of the frying pan, into the fire.

Still brimming with water, the raft barreled out of control through the rapid and headed downstream at a frightening speed. Grabbing the buckets, Yost and Bangs bailed like madmen; Mitchell Shields used his hat, while Kramer rowed and kicked water out with his feet at the same time. Another rapid lay downstream, hurling spray into the sky and roaring thunderously as the raft approached closer and closer. Kramer's most powerful strokes were of little effect on the swamped, ton-heavy boat; and 200 yards upriver of the rapid, with the boat still midstream and out of control, John Yost acted.

Leaping from the raft with bowline in hand, he swam for the crew on the left bank, hoping to salvage the raft before the big drop ahead. The only problem was that his dive had the effect of pushing the raft toward the right bank: at last the raft was moving toward shore, the opposite one toward which Yost was frantically swimming. Hearing warning screams behind him, Yost looked over his shoulder, saw what was happening, dropped the bow-line, and swam for his life. Both the raft and Yost made it to shore—on opposite sides of the river—at the lip of the rapid. Witnesses to this drama, Slade and the crew of the second raft decided to portage.

For the next few days the pattern alternated between grueling, body-beating portages and thrilling rapids of huge standing waves, with just enough of the latter to keep spirits alive. Then one afternoon loud rumblings rolled out of the distance at dusk. Avalanches? Glaciers groaning? A renewal of the Pakistan-India border conflicts over this region?

The next morning the small flotilla ran into the source of the noise: a Pakistani army road crew, blasting cliffs 400 feet above the northern bank of the Indus in an effort to construct an all-weather highway connecting Skardu and Gilgit to Rawalpindi. Some 10,000 troops were involved in this massive task, evidently motivated by the necessity of securing Pakistan's claim to this isolated region. The road's route was along a sheer rock cliff plagued with landslides, and one officer told Iqbal that two men were lost for every kilometer of progress. He agreed to hold up blasting for four days, to allow the party to pass beneath the area of blasting, but warned that he would start up again on schedule, regardless.

For four madcap days we unloaded the rafts, enlisted jeeps to take equipment to a downstream campsite, portaged as few rapids as possible, and ran others we could attempt only with the lighter boats. On the fifth day, as the expedition was fully loaded and on the river again, a peal of thunder split the air. An entire cliffside was blown across the river just upstream; dust billowed hundreds of feet into the air, and rock shrapnel sprayed the river like machine-gun fire just a hundred yards away. It was like rafting through a war zone.

■ ■ ■

Day followed day in the fantastic, yet finally oppressive, confines of the gorge. After almost two weeks on the river, the pattern of two portages for every rapid run was still unchanged. On the twelfth day another tortuous stretch of whitewater was confronted: a maze of boulders ringing the river like ramparts, followed by a twenty-foot falls, with razor-backed rocks at its base. After the portage of the first raft—a near debacle during which the bag containing the paddles was washed overboard in the confusion and lost—we all took a much-needed break and lunched on mutton and goat cheese. John Kramer didn't join in, however. He spent the repast staring at the rapid. When it came time to portage the second boat, Kramer made an announcement. "I don't want to jeopardize the expedition, but I'd like to try running this rapid. I think I can do it . . . alone."

Looks of surprise were exchanged, but no one protested. Nobody wanted to portage if they didn't have to.

"I'm worried about you," Helen finally spoke up.

Tibetan Buddhist prayer wheels, which are inscribed with invocations or *mantras* and, when spun, send the prayer to the gods as many times as the wheel turns.

72

"Hey, none of us is going to die of old age," he smiled back; then he bounded off toward the boat.

The rest of us set up safety lines at the rapid's finish or clustered with Nick around a good photographer's vantage. Kramer prepared himself out of sight upstream; the winds keened across from the rapid and paradoxically emphasized the silence that had settled over the moment.

Then, from around the bend, the raft came flying in midcurrent, Kramer whooping as he executed perfect pivots and pirouettes between the waves and holes, moving every bit like the dancer he was in college. As he arabesqued toward the rapid's end, jaws dropped along the shore: John wore no clothes, save for his underwear and lifejacket. Normal attire for the expedition had been either a full wet suit or baggy wool overclothing to guard against hypothermia in the frigid waters of the Indus. But Kramer had decided all this outerwear was too cumbersome for his dance and too dangerous should he need his strength and agility in a swim. He slid between the sharp rocks at the end of the run—an ace.

After a few more bends in the river downstream, another curious sight appeared: a sign held high by a Pakistani in Western clothes: "Pakistani TV Welcomes Sobek." Khalid Zaida, a television producer from Rawalpindi, had heard about the expedition and, eager to capture on film the inside story of this adventure, wanted to ride along down the river. After his enthusiastic welcoming, it was hard to deny his wishes, and he joined the group to film rapids and portages with his brand-new Bolex.

Late in the afternoon of his second day on the river, Khalid got more than he bargained for. He was riding in the raft with Helen, Mitchell, and Bangs as John Yost rowed; a slight miscalculation, coupled with the inexorable power of the river, caused the boat to drop into a huge hole and flip. Mitchell Shields wrote about the moment later in his *GEO* article.

. . . and the light died. It was as if the universe had ground to a halt. I heard no sound, felt no sense of motion. I was removed from time, my thoughts and actions coming minutes apart. The realization that we had overturned, that I was in the water, that the sheet of rubber above me was the raft, that I might drown, dawned slowly. I was part of the river, part of the flow, sweeping through the rapid. Gradually, wonderingly, I pulled myself back into the air, back into the light.

The two experienced boatmen surfaced immediately and pulled the raft to shore; slowly others emerged from the rapid, but two were missing—Helen Clyatt and Khalid Zaida. We ran down the bank after securing the raft and finally found Helen climbing exhausted to shore and Khalid floundering in an eddy below the next rapid, apparently blind.

Khalid had not bothered to tell anyone he couldn't swim, though in a capsize it sometimes makes no difference. He had been sucked to the river's bottom and spun rapidly; and he had temporarily lost consciousness owing to lack of oxygen. When he surfaced, he was blind, but it was temporary, and a few minutes later his sight returned. On inspection it was found he had also burst an eardrum, but for him the worst loss was his $1,800 Bolex, for which he had saved for three years.

The continued savagery of the Lion River finally wore down the resolve of us all, and the rumors of a monster rapid downstream, called Malupah, prompted a jeep scout along the new army highway now paralleling the river.

The river was, indeed, runnable to Malupah, but an unwilling swimmer could be swept into the deadly millrace unawares. Malupah itself was hideous beyond description. A granite wall, the size of El Capitan, blocked the river's passage. Twisting and turning to find a way out, rushing down one ravine to throw its spray high up the cliffsides that balked it, foaming down the next ravine in futile search, the Lion finally found release in a fissure barely a boat's width that hurled the angry, raging torrent twenty-five feet to a trough below. Nothing water-borne could survive Malupah.

As we bumped farther down the road, scouting the run as far as the Gilgit confluence, passing all too frequently small stone monuments to victims who had plummeted off the cliff, I became nauseated. Not with the drive, nor with the constant reminder of how near death was with each monument, but with the Indus. The rapids got worse, not better: narrow gorges, no place to portage, sheer walls, waterfalls, unrunnable, impossible. There was no way we could run this section. (RB)

It was time to concede. The two rafts floated down

OPPOSITE, TOP The Indus River as it pours out of the world's highest mountains (Jim Slade). BOTTOM Into the jaws of the Lion River (Michael Nichols/Magnum).

75

to just above Malupah, where we hired a transport truck painted like the walls of a cheap disco and left the Lion River roaring in triumph through the unrunnable gates of Malupah.

It was a thirty-mile portage to the confluence of the Gilgit, where we put on to float the waters that had hosted the Hatches twenty-three years earlier on their Cinerama filming. It was clearly a terrific location for a wide-screen movie. Incredibly high above the blue foothills, almost floating in the sky, Nanga Parbat looked too beautiful, too detached, and too innocent to deserve either its Indian name (Naked Mountain) or its Western nickname (The Killer Mountain). It seemed the very emblem of purity, dignity, repose, a pure-white vision in a gauzelike haze of delicate blue. To the mountaineers who have come to grips with it, it has indeed been a killer, fighting off climbing assaults with avalanches, rock slides, unexpected freezing weather, and more deaths per attempt than any other major mountain in the world. It resisted conquest until July 1, 1953, when its summit was reached by Hermann Buhl, member of a German-Austrian team, who climbed solo to the top.

As the river swerved closer to the mountain, Nanga Parbat revealed its structure more clearly: rather than a single peak, it is an enormous mass of rock ascending in successive ridges and cliffs to culminate in an icy crest that stands in solitary nobility. No other peak within a radius of fifty miles reaches to within 10,000 feet of its 26,660-foot summit.

At the last camp on the Indus, within a few miles of the Rakhiot Bridge take-out, a local villager stepped out of the twilight. Dressed in the ragged clothes of the mountain native, he quietly told tales of the Naked Mountain. It was protected by spirits of uncertain temper, according to the ancient faiths; its snowy peaks were inhabited by fairies, and when the sun shone hotly, the smoke at the mountain's crest was that of the fairies cooking their bread. He spoke of demons, of giant frogs whose croaking shook the snows, of snakes a hundred feet long hidden in the glaciers. Then he took his leave and disappeared in the darkness.

Just shy of the Rakhiot Bridge, where Jimmy Parker's name is inscribed with those of the climbers lost on Nanga Parbat, the canyon squeezed together and presented a series of three rapids, all of jawbreaking difficulty. Neither Hatch nor any of his party had left a detailed description of where the fatal accident had occurred, but common sense said it must be here. After more than three weeks on the Indus, with superstition in the air, a quick vote ended the expedition here, at the head of the final gorge. We weren't superstitious, but the Lion River had proved that its purpose was to take the waters from the center of the universe down to the sea, and men of reason were not necessarily invited along for the ride.

Apurímac

IT IS THE GREATEST RIVER in the world. Over 4,000 miles from source to sea, it may be shorter than the Nile by only a couple hundred miles. But by including its 1,800 known tributaries (7 of which are over 1,000 miles in length), its watershed leaves the river of Pharaohs in the desert dust. One-fifth of the world's freshwater flow runs to the sea from between its banks. It drains the world's largest forest, a body of biota some say provides the planet with over half its plant and insect species and a substantial portion of the world's oxygen production (through the photosynthesis of its plant life). It is 150 miles wide at its mouth, bearing 170 billion gallons of water to the sea every hour at a rate of over 6 million cubic feet per second. Its nutrient-rich flow stains the Atlantic more than a hundred miles from the Brazilian coast. If rivers have a pantheon, this is Zeus. We call it Amazon.

We can approach a river of this magnitude only with humility. It is too big to conquer, too mighty to restrain, and, like the sky, too vast to comprehend. All we can do is grasp it by a fragment of its length, the tail of the dragon: its source. We will find the stream farthest from its outflow, unravel the uttermost corner of the maze. By tracing the river those 4,000 miles upstream, across Brazil's narrowing basin, beneath the tiered canopies of rain forest, past tributaries and frontiers, into the eastern flank of the Andes of Peru, we finally reach the Apurímac, source of the Amazon.

When Francisco Pizarro, three of his brothers, and fewer than 180 Spanish soldiers of fortune began their assault on Peru in 1531, they marched on an empire far larger than they imagined. Then near its height, the realm of the Incas stretched along the greater part of the length of the Andes, from the Patía River in what is today Colombia southward to the Maule in central Chile. It was a distance equivalent to Rome's hegemony at its peak, the 2,500 miles from the British Islands to Iran; and it was a realm as rich as any in history. Already the discovery of the New World had spawned legends of cities of gold, of El Dorado, of fabulous riches waiting to be freed from the pagan's grasp. The legends were about to be tested.

Headquarters of this empire nestled between two of the loftiest and most remote headwaters of the Amazon, the rivers Urubamba and Apurímac. This was the physical and spiritual center of the Incan world, and the capital city—located in an inter-Andean valley at over 11,000 feet in elevation—was accordingly named Cuzco, the "navel," in the Quechua language the Incas spoke. The city was founded by the first Inca of legend, Manco Capac, said to be sent by the sun god Inti to teach humans the ways of civilization. The Moon in turn sent her daughter, Mamá Ocllo; together, the two journeyed from Lake Titicaca to the north and finally founded their dynasty in a valley where the soil was so rich that Manco Capac's golden spear sank from sight into the fertile earth.

Since Manco's descendants were said to be directly related to the god of the sun and the goddess of the moon, they ruled with divine guidance as gods in their own right. The term *Inca* refers not to the people of Peru or even of Cuzco but originally to the deified ruler himself, then by transference to the dynasty that governed Cuzco. They created a theocratic state that developed skills of engineering, agriculture, masonry—and warfare.

Less than a century before Pizarro landed at Tumbes, on the north coast of Peru, the power of the Incas was still wielded only along the upper stretch of the Urubamba River (also called Río Vilcanota in that region), with Cuzco as its center. The Incas had by this time developed a sophisticated oral tradition, though the only "writing" they had was a unique system of knotted ropes called *quipus* that recorded information on the economy and taxation, and, possibly, on genealogy as well. As recorded by the Spanish in their first century after conquest, the Incan

PRECEDING PAGE Salcantay, tallest peak in the Vilcabamba, realm of the "lost city of the Incas" (Brian Clark).

OPPOSITE, CLOCKWISE FROM TOP Sunrise at Machu Picchu, "door of the sun," and the funerary rock (all by John Tichenor).

Suddenly I found myself confronted with the walls of ruined houses. . . . In the dense shadow, hiding in bamboo thickets and tangled vines, appeared here and there walls of white granite. . . . Dimly, I began to realize that this wall and its adjoining semicircular temple were as fine as the finest stonework in the world. . . . I could scarcely believe my senses. . . . Would anyone believe what I had found?
—Hiram Bingham on his discovery of Machu Picchu in 1911

81

OPPOSITE, TOP Camping in the high Vilcabamba (Brian Clark). BOTTOM A paddleraft exploring the narrow waters of the Apurímac on second expedition (Jim Silva).

legends tell of the origin of Cuzco and the first eight rulers of the budding empire. Then in 1438 the ninth Inca came to power: Pachacuti, Quechua for "cataclysm" or "overturner of the world."

While still a young man, Pachacuti led Cuzco's defense against an invasion by Chanca warriors from the west and chased them over the Apurímac River, the traditional boundary of Incadom. Then, feeling flushed with a vision of possibilities, he embarked on a campaign to rebuild Cuzco, solidify his control of the region between the Vilcanota and Apurímac rivers, and expand his domain to the far corners of the world, as he knew it. With all the ambition and skill of a New World Napoleon, Pachacuti marched southeast to Lake Titicaca (*Collasuyu*), southwest to the Pacific coast (*Condesuyu*), northwest to the Peruvian highlands (*Chinchaysuyu*), and northeast to the remote cloud forests of La Montaña (*Antisuyu*). Almost single-handed, he thus created the empire of *Tahuantinsuyu*: the four united quarters of the world.

His son and grandson, Tupa Inca and Huayna Capac, solidified and expanded Pachacuti's empire, and by the time of the Spaniards' first contact with Peru, the empire was at its height. A 10,000-mile-long network of stone roads had been built throughout Tahuantinsuyu, some of them as wide as twenty-four feet; official runners kept the empire in communication, carrying the *quipus* from the outposts to Cuzco. The language of Cuzco, Quechua, was made universal throughout Tahuantinsuyu. A priestly class appropriated a third of all cultivated produce, crafts, and livestock, while the Incas themselves appropriated another third, leaving the rest for the people who produced the goods. In return, the empire provided protection and stability for its subjects: food, shelter, and land were available to all. The result was a domain as rigid and glorious as any in history, squeezed within the single century between Pachacuti and Pizarro.

Also constructed in that century of conquest was a legacy of stone that has long outlasted the last Inca: thousands of shrines, dozens of temples and defensive outposts, and more than a few cities of incredible complexity and beauty. "The only remarkable part of these buildings was the walls," wrote Bernabe Cobo, one of the Spanish conquistadores, "but the walls were so amazing that it would be difficult for

any who have not seen them to appreciate them." Their skill with hand-cut stone has never been surpassed. Beveled edges, tapered columns, and even blocks of granite hewn into a dozen or more corners to fit complicated puzzles of masonry were some of the flourishes in which Incan engineers seemed to delight.

The Incas succeeded in their quest for empire by doing what no other civilization had been able to do in Peru: unite highlands and lowlands, coast and jungle, north and south. This called on all their engineering skills, especially in bridging the mighty Apurímac River. Rising from a series of high glaciers and peaks that were worshiped as *apus* (lords) by the mountain people, the river united the diverse dialects of the channels and streams of these *apus* into the single voice (*rimac*) of a river: the Apurímac, Great Speaker, or Lord Oracle. In the 9,000-foot-deep Apurímac gorge, uniting the upper and lower realms of the empire, the Incas built a rope suspension bridge buttressed by stone and easily defensible from attack (as were nearly all Incan bridges). The Incas gave the native people of their remote domains the charge of maintaining and rebuilding the roads and bridges of Tahuantinsuyu; the bridge in this region was still maintained over three centuries later by the village of Curahuasi. Its collapse, in the 1890s, provided the drama of Thornton Wilder's *The Bridge of San Luis Rey*.

Under Francisco Pizarro, the Spaniards initiated their campaign against Peru by sailing from Panama in December 1530. Two years earlier a small party led by Pizarro had reached an Incan city at Tumbes, on the Peruvian coast near where the border with Ecuador is today; there they heard of the wealth and enviable order of the Incan domain. But when they again landed at Tumbes, in 1532, they found the city in ruins, destroyed by a civil war that two brothers were fighting for the title and authority of Inca. Divide and conquer was the motto of Spanish conquest; here, as Cortez had found in Mexico in 1519, the native empire was already in disarray.

In November 1532 Pizarro's army boldly captured the victor in the struggle for Peru's leadership, the thirteenth Inca, Atahuallpa, in the valley of Cajamarca west of Cuzco. As ransom, they demanded a room filled once to capacity with gold and twice with

Quipus were knotted ropes or strings that served as mnemonic devices or codes in the absence of a written Incan language. The type and sequence of knots, various objects contained in them, and the color of the ropes all had significance. A trained class of accountants, the *quipucamayoc*, kept track of crops, troops, taxes, and other numerical matters using the devices.

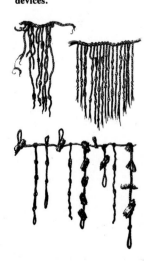

silver. The Peruvians had long believed in the significance of these two metals, so beautiful and suitable for artistic and religious works, as the "sweat of the sun" and the "blood of the moon." Still, the hunger the Spaniards showed for gold and silver convinced some natives that the invaders must find them edible. The Peruvians brought some $30 million worth of riches to the Spaniards as ransom for Atahuallpa; but it failed to satisfy the cravings of the conquistadores. The Inca was garroted in a public square on August 29, 1533. Thus began the pillage of the Andes.

The Spanish found that ending the line of Incas was not as easy as a few executions. Rebellions against the Spanish by the indigenous people—who had originally welcomed them as reincarnations of the mythic white savior Viracocha—persisted, and the people of Peru turned again and again to succeeding Incas, some of whom wore the red-fringed crown of Inca with the approval of the invaders. Sons, brothers, and nephews of the Incas—most notably Manco Inca, who ruled from 1533 to 1544—rose to regency even after the Spaniards took over the "world navel" at Cuzco. The royal Incas set up their court at ever more remote outposts: Manco Inca led his followers first to Ollantaytambo down the Urubamba River from the capital, then to Vitcos, and finally to Vilcabamba, far into the mountainous region northwest of Cuzco. Once again the empire of the Incas became restricted to the region embraced by two rivers, the Urubamba and the Apurímac.

■ ■ ■

The centuries pass, flowing between the banks of day and night like the eternal river's floods; yet some things remain the same. The weathered Volvo lorry that clattered and shook over a washboard road in 1974 was following the route of an old Incan highway, built five centuries earlier in the first flush of Pachacuti's triumphs. Aboard the truck was a young American traveler, John Tichenor. A river guide from California and a student at Yale University, Tichenor was carried by his curiosity to South America during a winter break from college, where he had read about Hiram Bingham, who discovered Machu Picchu. As a river rafter, he also knew about the Urubamba and its dangerous passage at Pongo de Mainique, which prevented an Andes-to-Amazon run. Perhaps he could find another river to explore,

one with the mystique of the Urubamba and which could carry him from the breathless heights of the alpine zone to the depths of the Amazon rain forest.

The road between Lima and Cuzco descended down and down from the Andean crest: as a waxing moon rose over the high ridges, the truck finally leveled out and crossed a narrow bridge. Down below, gleaming like the molten flow of liquid silver, a great river churned. "¿Que río es este?" John asked of his neighbor on the narrow bus seat.

"Ah, es el Apurímac." The name clicked: the source of the Amazon.

It had been only in 1971 that Loren McIntyre and a small National Geographic expedition trekked up the highest reaches of the Apurímac to a pond in the shadow of the Andean peak Choquecorao, and determined they were at the ultimate source of the Amazon. West of Choquecorao, the Colca River cuts its way to the Pacific just 100 miles away; on the eastern side, the Apurímac begins its flow as the Amazon's most distant tributary. To run the Amazon 4,000 miles from source to sea was but a dream and remains so; to this day, no single party or individual has made that historic journey. Nonetheless, as John Tichenor looked down to the moonlit flow of the Apurímac that night in 1974, the idea of being the first to raft a distant, heretofore unrun stretch of the Apurímac began to take hold in his imagination.

Three years later the goal came within reach. John became the field organizer for a California-based travel company that had started to conduct adventure trips in Peru. Such outdoor programs were then a new development of the tourism that had been an economic factor in the Andes since the 1950s. Cuzco itself became a "must-see" tourist stop, especially its ancient *Inti Raymi*—Festival of the Sun. The annual celebration, held every June 24, near the winter solstice in the Southern Hemisphere, recalls the Incas' power and the return of the sun's ascendancy. Machu Picchu, the most famous ruins in the New World, was but a half-day's train ride from Cuzco. Even the usually restrained Peter Matthiessen, in *The Cloud Forest*, declared of Machu Picchu, "it is the principal sight of South America and sufficient justification in itself for a visit to that continent."

As adventure travel became popular, some travelers preferred to forsake the train and take the more

The Incas were not the first empire to rise to prominence in the Andes; the Chavin (c. 300 B.C.), and the Mochica and Nazca (c. A.D. 300) all preceded them. Many of the silver and gold treasures for which the Incas were famous were made by the Chimu, a north-coast civilization of the centuries just prior to the arrival of the Spanish. But most of these predecessors to the Incas were best known through their pottery, which represented the gods, demons, and rulers of their lost empires.

colorful rafting route down the river, along the upper stretch of the Urubamba, through what is today called the Sacred Valley of the Incas. The stretch is between Huambutio, to the east of Cuzco, and Ollantaytambo, the formidable fortress that once served as Manco Inca's capital in his flight from the Spaniards. Rafters find that the river courses between terraced fields and small Quechua villages on a lively run past the Incan ruins of Pisac and Ollantaytambo.

John and his companion, Cheri Gleason, led a two-week rafting and hiking trip every month during the summer of 1977, rafting the Urubamba, visiting the ruins of Machu Picchu and Ollantaytambo, and trekking along the historic Inca Trail, part of the network of stone roads built to unite the far-reaching empire of the Incas. Between trips, John planned a first rafting descent down a stretch of the Apurímac; in September of that year his chance came.

John and Cheri were joined by Hugo Paullo, a close friend from Cuzco, and Steve and Jerry, two young American travelers eager to find adventure in Peru. The route John chose started at the Cunyoc Bridge, the same one from which he had had his first moonlit glimpse of the Apurímac three years earlier. The run was only twenty miles, with an average drop of sixty feet per mile, according to the often-spotty Peruvian maps. Take-out would be near Choquequirau ("cradle of gold"), one of the first ruins explored by Hiram Bingham in 1908, and for a time supposed to be the legendary lost city of the Incas, Vilcabamba. Somewhere in the 9,000-foot-deep canyon of the Apurímac, between Cunyoc and Choquequirau, was the celebrated Bridge of San Luis Rey.

This stretch had in fact been run once before, in 1975, by a small kayak party led by Cal Giddings. The five-member group took eight days to run the stretch from Cunyoc to Choquequirau, in the midst of their thirty-three-day expedition from Puente Pillpinto to Luisiana. Tichenor felt that with a distance of only twenty miles or so to cover and five people to share the labors of portaging the one boat (a single Avon Adventurer raft, thirteen feet long and correspondingly narrower than the sixteen-foot Professionals), five days would be the maximum time they'd spend on the river—and three seemed quite possible.

Indeed, on the first day all things seemed possible, despite some good-natured warnings from the Quechua villagers at the put-in. They had told of "pools down there that could swallow you"; but that is one of the common fears of native people the world over toward the wild rivers that race through their own countryside, and Tichenor easily calmed his group's apprehensions. Then one villager remembered the kayakers of two years before and told how impressed he was that they could run the river "both right side up and upside-down." But their main warning about the river—of *piedras grandisimas*, or huge boulders, in the canyon—would prove to be chillingly accurate.

From the Cunyoc Bridge the party raced a quick seven miles through the beautiful Apurímac canyon, at first a placid, broad run, with football-size quartzite crystals of different colors poking out of the andesite walls. When they came to the first rapid, however, the voices of the *apus* were raised in an ominous prophecy.

We began to hear the roaring of a rapid, which turned out to be just a very large shoal. The river

Nineteenth-century representations of the natives of the Amazon basin.

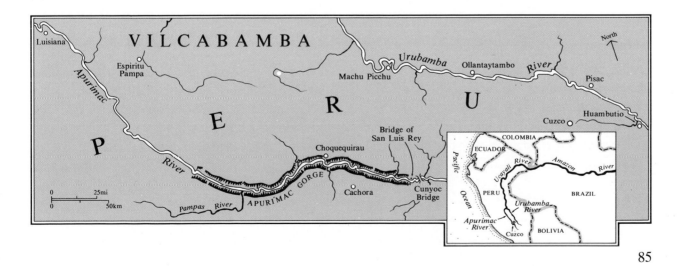

OPPOSITE, TOP The howler monkey, denizen of the Amazon rain forest, roars loudly enough to be heard a mile away (Jack Morison). BOTTOM The shaggy-coated alpaca, first cousin to the llama, on the ancient Incan highway north of Cuzco (Bett Lonergan).

wasn't flowing by the shoal that fast, but it was spreading out over a big wash of hand-sized boulders, making an enormous sound as the water gurgled between every rock along the curve. We stopped and scouted and found that it looked like a difficult little run. There were some very large boulders in the middle, and just where the river surged as it turned the corner, it undercut a big cliff. Worst of all was a whirlpool off to the side that would be impossibly difficult to escape. It took a couple of hours to get ready to run the rapid; finally, we made our entrance, and almost at once Jerry was thrown out of the boat, landing painfully on his tailbone, losing his new Peruvian tire-tread sandals. Otherwise the run was a complete success; but barefoot Jerry soon had reason to wish he had walked around. (JT)

Jerry, one of the American fellow travelers, made it to shore without trouble—he had been an Olympic swimmer in Tokyo in 1964 and was still a strong swimmer. Even so, they decided to set up camp there at the head of a narrowing canyon. They had already covered about seven of the twenty miles they estimated the run to be, and while they had packed enough food for five days, they estimated that at this rate they would finish in three. Besides, the wind had picked up, making downstream progress difficult; and blackflies were attacking every square inch of exposed flesh, eating away the group's patience.

Hugo Paullo, who claimed to be descended from the Incas, was working busily around camp, setting up the tents for the night. He finally sat down for a breather, looked around, and said, "Well, here we are. This is the Bridge of San Luis Rey!" Right across the river were the old abutments of the famous bridge: Incan stonework on the bottom, Spanish stonework on top of that, and pillars on the very top that had held the suspension spans. The villagers of the region had rebuilt the span for centuries, until the road veered off to cross the Apurímac at the more accessible Cunyoc; but it was still a dramatic construction.

One of the ironies of the Spanish conquest of Peru is the incredible good luck Pizarro and his troops had as they marched on Cuzco. In the first place, there was a power struggle going on between Atahuallpa and his half-brother Huascar, over who would succeed Huayna Capac, who had died in 1527; so inter-

The bridge over the Apurímac, as it appeared in the late 1880s, shortly before its collapse in 1897. The bridge, some 135 feet long, spanned the river about 45 feet above its currents.

nal strife had compromised the commitment of the Incas' troops. In addition, here at the Incan bridge over the Apurímac—which had long been the symbolic border of the land of the Incas and was one of their most secure frontiers—the Spanish troops crossed uneventfully in 1533. Although the retreating Peruvians had wisely burned the bridge, the mounted invaders easily forded the Apurímac, which was by chance at the low ebb of its flow. None of the Incas' troops was there to defend the ford; they had not thought it necessary. They were converging on Cuzco for a final defense. Within a month, however, the Spaniards took Cuzco—on November 15, a year to the day after they had captured Atahuallpa.

■ ■ ■

The next morning the rafters put on the river early to avoid the irritation of the blackflies; but just as the Bridge of San Luis Rey provided protection and security for the Incas, it marked the mouth of the narrowest part of the Apurímac gorge. It had spanned the throat of an incredibly steep and vertiginous canyon, one shaped neither like a river-cut V nor a glacier-cut U, but like a unique exclamation point. It was clear the river could become only more difficult from here on. And indeed it did: almost immediately after passing the abutments of the historic bridge, another graveled drop bisected the current, roaring with the threats of the Lord Oracle.

The pattern for the day was set: run a few hundred yards, scout a rapid carefully, run it with apprehension, and start the process over. Only five or six miles were made that day, and camp was set up opposite a feathery waterfall spilling from a travertine apron. It was a beautiful location and was to be one of the last chances the five rafters would have to calmly appreciate the canyon's scenic qualities. Ahead, the canyon narrowed to as few as twenty-five feet across, which could only mean more portages and less shore along which to carry the gear. Curiously, the narrowest part of the canyon was actually *above* the high-water level, as narrow as fifteen feet from side to side. The current had cut into the walls of the canyon at a faster rate than erosion had cut away the banks.

With the increasingly claustrophobic atmosphere of the inner gorge, the river itself seemed to play games of mockery: the main portion of its flow sometimes disappeared beneath the huge boulders that

choked the channel. It was not that rapids were portaged because the drops were too dangerous; they were simply too narrow for the five-foot-wide craft. Progress was further slowed when winds came screaming up the canyon at an estimated thirty miles per hour, making progress in the afternoon nearly impossible. The winds, thankfully, served to blow away the irritating flies; but they also knocked stones off talus slopes 150 feet above the river, sending down a deadly hail of rocks, from fist to melon size. Even the clean sand beaches at the bends, left by the winter flooding of the river, were littered with sharp rocks. The gorge of the Apurímac was losing its hospitality.

There were, nonetheless, moments of surprise and beauty to counter the dangers and disappointments. River otter slid into the stream, only their dog-bristled muzzles showing as they cautiously eyed the boat; at one bend a small suspension bridge linked two haciendas, a bridge that John had neither heard of nor seen on any maps. There were views of 18,000-foot peaks towering over the gorge to the east, in the remote fastness of Vilcabamba. Then, as the portages became more frequent toward the end of that third day, the canyon seemed to collapse on itself. Huge smooth granite boulders were anchored in the river like ships: thirty feet wide and sixty feet long, looming thirty-five feet high, yet completely rounded from the force of the flooding Apurímac. Several times the huge boulders filled the gorge to such an extent that the widest point in the river was only two-and-a-half feet—the rest percolated through and beneath the rocks in small rivulets, whispering and mumbling with derision.

Scouting the route can be one of the joys of exploration, but to spend six hours on the rocks for every hour on the water was becoming discouraging. As the only one with the experience necessary to determine if the rapids were runnable, I had to scout them all. I wound up clambering all over the steep insides of this clearly uninhabitable canyon. At one point I had to climb about 250 feet up a cliff and was just barely able to see that the narrow canyon we were in at last became calm only a short distance downstream. It even opened up to a very small beach at the end. So I would be able to find my way back down this cliff face, I turned at one point to mark my trail. Right behind me was a stack of three rocks, marking the very route I had climbed up.

Suddenly I remembered a description in Cal Giddings's article about his kayak trip. At one point, he said, you had to climb a cliff face hundreds of feet to see if it was passable down into the canyon. These could only be Cal's own rock markers. Then I laughed out loud, realizing that the last folks through here had made it, and everything would probably turn out just fine. (JT)

The small group managed to wrestle through only three miles that third day; it was clear the five days of food they had packed would be barely enough, if they were lucky. A more difficult day on the river would be hard to imagine. Indeed, as they started up the next morning, they proceeded a good mile downstream without incident. Then another belt of boulders, a veritable dam of difficulties, split the river—the first of five major portages in less than a mile. The fourth day was capped when the bottom dropped out of the canyon and the river crashed down a half-mile-long rapid, either a tremendously exhilarating and dangerous ride or the longest single portage yet. A quiet night of calm resignation at the head of this horrendous rapid stood between the small party and the travail of tomorrow.

The next morning they divided up the remaining food—three dates each for breakfast and a last few spoonfuls of mayonnaise, their carbohydrate and protein. And then began the worst portage any of them had ever faced.

It was a half-mile long. The only way along the bank was not beside the river, but crawling through thorny acacia bushes for hundreds of yards at a time. Our clothes were ripped and tattered, our skin was welted with fly bites, the boat had to be dragged under bushes the whole way. It was horrible, but we knew our only hope for exit still lay somewhere downstream, at the bridge to Choquequirau. Finally we put back in, floated around the bend, and, at once, there was another portage. Almost wordless now, worn down by the river and the portages, we hauled the raft over this narrow range of granite boulders and headed for the turn around the next bend, full of hope and apprehension. A big beach opened up ahead of us; at the same time, Cheri and Jerry screamed. (JT)

They were joyful screams, for there above the river was a cable span, which had to mean that an unexpected trail led out of the Apurímac gorge. By

OPPOSITE Quechua merchants and weavers, direct descendants of the people of the Peruvian Andes ruled by the Incas (clockwise from top: Virginia Ferrero, Cheri Gleason-Tichenor, Skip Horner, John Tichenor).

Clay pots from the Peruvian Andes.

89

OPPOSITE Following the ancient Incan footpaths through the Vilcabamba, one of Peru's most remote regions (John Tichenor).

eleven in the morning on that fifth day, the boat was at last deflated, the tent was set up—Cheri, Jerry, and Steve's shelter from the blackflies—and Hugo and John were on their way up the cliff to find food and horses in the nearby village of Cachora—some five miles short of their goal, the ruins of Choquequirau. Still, it was not until late the next day that they managed to barter for a small horse caravan to trek down the steep path to the river to rescue the first Tichenor Apurímac Exploration.

■ ■ ■

Needless to say, John Tichenor regarded his first Apurímac excursion as less than a success. He had been looking for an avenue from the scenic Andean valleys, the traditional seat of Quechua villages and Incan influences, down through the steep gorges that divided the mountains from the lowlands to the lush jungles of the Amazon basin. The run from Cunyoc to Cachora was clearly not it; faced with the choice of giving up or trying again, John was never in doubt.

The next year John and Alfredo Ferreyros, a Peruvian with Explorandes, an adventure travel company based in Cuzco, chartered a helicopter to take them along the Apurímac River in search of an ideal run. They flew above the narrow canyon, looked down on the short stretch that had taken so much effort and hope out of John the year before, and continued farther downstream to the north. John thought he saw possibilities from the Río Pampas tributary down. Finally, running low on fuel, they turned and raced across the uncharted ranges of the Vilcabamba region back to Cuzco.

Even four centuries ago, when the Incas were pushed ever farther into retreat by the Spanish, the Vilcabamba was not a very hospitable place. And when Manco Inca, the first popular successor to Atahuallpa, adopted a stance of open rebellion against the intruders in 1536, he was forced to lead his nation into exile. He set fire to Cuzco and retreated to Ollantaytambo, an incomplete resort for the royal Incas. There he held off an initial assault by the Spaniards under Hernando Pizarro, the commander's most trustworthy brother. But when the Spanish held on to Cuzco for more than a year, despite harassment and attacks from the Incan forces, Manco Inca fled to Vitcos, a small settlement in the remote mountains of the Vilcabamba. The next year the Spanish pursued

him even to Vitcos; the Inca fled for his life and set up his ragged court in a region even more remote than Vitcos, establishing a fortress at what became known as the lost city of the Incas.

The Vilcabamba—Quechua for "domain of the prince"—is today sparsely inhabited; it is a series of precipitous ranges running between the two major drainages of central Peru, the Apurímac and the Urubamba, tapering down to end at the confluence of those two rivers as they unite to form the Ucayali. Much of it is too steep for easy passage; contemporary records of the Spanish attempt to capture the exiled Inca tell of quagmires and trails too slippery for mounts. And while the Incas had ruled for generations from the 11,000-foot mountain valley of Cuzco, during their retreat into the Vilcabamba range they were forced to descend ever deeper into the thick, humid jungle of the Amazon, to their final refuge at barely 3,000 feet.

Perhaps only the dispute between two factions of the Spanish conquistadores prevented their taking Vilcabamba earlier than they did. One faction, led by the Pizarro brothers, was awarded the northern half of the Incan empire of Tahuantinsuyu by King Charles V of Spain; the other group, under Francisco Pizarro's original partner, Diego de Almagro, was awarded the southern half, including present-day Chile. Which party was to rule Cuzco was not established, and that almost at once became a bone of contention. The Spaniards proved to be almost as murderous toward their countrymen as they were toward the Peruvians: Almagro was executed in 1538, and Francisco Pizarro was assassinated in 1541. As it happened, one of the men who killed Pizarro was on the scene three years later when Manco Inca was stabbed in the back in his Vilcabamba retreat. He had ruled for nine years, at the end of his empire's age, leading his countrymen from an uneasy truce with the bearded invaders, through a hopeless rebellion, to a dead end in the unwelcoming Vilcabamba.

■ ■ ■

In July 1978 Tichenor began another trip on the Apurímac, down a lower stretch, following a steep one-day descent from the Ayacucho region to the west of Vilcabamba. Again Hugo Paullo joined him, this time because the river would take them to the village where he had been born, and which he had

90

left nearly twenty years earlier. Two rafts were carried in by horseback, through farming communities and across a region that descended 8,000 feet, from forest-lined valleys to a harsh acacia desert to the familiar granite canyon of the Apurímac.

Again the river portion of their trip was planned for three days, but this time the trip went smoothly: the twenty-five-mile route was covered in good time with just one portage. Most of the rapids were big waves, rolling past waterfalls and an occasional homestead deep in the forgotten canyon; but the blackflies were just as hungry, and the transition that John was looking for—from Andes to Amazon—was not found on that short stretch.

They packed out across the Vilcabamba, still an all-but-unexplored quarter of Peru. Many small outposts can be found throughout the area, and ancient Incan roads link the valleys and towns in every direction. The Incan roads still survive intact in many areas, with fitted stone paving more than six feet wide, sometimes even raised slightly from the nearby terrain to prevent puddling. Native villagers—Hugo Paullo's cousins and long-lost friends—pointed out the way back to Cuzco. The regular outlines of a classic Incan paved road led through the isolated valleys; watchtowers above the trail still stood on their stone foundations; functional bridges were still supported by their ancient abutments. The uncharted road led through villages made of stone and thatch, over a pass known only to the natives of the Vilcabamba, and back to the main road to Cuzco.

A year later they returned, taking the train from Cuzco to Chaullay, then trucking along the Vilcabamba River to the end of the road. There they packed all their gear on mules and set off on a much slower crossing of the Vilcabamba region to the Apurímac.

In the next six days we retraced our earlier route across Vilcabamba, over the passes and through the villages, but this time we detoured. Children tagged along through the farms near Lucma and Puquiura, giving us handfuls of oranges and field orchids as we left. One boy about eight years old led us up a side trail to the ruins of Rosaspata, an orderly hilltop complex with a panoramic view of the valley. He then led us through doorways and stone passages and turned down to a gentle draw behind the hill. As he walked up

a stream, we followed him through the sloping pasture to its source.

The spring surrounded a great carved stone, which emerged like a whale's back from the meadow. A carefully fitted wall had been built to retain the seepage, forming a garden of succulents and moss beneath the monolith. The spring water collected in a canal beside the pool, flowed through a pair of conduits, spilled through a matched pair of spouts, and splashed from a flat stone in interlocking rings of spray. (JT)

Hiram Bingham had found this site shortly after discovering Machu Picchu. He recognized the "great stone over a spring" from the Spanish chronicles and identified the nearby ruins as Vitcos.

After passing through the higher valleys, where villagers survive by herding horses and sheep, raising potatoes, and trading with the travelers along the old Incan highways, the Tichenor party continued down through lower grasslands to warmer altitudes, where the tropical forests began to take over. Orchards were replaced by acacia forests, cactus began to appear, and flocks of parrots screamed overhead. By the time they reached the Apurímac, the landscape was once again desert.

This time the surprises the river had in store were, for the most part, pleasant. The first morning everyone noticed the complete absence of blackflies, the greatest gift the river could offer. Jim Silva, one of the expedition members, celebrated by catching trout for breakfast, and gentle swells and sparkling water welcomed the boats onto the Apurímac. In the long pools between rapids, the canyon was cathedral quiet: sculpted granite arched in abstract alcoves, and swallows nested in the high corners of the canyon walls.

Before noon the river carried the two boats down to the falls at Pawac, which on the aerial scout the year before appeared to be the only major obstacle in this stretch. From river level it was clear that a portage was in order: the entire river was compressed to race through a gap of less than twenty-five feet, where a huge double wave was followed by a long riot of whitewater that curved out of sight. It might have been fun, but on exploratory expeditions caution is sometimes the better part of valor.

Two hours later both rafts were loaded and ready to continue. A long set of rapids stretched out just down-

93

OPPOSITE At the ancient ruin of Sacsayhuaman, near Cuzco, celebrants recreate the reverence for the Inca, "The son of the sun," by bowing before his golden ax (John Tichenor).

stream, so we pulled into the current and crossed to the other bank for a better look. We landed at a sandy grotto, with a spring streaming down its deepest face and a terrace filled with sandy hollows reaching to the current below. A better camp couldn't be imagined, so we spent the rest of the afternoon here, quietly reading, writing, and poking along the shore. Three boys spotted us from a trail above and brought down papayas and bananas to share. We feasted together, and at dusk they ran home with a batch of cinnamon rolls left over from our breakfast. (JT)

The next day the voice of the Apurímac roared once again in the big waves and the crash of whitewater, but everything was easily runnable. For the next four days the river became increasingly relaxed, the rapids ever shorter, and the quiet pools ever longer. The threats and taunts of the Apurímac had finally given way to the gentle murmurs of welcome and approval as the rafts floated quietly through a canyon already greening with the approach of the jungle. Somewhere above this stretch of river, in the forested steepness of the Vilcabamba, the Incas made their final stand in a modest capital city far removed from the glorious ease of their palaces at Cuzco.

When Hiram Bingham discovered Machu Picchu in 1911, he was certain he had found the lost city of the Incas. His certainty, in retrospect, was based more on his desire than on fact; a careful reading of the Spanish chroniclers shows that the city of Vilcabamba lay much farther to the northeast and much farther from Cuzco. Certainly Machu Picchu is an impressive ruin, and its location along a ridge spine made it naturally defensible against Spanish invaders. But it was not designed as a fortress, and, in fact, the Incas appear never to have used it as such, even in their retreats from Cuzco and Ollantaytambo. Its excavation and reconstruction have provided no justification for Bingham's thesis that it is the lost city, where Manco Inca led his followers into a final exile, and where Manco himself was killed in 1544.

Following Manco's death, his five-year-old son, Sayri Tupa, was named Inca, and the loyalists continued to preserve their mountain kingdom. But Sayri Tupa was not destined to lead a decaying empire; when he came of age, he chose to leave Vilcabamba and, ironically, to seek the approval of the Pope and the Spanish authorities in Cuzco for his

marriage to his sister, the traditional alliance of the Incas. His half-brother, Titu Cusi, took over the red forehead fringe that crowned the Inca.

Although Tahuantinsuyu had long since fallen into the hands of the Spanish, Titu Cusi continued to harass the invaders from Vilcabamba, justifying his actions by citing the history of Spanish abuses against his people and the poverty of his new domain. For thirteen years, in fact, Titu Cusi played a game of cat and mouse with the Spaniards, as both a guerrilla leader and a diplomat, making promises and treaties but never forsaking his diminished empire.

Finally in 1572 the new Spanish viceroy of Peru, Francisco de Toledo, vowed to end the Incan problem once and for all. He gathered information on the short life of the Incan empire and its abuses against the native people of Peru as justification for his planned assault; he then outlawed the puppet Incas who had been allowed to maintain royal living standards in Cuzco. At last he raised an army of 1,500 men, including local Indians and colonial gentlemen of Cuzco, and set out toward Vilcabamba.

The army was led by the villagers of the mountainous region and defectors from the humble Incan capital. After eight days of marching through thick forests of thorns and suffering attacks from Incan guerrillas, the Spanish finally marched into the capital to find it deserted, sacked, and burned by the fleeing Incas. The date was June 24, 1572—for the Spanish the feast day of John the Baptist, for the Incas the traditional date of the Festival of the Sun.

In the ruins of Vilcabamba were found the mummified remains of both Manco Inca and Titu Cusi, who had died just months before. But, once again, the reigning Inca had vanished into the forests, just as Manco had done in 1537. The new ruler was Tupac Amaru, one of Manco Inca's legitimate sons; but Toledo was not to be defeated by flight. Tupac Amaru was chased down and captured at a jungle campfire with his pregnant bride. He was led back to Cuzco and beheaded in the main square, thirty-nine years after the death of Atahuallpa introduced the Incas to Spanish justice.

■ ■ ■

Today most authorities believe that the fortress of Vilcabamba was at a site called Espiritu Pampa, at the low edge of the Cordillera Vilcabamba, between

94

the watersheds of the Urubamba and the Apurímac. Although Hiram Bingham, who so earnestly searched for the lost city of Vilcabamba, had actually investigated one portion of the ruin, a Spanish-style palace he called Eromboni, it was left to American explorer Gene Savoy to rediscover the site in 1964 and to recognize it as a large city buried in the jungle. The location of Espiritu Pampa answers to the description in contemporary accounts of the Incan fortress, in terms of altitude, climate, topography, and landmarks along the route Toledo's armies followed to reach Vilcabamba. Although the site is near navigable stretches of the Cosireni River, a tributary of the Urubamba, Espiritu Pampa is on a ridge that rises above the Apurímac as it reaches the warm low forests of the Amazon basin.

First the fern thickened on still-vertical walls, then agave replaced the cactus, and Spanish moss thrived as the air became moist. For nearly a full day the impending change was in the breeze; then in three quick turns of the river we were in jungle. The canyon still formed a gorge where trails couldn't follow, but the forest was rich and luxuriant. Weaverbirds and kingfishers slashed through the canyon, and we saw houses made of fronds instead of stone. Even the solid rock changed. In the desert we had drifted among granite boulders and cliffs of schist, but suddenly we were finding great masses of stone that seemed almost like clay—huge blobs of basalt wadded together like honey buns in a bakery. (JT)

For three more days Tichenor and his party floated through the ever-greening Apurímac valley as it ran northward toward its confluence with the Urubamba and the creation of one of the Amazon's two main forks, the Ucayali. Homesteads typical of the upper Amazon appeared: small farms raising fruit, cacao, and manioc root. As the river widened to several hundred yards, its flow swollen by the tributaries that came out of the Vilcabamba to the east and Ayacucho to the west, dugout canoes plied the waters in commerce between the homesteads and villages.

Finally, as monkeys scrambled noisily in the forest canopy and small colorful squalls of butterflies swirled along the shore, the two rafts pulled into Hacienda Luisiana, a classic cacao plantation and rum distillery. There began the road that carried rum and, this time, river rafters to the highlands of Peru. The Apurímac, its voice hushed in the deep, silently swept on, carrying the waters of a lost empire toward the distant Atlantic.

OPPOSITE The Apurímac, flowing wide and slow into the Amazon basin near Hacienda Luisiana (John Tichenor).

97

Bío-Bío

CHAPTER SIX BÍO-BÍO *River of Song*

IT WAS A LONG SHOT. We knew practically nothing of the river, only that it was Chile's second longest. Yet in a country measuring 2,600 miles long and just 113 miles across at its widest, the odds of finding a navigable whitewater river of any length seemed poor. We had no hydrological data, no flowcharts, not even good maps. For all we knew, the eddies south of the equator spun counterclockwise. But Chile did have a promising source of whitewater: the Cordillera de los Andes, the world's longest mountain range and one of its highest. And the name of our target river, the Río Bío-Bío, had a fanciful lilt that put a smile on everyone's lips. After struggling with names like Çoruh, Tuolumne and Tatshenshini, this river sounded like a song.

And that is just what it is: the Mapuche Indian word for the song of a local flycatcher, the Chilean elaenia. The Bío-Bío (pronounced bee-oh bee-oh) springs from Lago Galletue, a shimmering alpine lake at the foot of the 10,000-foot peaks a few miles from the Argentine border. The river flows from near a town called Sierra Nevada in a grand arc, skewing south, then dodging off to the west, passing through the village of Santa Bárbara and the town of Los Angeles (near San Fernando) before finally spilling into the Pacific. It all sounds hauntingly familiar to a Californian.

The Bío-Bío had been called to our attention by Bill Wendt, chief ranger at Yosemite National Park. He had spent three years in the area on a United Nations project and had flown over and hiked a portion of the river. Although he knew little of river running and had seen only a fraction of the Bío-Bío, he spoke glowingly of its clear gushing waters and the landscape through which it flowed.

While making plans to run unrun rivers was no longer new to us, committing the time, money, and energy on the basis of so little information made us a little uneasy. Nonetheless, Bill's confidence and excitement were contagious; and six of us were gamblers enough to throw our hats into the ring, including Bill and his cousin George Wendt, owner of a California river-rafting company and a Sobek partner from the beginning; Mike Cobbold, a seasonal Yosemite ranger who also had worked for the Park Service in Chile; and three Sobek river guides: Bruce Gaguine, Jack Morison, and Rich Bangs.

In December 1978 we flew from San Francisco over the equator, reaching Chile at 17 degrees south, well within the tropic zone. The country we saw below us was barren, sparsely inhabited desert spreading across the western flank of the Andes. By the time we landed at Santiago, Chile's largest city, we had reached the more comfortable temperate zone, and the plain between the Andean peaks and the Pacific tides was full of angular fields devoted to grain and grazing. Santiago is only half-way to Chile's southern reaches, the land's end of South America.

In Santiago we transferred all our gear to the train station: two fat rolls of neoprene that would inflate to Avon Professional rafts sixteen feet long, nine ten-foot-long ash oars, a dozen metal ammo boxes (which never fail to raise a few eyebrows at the customs lines) to keep our gear dry, a couple of eighty-quart coolers, and the six-foot-long aluminum alloy pipes that fit together to form rowing frames. We enlisted a few eager teenagers at the train station to help us load it aboard and took the modern diesel train south to Victoria, a small farming village in the Andean foothills. There everything was unloaded onto the old wooden station platform, and we sat down on the pile of equipment to wait for the arrival of the steam-powered, narrow-gauge engine that would take us up the old spur railroad into the Andes. Finally it arrived, smoking down the tracks like the long-awaited rendezvous with destiny in *High Noon*. We hefted all our gear into a baggage car and took our seats on the antique red leather bench seats. Then the steam engine belched a cloud of dark smog, sending sparks scattering over the tracks, and lurched and staggered its way out of the station, plunging almost at once into the Andes.

The Andes are one of the most impressive geologic formations on the planet, a single mountain range, predominately volcanic, over 4,000 miles long, created along the entire west coast of South America, from Colombia to Patagonia. While its highest mountain, Aconcagua (just to the northeast of San-

PRECEDING PAGE Volcán Callaqui, whose sulfurous crater keeps watch over the Río Bío-Bío (Skip Horner).

OPPOSITE, TOP Peaceful upper waters of the Bío-Bío (George Wendt). BOTTOM The Bío-Bío in its canyon at the entrance to the Queen of Hearts (John Kramer).

OPPOSITE, CLOCKWISE FROM TOP
Chilean market scene from a
hotel window (Peter N. Fox).
Chilean *huasco* wearing
traditional woolen *manta*
(Jim Slade). Ducklings at a
local market (Peter N. Fox).
Savoring the fruit of the
Andes (Mark Jensen).

tiago, in neighboring Argentina), measures 22,831 feet, which barely joins the top twenty summits, the average altitude of Andean peaks makes it the world's second highest range, behind the Himalayas. A range that long and that high has just about every possible mountain phenomenon: remote and rugged summits that defeat the best mountaineers, sharp glaciated ridges that forbid overland travel, and popular ski resorts surrounding pristine alpine lakes.

The railroad into the mountains followed the line of least resistance and, avoiding the peaks and ridges, took us to Temuco, a small town in the heart of Chile's wine-growing region. Today Temuco is the northern limit of the Araucanians, a native people who have been singularly successful at avoiding conquest. The people derive their popular name from the *araucaria*, or Chile pine, known also as the monkey-puzzle tree because its long spidery branches are covered with stiff green needles that remind some people of monkey tails. The Araucanians call themselves Mapuche, however, which means "people of the land." They are for the most part a sedentary, agricultural people who in centuries past hunted guanacos, pumas, and armadillos—and, when their security was threatened, invaders.

In the years of the expansion of the Incan empire, under Tupa Inca's leadership during the years 1463 to 1493, the Incas were stopped in their conquests at the Maule River, some fifty miles north of the Bío-Bío. There fierce Mapuches armed with bows and arrows showed the Incas that they were, at last, too far from their homeland. In the century that followed, the Mapuches resisted conquest by Spanish forces under Pedro de Valdivia, who solidified the conquest of

Chile. Valdivia was slain in battle against the Mapuches in 1553. For 300 years after that, the Mapuches continued to resist conquest and assimilation; until 1882, in fact, the region of Chilean national authority ended at the Bío-Bío, despite the maps that showed but one country. Below that river the Mapuches continued to live apart.

While no Incan, Spaniard, nor Chilean has ever conquered the Mapuches, the slow but inevitable effects of contact and commerce have brought them closer to the modern age. Now they raise wheat and barley as well as the traditional maize and potatoes, and breed cattle and sheep, like much of Chile's rural population; but the Mapuches continue to be one of the largest functioning indigenous societies in South America.

In Temuco we picked up a seventh expedition member—Alejandro Sepulveda, an administrator in the Chilean Park Service and an old friend of Bill Wendt's during his Chilean sojourn. Alejandro had set up a flight over the Bío-Bío so we could evaluate our destined course before it was too late. We flew from Temuco over the river, soaring over nearly 200 of the river's 240 miles, from Santa Bárbara up to its source at Lago Galletue, searching for obstacles that might end our expedition before it got on the water. The river did look runnable, with one series of four big rapids that promised excitement, but no major waterfalls or other impassable obstacles. None that we could see, at least, for the river at one point played hide-and-seek in the narrow canyons of the Andes. We congratulated Bill on his choice.

That evening we finally reached the river's source after a half-day's ride in the rear of a cattle truck over

With the conquest of the Incas in Peru, Charles V of Spain awarded the northern part of the Incan lands to Francisco Pizarro and the southern part to his partner, Diego de Almagro. In 1535 Almagro went to the south with 570 Spaniards and 12,000 Inca warriors; but few riches awaited the eager conquistadores in Chile, and their greed turned easily to cruelty. Robbery, slaughter, and rape were the modus operandi of Almagro's expedition; soon the native warriors and servants abandoned their Spanish leaders, the high Andean passes claimed victims, and the barren deserts of Atacama further disillusioned the troops. Almagro proceeded as far south as the land occupied by the powerful Mapuche tribes but, failing in battle against them, returned to Peru in 1536.

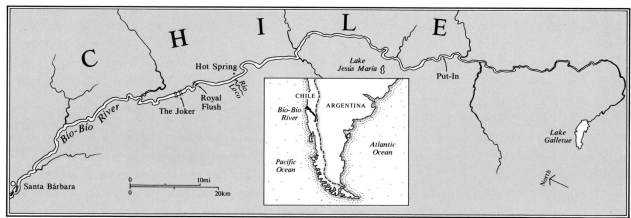

Chile's back roads. Some Lago Galletue residents killed a lamb, cut its throat, collected the hot blood in a wooden bowl, and dropped in a lemon wedge, which coagulated the blood into chunks that looked like four-day-old cafeteria Jell-O. It is called *nachi*, a delicacy reserved for special occasions. We were honored, and rushed to wash it down with *pisco*, the clear brandy of the Andes.

We spent much of the next morning rigging up for our expedition. The rafts were rolled out and, with the help of a high-volume pump, assumed their familiar shape. Four separate chambers create the oblong perimeter of the rafts, with two thwarts placed in the center to add stability. Each chamber is inflated to drum-hard tightness, so the raft rides high and firm in the water; the chambers are separated by baffles so that, in the unlikely event one should pop because of a sharp rock, crocodile teeth, or overinflation, the other three will keep the boat afloat. During the twenty-five years of professional river rafting, the standard configuration of the raft—its dimensions, including tube diameter, uplift at bow and stern, and placement of D-rings for tying on gear—has been refined to a very specialized level. Today's riverboat is a far cry from the surplus landing craft that first found its way downriver in the years following World War II.

Next, the two-inch-diameter aluminum tubing was assembled into the rowing frames. They are equipped with the essential oarlocks and also supply stability and rigidity to the raft. When lashed securely into the midsection of the craft, the frame allows gear to be tied onto a wood panel floor section that is dropped between the thwarts. Coolers, ammo boxes, stove, fuel, water jugs, heavy cast-iron Dutch oven, and other paraphernalia are then all secured to the deck, while the water-tight black bags containing dry clothes are tied into the rear bilge section. The weight of the gear, riding low in the boat, adds further stability to the raft in the torquing and twisting of powerful hydraulics. Everything is lashed down securely, either to the boat or frame or both, to prevent its loss in case of a flip.

Finally all was ready: the oarsman was braced with his feet between the gear on the floorboard, with a spare oar tied by slip-knot within easy reach; passengers took their places in the front section for weight balance against the black bags in the rear—and for a thrilling, wet, front-row seat. All the tied-in gear was checked and doublechecked; lifejackets were pulled snug. Upstream, the snowy crown of Volcán Llaima, scraping the skies above Lago Galletue; downstream, the river.

As a condor caught an air current overhead, we shoved the rafts into the water, spun into the current, and whirled downstream. The first rapids were shallow, rocky, and couched in a small canyon topped with thick araucaria *trees, which cast a magical aura over the river. Twisting through this watery maze, I was struck with the ghostly feeling of unfamiliarity. The river seemed like none other I had experienced. The River Styx, I felt, might bear some resemblance.*

The water was crisp, clear as pisco. *It almost crackled with each stroke. We pumped and shot through channels and chutes and drank in the scenery. The area we were traversing was called the Switzerland of South America. That does it an injustice. The backdrop was the unique snow-capped Andes, an endless phalanx of three-dimensional points that blends with sky and clouds without clear definition. Closer stood the perfect, snow-dripped cone of Volcán Llaima, poking 10,000 feet into the clouds.* (RB)

In those first twenty-five miles the river left the alpine Andean forest of *araucaria* and flowed across a broad foothill plateau; above the gentle banks, green fields sloped gradually to the bases of the surrounding mountains. Our aerial survey had given us the foreknowledge that later, when the river poured off the escarpment, we would plunge through dark gorges in a fierce region—a junkyard of the spare parts of mountain building. But for now the landscape was smooth and sweet, and we savored its comfort.

Horsemen decked out in silver spurs and leather rode to the edge of the river and gaped at the *gringos locos*. Horses, pigs, and sheep wandered along the cobbled banks, and at one small farm along the river a local cowgirl tried to sell us a live goat for dinner. It was like being in the real Wild West, from the steam engine burrowing into the mountains to the broadchapped cowboys waving their laconic greetings. And, from what we'd seen of the river from the air, the broncobusting was yet to come.

Our first night's camp was on a broad green velour-

OPPOSITE, TOP Portaging Jugbuster, at high water one of the Bío-Bío's most severe rapids (Curt Smith). BOTTOM Ferry boat on the upper Bío-Bío, near the beginning of the river trip (Mark Jensen).

A Chilean rancher of the southern part of the country, where much of the land has been given over to grazing. The large hacienda system that the Spanish founded in Chile has broken down in the twentieth century, largely at the will of the ranchers themselves, who have found it very lucrative to subdivide their enormous holdings and sell small parcels to families or ambitious stockmen.

105

textured embankment with a downstream vista of saw-toothed, snow-draped peaks. The night was our real introduction to the Southern Hemisphere: our latitude was about 36 degrees south—the southern equivalent of Carmel, California. We savored a dinner of fresh vegetables and fruit, bantering in shirt-sleeve warmth and familiarity beneath a crisp sky speckled with unfamiliar stars.

As we lost elevation, the flora and geology began to change. The towering *araucaria* pines—which can grow to 150 feet high—gave way to groves of cedars, Lombardy poplars, and cyprus festooned with long shags of Spanish moss. The river began falling into a burnished gorge. Evidence of human habitation began to disappear, and the roots of the Andes were revealed in layers of basalt, pumice, and andesite—the igneous substratum of the great range. There was a sense of leaving behind the commonplace, of gliding toward the unknown.

As we passed a creek mouth, we saw a lone fisherman working a line with a crude sapling pole. This prompted Bill Wendt to try his luck, and he cast his nylon line over the stern. Seconds later he brought a five-pound brown trout flopping into the bilge. He whooped and hollered and threw the line in again. Within seconds he had another strike, and another five pounder.

All this served to fuel the predator instinct in Bruce Gaguine, and when we passed a giant European hare (the size of a cocker spaniel) loping through the bush like a target waiting to be hit, Bruce got an idea. He had us pull to shore, where he filled the bilge with golf-ball-size rocks; then we pushed out into the river again, creeping stealthily downstream looking for prey. We saw no more hare, but geese were everywhere. With every turn Bruce sprang to action, spitting rocks from his hands like gunfire.

Preoccupied with the hunt, he didn't notice when the boat was sucked into a rapid littered with boulders and chopped with three-foot drops. While novice river runner Mike Cobbold was at the oars, Bruce was crouched in the bow, still clutching ammunition. Suddenly Mike lost control: the boat rode up on a rock, waffled, and turned on its side, and the river started flushing in. Bruce leapt to the oars and wrestled the raft off the rock and through the rest of the rapid. Since we were the first to negotiate this

river, we had the prerogative and privilege of naming rapids. This one became Gaguine's Gauntlet.

We purled past Chilpaca, a ghost town that thrived during a gold strike in 1932. Then we left the inhabited regions behind and were drawn into a forested whirlpool as the sun dropped behind a distant volcano. Camp was at the foot of a tremendous, frothing, white cascade of a tributary.

The next morning was Saturday, and we decided to treat it as such. Scanning our maps, we found a lake just two miles up the tributary, Lago Jesús María. We decided to investigate and scrambled up the rocky stream. Before long we reached it, and it was beautiful. The deep-blue, sun-dappled glacial basin was encased by 6,000-foot-high granite points, spires, and flutes, with tears of snow running down steep valleys on its flanks. It looked very much like one of the Twin Lakes at Yosemite, except for the absence of campers. We reveled and sunned in the wildflower meadows; but the promise of rapids downstream on the Bío Bío called, and we returned to its banks before noon.

Running downstream once again, we splashed and careened through scores of rapids, naming them all as we went. With every passing mile the river was showing us a combination of the best features a river can have: resplendent scenery, powerful rapids, clear water, and good fishing.

That evening we feasted and fested. Bruce got lucky, so a local goose was roasted while the hunter-chef prepared a liver pâté. We mixed *pisco* sours for cocktails and spread coals from our campfire beneath and on the lid of the Dutch oven. While heat surrounded the pot and radiated through the cast iron, we awaited the exotic concoction for dessert. Finally dinner was ready: we uncorked a bottle of Chilean wine (70¢ for the wine, $1.70 for the returnable bottle) and ate corn on the cob, chicken soup, barbecued goose, and, finally, fresh cherry-vanilla pudding—the product of our Dutch oven.

On Sunday, distended bellies notwithstanding, we rolled onto the river at 11:00 A.M. At noon we pulled over to a cascading tributary with a promising name, Río Loco, and noticed some strangely discolored rock: mineral hot springs. "Doesn't this river ever stop?" Jack asked in wonder as we lay back for a soothing soak. "What more can it give us?" If the

Chilean pots of the central Andes.

Bío-Bío heard that question, the river took it not just as a compliment, but as a challenge. Downstream we hit the first of the big rapids.

We were suddenly in water as violent and complex as any we had met, and it sent pulses thumping and spirits soaring. One rapid had a hole a small hotel could get lost in, in river dead center. Another had a glassy chute that slid over a twelve-foot drop and ended in a back-rolling column of water, a horizontal tornado. Another was a 500-yard labyrinth, through a team of basalt rock bone-crunchers positioned like a defensive line.

In the middle of the rock maze, a glacial stream, gray with silt, spit into the river. As we scrambled up the bank to scout, we could see the source of the stream—a fantastic glint of ice, pouring down through a mammoth mountain cleft like a huge strand of frozen molasses. It was an unnamed glacier, a stream of brilliant blue light carving through a realm of black basalt and ash. Ignoring for the moment our scout, we climbed higher, and the view got better. The glacier hung from the 10,000-foot cone of an active volcano, Volcán Callaqui, a belching, smoking, snow-creamed peak that loomed directly over the river. We paused in amazement and excitedly pointed a route up the broad snowy flanks of the volcano. Perhaps another day; this one was for running the rapids.

Reluctantly we turned our attention to the rapid and descended to walk along its banks. We shook our heads in dismay, then paused in concentration, and finally nodded with understanding. It was, perhaps, possible, and a portage would not be easy. It took half an hour to memorize the run, which zigzagged through the rocks in a broken course. At last we walked quietly back to the boats, checked the rigging, and pulled tight our lifejackets. The oarsman slipped on his soft leather gloves.

I began the run, drawing on the oars methodically, trying to match the map in my mind with the frothy view crashing down my bow. The current was fast, and from the river the perspective was disorienting. Almost at once I lost my way. I fell back on my instincts and had to rely on snap judgments and quick action. As I pulled to miss an approaching rock, I suddenly realized I would not make it. Whack! The collision felt like a VW bug in a head-on with a Mack truck. The boat buckled, rebounded, fibrillated, then snapped around the wrong side of the rock, straight toward a deep-throated hole. Miraculously we were all still in the boat, and we braced for the hole.

We were flushed out immediately and couldn't believe it. But once we were out of the rapid and around the river, before our blood vessels got a chance to relax, the view downstream sent our hearts into our throats. Just 200 yards away was one of the most incredible river sights I have ever witnessed. A 150-foot tributary waterfall leaped in a show of shimmering, reflected light off a sheer cliff of columnar basalt and described a gentle arc as it crashed directly into the river. Most rivers of appreciable length offer tributary waterfalls that can knock the breath out of any mortal; but such falls are usually a long way off the mother river, sometimes a hike of many miles. Never had I seen such a dazzling display of water and light spuming and mixing into a main river. It would have been a crime to continue, so we pulled in directly across from the waterfall to make camp. (RB)

After a hypnotic dinner, with the eyes of seven chewing heads trained on a common spot across the river, a small group managed to break loose to hike downriver. It was a mistake. The next rapid was the biggest yet, a fuming, frothing, mad jitterbug of big water dancing and tripping through king-size holes and against Statue of Liberty boulders. We continued downstream to see if there was a calm stretch into which we could pull flipped boats, should we attempt the rapid. There wasn't. After 500 yards of fast, eddy-less water, the river pinched against the south wall and created a quarter-mile-long toboggan run that dumped through a half-dozen major souse holes and twice as many pressure waves. Finally, far below, a long, sleepy stretch of water waited, where the pieces could be picked up.

We couldn't remember spotting these rapids from the air, and we had seen some bad ones. But a worse rapid than this seemed unimaginable. To climb out of the canyon would be less than easy, and to portage half a mile over slippery, uneven terrain would be just a hair more fun than rolling boulders uphill all day. No one slept well that night. Only the spectacle of a shaft of moonlight playing on the milky waterfall across the river distracted us from our worries for a while.

Mapuche family and homestead in Araucania, the region of southern Chile between the Bío-Bío and Toltén rivers, which never fell to the Spanish conquerors.

OPPOSITE Caught in the maelstrom of Lava South (Bart Henderson).

No one was hungry the next morning, so we skipped breakfast and marched down, a funereal procession, to the first rapid. Jack Morison, a ten-year Colorado veteran, commented with a grating crack in his voice that this was the first rapid he had seen that was more difficult than Lava Falls on the Colorado—a rapid considered by many to be the toughest piece of whitewater in the U.S. After eyeing the stretch in the warming light of morning's optimism, we decided it was just possible to make the run down what we were now calling Lava South. Besides, it would be far preferable to run it than to portage, though the consequences of a mistake could be dear.

Alejandro looked at it and told us he could round up horses to get us out of the canyon. When we didn't respond to his offers, he told us he had two kids, cute with brown eyes, and he elected to walk the rapid.

Bruce rowed first, as Bill and I rode the bow. We pivoted past the tributary waterfall, a grand, miraculous sight, but we couldn't dwell on it. Survival superceded our sense of aesthetics, and all attention was directed downstream.

Bruce made a good entry, but smacked into a lateral wave that turned him the wrong way. The path devised while scouting from shore was the path not taken. We suddenly washed broadside against a boulder bar bisecting the river, and the boat started to ride up on its side, the first stage of a flip. Bill and I threw our weight on the rising tube, and the boat slid off the rock, around the far side into a channel we hadn't been able to see from shore. We were out of control in unknown water. We careened toward a pair of basalt slabs, smashed into one, spun on our side, and flopped down to the rapid's end, right side up. The bilge was brimming with water, and as Bill and I frantically bailed, Bruce pulled to shore on a broken oar. But we made it! (RB)

The day continued with a seemingly endless cascade of rapids. At one, Alejandro met a Mapuche Indian who described a recent drowning; and, as it turned out, the victim had been a friend of Alejandro's. At the next rapid, Alejandro explained he had three children, just school age, and again he volunteered to walk.

At another sharp rapid, Jack and George were kicked out of the boat. As Jack was thrown out, his tennis shoe caught on the oarlock, and he ended up dangling helplessly upside-down in the water, dragged along like a stunt man behind a horse. But this was no stunt: he struggled to keep his chin above water and to wrench his shoe free while the boat drifted toward the next cataract, a bad one.

The scene seemed too melodramatic to be real, but a watery scream from Jack dispelled the theatrical illusion. George Wendt splashed back into the bilge, grabbed the oars, and wrested the raft back to shore, while Mike plunged out of the boat next to Jack to help pull the caught leg free. Coughing and sputtering, Jack dragged himself up on the beach, a vacant, hurt look in his eyes. He'd come close; it was a freakish close call. Some nasty bruises and a deep cut testified the river couldn't be messed with.

Later that same day Bruce, too, paid his dues. After several cautious, successful runs, Bruce decided to run left through a rapid Jack had already run down the right. It was a mistake.

We suddenly plummeted through space toward a rock at the bottom of a fifteen-foot hole. We smacked, buckled, twisted, and almost flipped, and Bruce hurtled overboard. I sprang to the oars just as the raft slammed into a cliff. We bounced off, and a few hard pivot strokes spun us into an eddy. No sign of Bruce. A few seconds passed, those steel-cold seconds in which everyone wonders if the worst has happened, then we all broke into a chorus of screams. I felt the floor of the boat bump twice and realized Bruce was stuck underneath. I jumped to the side, about to dive in, when a blue-faced Bruce popped up, alive and sputtering next to the boat. (RB)

The day had been too intense to continue any farther. We'd run more big rapids in a single day than are run in twelve days on the Colorado, and a couple were as big as the biggest in the Grand Canyon. We camped across from another 100-foot tributary waterfall, one of dozens that grace this canyon, but we were too weary and jaded to give it proper attention. It was like trying to admire a beautiful painting after having been mugged. We slept in exhaustion, unable to worry about what tomorrow might bring.

The next morning, our sixth on the river, was crisp and clear as a bell. Alejandro went for a hike during breakfast and came back with information some Mapuche Indians had passed on to him. They said there were twenty-three miles of bad rapids ahead,

OPPOSITE, TOP Entering Lost
Yak Rapids, with tributary
waterfall just upstream (Jim
Slade). BOTTOM Punching the
hole in One-Eyed Jack (Skip
Horner).

worse than what we'd been through, including a major waterfall. He'd also heard a rumor that another group had tried to raft the river five years earlier, but they had lined their boats for days down to the first big rapid (which we had hit two days earlier) and there they walked out. Prudent, sane men. He concluded by relating the popular local legend of *chenque*, a cave deep at the bottom of the river where those who drown go. There they live forever, a very good and happy, though perhaps soggy, existence, but they can never resurface.

As was by now the pattern, the morning unrolled a stream of thrilling rapids. At noon, after a surprisingly nasty rapid that we navigated without mishap, we reached a red light. The river pinched into a sliver, barely fifty feet wide, and zigzagged through two tortuous right-angle turns. Most of the water jetted around the first corner, slid down an eight-foot sluice, and crashed into an overhanging cliff on the right. Overhangs—wedges of rock just above the surface—are major risks. Each year they drown a few hapless kayakers and occasionally some rafters. If a boat or body gets swept into an overhang, it easily can get pinned by hundreds of pounds of water pressure, making it impossible to escape.

The overhang ahead of us, coupled with the fact that the next three rapids, all in close succession, were horrendous, gave us pause. We were certain we had now reached the series of difficult rapids we had spotted from the air. From high above, they had all looked runnable. Ground level had a different story to tell. After an hour of scouting through the virtually impenetrable brush and after much deliberation, we decided to portage one boat and position it in the water downstream from the falls. There, we hoped it could catch the other boat, should it capsize.

Alejandro had taken little time to decide to walk out to the road and hitch to Santa Bárbara, our take-out point. He felt sure his four hungry children would want to see him again. So Jack Morison, who had not upset a boat in ten years of river running, started into the rapid with only one crew member. All the others, save Alejandro, were stationed in the other boat below, with coiled safety lines in readied hands.

"Whatever you do, Rich, stay away from that wall," Jack had warned as we pushed off, as if I might skip out of the boat and splash over to the wall for a playful inspection. Still, the tension in his voice put a lump in my throat.

His setup was perfect. He made it all the way to the top left, where the water was safest; but too quickly the current changed and pushed the raft into the right sluice that rammed into the overhang. The wall bore down on us at an alarming speed; I could see the dark recesses of the overhang getting bigger, enveloping the total picture of possibilities. I jumped back, and bam! We hit the wall at a forty-five-degree angle, and the boat ever so slowly slid up the wall, wedged briefly in the overhang, then tipped over. I jumped clear, as did Jack, and we were flushed safely to the eddy below. His first flip—after ten virtuous years of rafting.

Instinctively Jack and I grabbed the D-rings of the boat and tried to drag it to the right shore. It was as cumbersome as a pregnant hippo, and I found myself quickly exhausted. We made one small eddy, but couldn't find a handhold or break in the rock to climb out, so we slid back into the current and down around the corner toward the next rapid. The other boat showed in the nick of time and pulled us in barely twenty-five feet above the angry water. Had we been sucked in, we probably would have lost the boat and gear forever, to say nothing of Jack and myself. Luckily we hadn't sent both boats through the rapid back to back, as we had talked of earlier. The cost would have been high. (RB)

This sequence of rapids, each of which was a gamble, was later given the name Royal Flush. The first was the Ace; this second one we called Suicide King. Then we continued through the next rapid, the Queen of Hearts, without mishap; if we hadn't been scared to death, it would have been fun. Shortly thereafter we came to the fourth big one of the day. It was the legendary falls, or *salto*, that the Mapuche had warned us about, and it deserved legendary status. Briefly described, in this rapid—which came to be known as One-Eyed Jack—the river collides with a boulder as big as the Ritz, splits into two channels, then slices, spits, and erupts 15,000 cubic feet of water per second. We decided to portage.

We unloaded all the gear and lugged it 100 yards down the shore; then we lined the boats through the narrow portions of the river and pushed and shoved them through others. It was difficult to communicate because the roar of the rapid sounded like a rocket at

110

liftoff. In two hours' time we were back in the boats, tossing on white-capped water as we secured the gear. The lower half of the *salto* was run easily; the stretch is now called the Ten, to complete the gambler's hand. A mile downstream we made camp.

After a long, tough, but satisfying, day, we raised a few glasses of *pisco* and vermouth to the rapids of the Bío-Bío and toasted the looming beauty of Volcán Callaqui, still dominating our view to the south. Then we dined on spaghetti, soup, and pudding, and lay back for another starry evening with the sound of the river just a few yards from the security of our camp. Our aerial scout and every weary bone in our bodies told us the worst must be behind us.

We pushed off the next day and ran what we thought was a riffle, but it transformed into a Class V rapid (on a difficulty scale of I to VI). George, who was rowing, smacked into every big wave and reversal, and we came within inches of capsizing. Then, without warning, we were in another rapid. This time Jack was swept out of the boat but sprang back in as quickly as he had exited. Next, George repeated the act by being catapulted straight out of the bow. Had we again misjudged the Bío-Bío?

The wildness continued all morning, and despite seven days in the sun, our faces were wan and our knuckles blue. But then the rapids slowly began to ease, and the canyon walls began to taper back. Soon afterward the mountains began to recede and flatten. The first hour of our freedom from the uncertainties of the Bío-Bío's gorge was rich recompense for all the pain and terror. We were through, and the river now rolled in silent majesty.

Here, below the narrow gorge with its small strip of sky and the whitewater that had demanded all our attention, we had a chance once again to appreciate the Chilean scenery. Volcán Callaqui retreated into the maze of the cordillera, the soil around us grew rich from the sediment laid down by the Bío-Bío's floods, and homesteads once again appeared. The branches of the oaks were filled with the songbirds of the south—the Misto yellow finch, the brightly colored red-breasted starling, and the olive-green Chilean elaenia, the bird whose call resonates over the waters of the Bío-Bío.

At 4:00 P.M. we drifted into Santa Bárbara, where Alejandro, true to his word, was waiting with a pick-up truck. We derigged, loaded up, threw a few hands of Frisbee with the locals who had gathered at the small bridge, then drove into town for a final dinner at the firehouse, letting someone else do the cooking for a change.

After celebrating, we wandered to the town square, where we were surrounded instantly by dozens of children. They giggled and hovered around us, all smiles and good nature. As the first *norteamericanos* to ever visit their town, we were instant celebrities. They brought out a guitar, and we played American folk songs while they clapped and cheered; then they played and sang in the haunting accents of the loving tongue, and it was our turn to applaud. While the *pisco* flowed and the Southern Cross made its slow pilgrimage across the sky, the Bío-Bío sang its own soft song nearby, a gentle echo of the thunderous symphony of the Andes that had underscored our sleep for the past eight days.

OPPOSITE, CLOCKWISE FROM TOP Looking upriver toward the gorges of the Bío-Bío (Stan Boor). The river from the air, toward Lost Yak Rapids (Mark Jensen). Village inhabitants along the upper river (Curt Smith). Ferns and giant rhubarb plants line the banks in quieter stretches (Skip Horner).

Yuat, Watut, and Waghi

THE RED-BRICK, Tudor-style townhouse on East Seventieth Street in New York is undistinguished from the outside, but once one passes through its arched portal, another era is entered. It has a solid, masculine atmosphere: leather trim is everywhere; and mementos of Africa from when Burton and Speke tramped its interior, of the North and South poles, of the Andes, of the Himalayas lend its rooms historical resonance. The musty smell of rare and wonderful books wafts down the stairwell, and the members' book is signed by the Roosevelts, the Hemingways, the Hillarys of exploration.

We first entered the Explorers Club in the summer of 1973, having just returned from our first expedition—the first descent of the Omo River in Ethiopia. The tall man who greeted us in the dark, leather-trimmed halls was Lowell Thomas, the man for whom the building is now named. He listened carefully as we recounted our tales of high adventure on Ethiopia's great river. His attention was rapt, perhaps because he himself had organized a similar rafting expedition down the Indus River in Pakistan a few years earlier, an expedition that had ended in tragedy: one of his close friends had drowned.

When we concluded our tale, we turned to the man who for decades had broadcast reports from the far ends of the earth and asked him what he would recommend for the next great rafting expedition. "New Guinea," he said, his gravelly baritone cutting through the mannered atmosphere of the club. "New Guinea's got what you're looking for. Steep mountains, plenty of rainfall, and primitive cultures up every ravine."

He rose to leave early, shook hands firmly, then stood for a moment in the doorway, his tall, solid frame silhouetted by New York's dusty afternoon. "Go to New Guinea. That's the place," he repeated. Then he waved goodby. "And so long, until tomorrow."

Four years passed before we could follow Lowell Thomas's advice, but May of 1977 found us flying high over the new nation of Papua New Guinea, searching the landscape below. We had read of several expeditions on New Guinea's rivers and even had a couple possible expeditions of our own planned, on tributaries of the Markham and Sepik—two of the country's largest rivers. Yet it was an intimidating landscape we looked down upon. From the air the island looked like King Kong's habitat. The razorbacks and gorges of the island's massive cordillera rose and fell like the dark green billows of a frozen sea. A luxuriant carpet of vegetation, caused by the ever-present equatorial storms, covered the mountains with the dense foliage of a rain forest. And the wildest rivers found on any island twisted and raced through the jungle, carrying away the ten to thirty feet of rain that fell yearly on every square inch of the island's surface. It has been said that climbing a simple hill in New Guinea is more difficult than climbing a steep peak in the Alps. So, in such a steep and densely foliated landscape, where millions of tons of water flush through a tropical rain forest that remains but poorly charted over much of its area, what would rafting its rivers be like?

A multitude of waterways dissects Papua New Guinea's rugged limestone terrain into islands of isolation. Many of these rivers are muddy, flowing brown with silt off the forested mountains; many others are feathered and torn by rapids. As we peered out the window of the small coughing plane, searching out tributaries and main stems that we had earmarked for exploration by raft, two questions were foremost on our minds: How trustworthy is this plane? How trustworthy are the people down there?

The tales of cannibals, of headhunters, of missionaries and anthropologists lost in the hungry jungles, and of pockets of Stone Age tribes living in elevated valleys obscured from the outside world are, for the most part, true. At least in certain cases: the adventurer's tendency to exaggerate has no doubt added luster to the legends. New Guinea has long been one of the world's least-known regions, although it is the second largest island on earth, well behind Greenland yet comfortably ahead of Borneo. Its interior has been charted only within this century, making it one place where the prehistoric has survived into the present.

PRECEDING PAGE Profile of a Papuan (Michael Nichols/ Magnum).

OPPOSITE, TOP Flying over the mountains of New Guinea, near Lae; Watut River below (S. Kuwabara). BOTTOM Looking down on the Waghi River (Michael Nichols/ Magnum).

117

OPPOSITE Footpaths link clan villages throughout the New Guinea highlands (Richard Bangs).

New Guinea's first recorded contact with European civilizations came during that first flush of world discovery, when the Spanish mariner Jorge de Meneses landed on Waigeo Island, off the southern coast of the main island in 1526. He called it *Ilhas dos Papuas*, the island of the fuzzy-haired men. In 1545 Ynigo Ortiz de Retes sighted the 1,800-mile-long mainland and called it *Nueva Guinea* after the colony of Portuguese Guinea in Africa. Over the next 300 years, occasional seamen on their way to somewhere else—the rich trade routes with Siam, Malaysia, and India passed close by—charted the outlines of New Guinea; but cordial contact with its inhabitants was rare, and penetrations into the interior were unknown.

When explorers finally were motivated to explore the unknown land before them, they used the natural approach into the forbidding jungles: the rivers. In 1872 Italian naturalist Luigi D'Albertis began four years of scientific explorations on the largest, the Fly River, from its broad outflow at the Gulf of Papua (the scoop out of the southern coast of the island) to 580 miles upstream. On his final expedition, made with the young English engineer Lawrence Hargrave and a crew of Jamaican adventurers, the explorers were beset by malaria, attacks by native tribes of the cannibalistic persuasion, rebellion from the crew, shortage of supplies, wild fluctuations in river level owing to rainstorms, and finally by D'Albertis's own bout with feverish insanity and coma, induced by beriberi. It was the kind of expedition about which river runners have nightmares.

From that point on, forays into the interior were more frequent, though not exactly common. Missionaries and gold miners prospected for souls and stones up the major watersheds—the Fly, the Sepik, the Markham, and the Purari—but even as late as 1930, few had penetrated the precipitous mountain ranges that rim the heart of the 400-mile-wide island. The region was rumored to be uninhabitable, a wasteland of jagged limestone (termed "broken-bottle land" because of its sharp edges), impossible mazes of jungle and gorge, and rampaging rivers impossible to ford.

In 1930 two Australian prospectors, Mick Leahy and Mick Dwyer, put an end to those notions, though purely by accident. Taking a wrong turn in the irregular topography of the limestone regions, Leahy and Dwyer wound up making a complete traverse of the island, over hidden passes in the rugged high mountains, through tribes that had never seen white men before, and down the impossible gorges of the Tua and Purari rivers. At the time of their journey, tribal warfare was still practiced as a matter of course in the highlands, and they described seeing body after bloated body, some punctured by arrows, floating down the Tua River. Leahy ascribed their safe passage only to the temporary astonishment of the natives they met; they made it a practice to keep moving, to stay ahead of the natives' inevitable return to suspicion.

Finally, to prove his story to a skeptical outside world, Leahy organized an airplane fly-over of the heavily populated Chimbu and Waghi valleys in 1933. The flight "laid to rest for all time the theory that the centre of New Guinea is a mass of uninhabitable mountains," he crowed in triumph. [We found] "evidence of a fertile soil and a teeming population—a

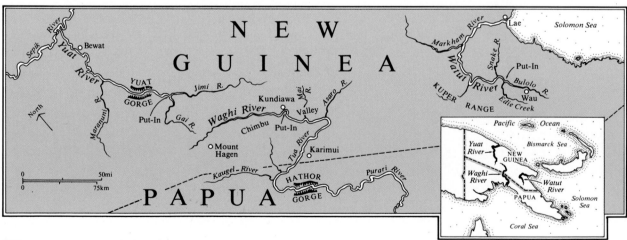

continuous patchwork of gardens laid off in neat squares like checker-boards, with oblong grass houses in groups of four or five, dotted thickly over the landscape. Except for the grass houses the view below us resembled the patchwork fields of Belgium." They estimated the population in the highlands of New Guinea at over a million people, who had never been touched by the modern age.

Aerial surveys and missionary zeal notwithstanding, the government maps of the highlands of New Guinea still show, in their 1973 printing, vast areas of blank space marked "Obscured by Clouds." Some 250 inches of rain fall each year in those remote regions, dripping from every wide leaf and long vine each day of the year. Across a broad belt of New Guinea's interior, from the Gulf of Papua arching northwest across the Purari River catchment into the Star Mountains in the island's core, there are no seasons but one: the rainy season.

Although the physical barriers of the island accounted in part for the slow progress of Western contact, so, too, did the fierce reputation of the Papuans. They were, after all, headhunters and cannibals: perhaps not as part of the daily routine, but certainly for those special occasions, such as tribal warfare and ceremonies. The recency of contact means that there are people still living in the highlands who were adults when the first whites came to their villages (and some who probably remember the taste of human flesh) and communities for the most part unchanged for several thousand years. As a result, New Guinea has provided the most pristine conditions for anthropological research on earth. Indeed, the list of influential anthropologists who have done fieldwork on New Guinea and its neighboring islands reads like a Who's Who of ethnology: Bronislaw Malinowski, Margaret Mead, Gregory Bateson, Roy Rappaport, and others engaged in over 400 research projects since 1899—to say nothing of Michael Rockefeller.

A fourth-generation Rockefeller, Michael had eschewed the worlds of investment and politics that made his family famous and wealthy and had taken up the career of anthropologist. He became involved in a .research project with Harvard's Peabody Museum among the Kurela tribes in the highlands of Dutch New Guinea (today's Irian Jaya, the western

The hatchet, or *ila*, and drum, or *gaba*, of the Motu people of the Port Moresby region—as well as the other implements used in food gathering, ceremony, and warfare—are still made of stone and wood in many parts of the island.

half of the island). The subject of that research was the rôle of tribal warfare in the social life of the natives, a spectacle not unlike a football match—full of high emotion, sound, and fury, but with few injuries and only an occasional death. Two influential documents resulted: the film *Dead Birds*, one of the first uses of cinema in anthropology, and Peter Matthiessen's book *Under the Mountain Wall*.

So fascinated did young Rockefeller become with Papuan cultures that he committed to a lengthy research project in the Asmat District of Dutch New Guinea, collecting artifacts such as intricately carved shields, canoe figureheads, and shrunken heads. He and his associate, Rene Wassing, a Dutch anthropologist, set out for the South Eilander River in their motorized catamaran on November 18, 1961. Against the advice of the natives, they took a coastal route instead of weaving through the intricate delta. A rogue wave swamped the boat, drowning the engine and sweeping their research notes overboard. Wassing and Rockefeller held on to the foundering craft, and the night's tide took them out to sea.

The next day Rockefeller strapped on two empty gas cans as flotation and slipped overboard, paddling for the coast. Wassing was rescued the next day, but search parties—including an effort by his father, Governor Nelson Rockefeller—found no trace of Michael Rockefeller. While the official explanation is that he drowned trying to swim to shore, some investigators suggest he made it to shore and encountered a tribe of warriors from the nearby village of Otsjanep. Unfortunately the warriors had been attacked recently by Dutch soldiers engaged in a "pacification" program, and they would have been unreceptive to a white man in distress. Michael Rockefeller may have become one of the last victims of cannibalism on the island.

Running the rivers of Papua New Guinea in the pursuit of pleasure, rather than science, was not new to the island. In the late 1970s John Blashford-Snell—commander of the 1968 Blue Nile expedition and subsequently leader of another military-style first descent down the Zaire in central Africa—tried to make the Strickland, a major tributary of the Fly River on the south side of the island, his third major conquest. His expedition failed because of the severity of the rapids and the impenetrability of the jungle.

In 1966 New Zealander Jon Hamilton tried a jet-boat ascent up the Yuat in the Sepik drainage; four years later a kayak team led by Australian Ross Allen tried to get down the Yuat. It was the only major defeat for Hamilton, who had forged up the Colorado through the Grand Canyon in 1960 and subsequently bested the Ganges, the Zaire (then called the Congo), and the Sun Khosi in Nepal, among others. Ross Allen's team had fared better. Going downstream, all they had to do was portage and patch their battered kayaks, haul their boats up a steep cliff, burn away the topside grass, and dodge three death adders and a python that scudded out of the blaze. But they made it.

In fact, it was the report of Allen's descent of the Yuat that drew us to Papua New Guinea, and we eyed the river carefully on our fly-over. From the air it looked runnable by raft, given a strong enough crew and a great deal of luck, so we decided to begin our river exploration of New Guinea by following Allen's route. We believed we had the technical expertise and equipment to run the river that had thwarted Jon Hamilton and given Allen a run for his money.

The river begins as a small stream on the northeast side of Mount Hagen, the centerpost of the central highlands. Feather white and torn by crystal cataracts in its upper reaches, the Yuat is joined by the Jimi and swells to a hundred feet in width. Several dozen tributaries later it is a roaring, chocolate-brown torrent, charging through scalloped limestone, spitting into glossy rain forest en route to its confluence with the Sepik, the largest river on the north side of the island. A hundred miles down its twisted path off the northeast side of Mount Hagen lies the Yuat gorge. Both Hamilton and Ross Allen had met their match there.

The members of the expedition—including John Yost, Jim Slade, Randy Simpson, Tom Cromer, and Rich Bangs from Sobek, and writer David Dworski—gathered in Mount Hagen, a frontier town in the western highlands, one of Papua New Guinea's eighteen districts. Since the nation is a new one and anxious to develop its natural resources, many of the highland valleys that were unknown a short forty years earlier are now buzzing with the activities of mineral researchers and other harbingers of the future. Our host in Mount Hagen was Hagen Hauliers, the sole commercial trucking firm in the mountains, run by a pack of adventurous Australians. Another adventurous Australian, visiting his friends in Mount Hagen, was Geoff Sadler; with a ready-for-anything attitude that would prove helpful on the expedition, he agreed to join the Sobek group on the first descent. Our last night in town was spent shooting pool and drinking beer with the local Aussies. They treated us like condemned men.

Launch day, sunny and scintillating. Tom Cromer caught a catfish for breakfast; we loaded and shoved off. A mile downstream the Jimi River joined us and turned the crystal water to a turbid malt. The current was fast and the jungle thick. But over the upper canopy of the rain forest the mountains of the Bismarck Range were magically verdant and cloud-swirled. We passed beneath hornbills, pelicans, lorikeets, herons, kingfishers, and other tropical birds.

While maneuvering around one sweeping curve, we were washed against a group of overhanging bushes, where a crocodile spilled from a high branch into the bilge, right at my feet. I almost dived in, but the reptile beat me to it. As it turned out, our hitchhiker wasn't a croc but a giant monitor lizard, common along the New Guinea rivers. The monitor, in fact, is the source of rumors in the 1700s that New Guinea harbored the world's only tree-climbing crocodiles. (RB)

The river swirled past a number of native vine bridges, supported by bamboo poles and woven in complex lattice designs. Close to the road, these bridges were bound together by cables, nails, and other modern materials; as we progressed downstream, the bridges became more primitive, built with only bamboo and vines. But there was no trace of their builders, or users. Ross Allen claimed to have seen pygmies in this area, which is possible—the range of physical types in New Guinea is broad, and one of them is a short-statured type common to the central mountains. Others look like bearded Assyrians, some have the hooked noses of Semites. Since contact with outsiders is rare even today, and contact with troops of white men who float the river in bloated boats is even rarer, we were no doubt seen without seeing for a good portion of the journey.

The second day on the Yuat began with a quickening current and sporting rapids, but suddenly the

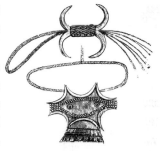

Youth and breast plates of southwestern New Guinea, in the region of the Watut River.

OPPOSITE, CLOCKWISE FROM TOP
Papuan man wearing
traditional penis-gourd (Dave
Shore). Women watch festival
proceedings in Watut village
(Richard Bangs). Beating
pulp of sago-palm bark to
produce the staple food of
the Sepik lowlands (Skip
Horner).

walls closed in: the Yuat gorge, bane of Ross Allen and Jon Hamilton. As we approached the first rapid, it became clear that the river went crazy. It dropped over a series of furious waterfalls, crashed into house-size boulders, and roared down an angry path to a pool half a mile downstream and several hundred feet below. We beached the boat and scampered down the rocky shore to scout. Our evaluation was immediate and unanimous: Allen and Hamilton were right. It was simply impossible.

The next day and the next and the next were spent portaging nearly all the rapids of the Yuat gorge. Halfway down the shore of the second rapid, one of the inflated boats fell on a sharp, pointed rock and exploded. Because it would have taken a day or longer to repair the boat, it was simply rolled up and placed in the second raft. Then Randy Simpson, at nineteen the youngest and strongest of the group, badly sprained his ankle on the irregular rocks. Finally, as the remaining boat was being lined down the shore, bearing its companion in its bilge, the force of the current pulled the bowline away from the three men holding it.

The boats were swept over a falls, where the rolled one sank like a stone into the bottom of the river. The good one was caught in the reverse hydraulic at the bottom of the falls, then spit back into the current to disappear downriver.

Jim Slade and I took off after it. The current was sprinting twice our land speed; nevertheless, we bulleted down the rocky shoreline with desperate abandon, hoping the boat might get caught in an eddy or against a snag. Then, out of nowhere, John Yost appeared next to us in the water, floating the fast but unobstructed main current. He overtook us and was soon out of sight around a bend.

When Slade and I made it around the corner, we could see nothing, and the hard reality of the situation began to sink in. The nearest village was a good two days' hike through dense, knotted jungle and across a raging river. One of our team already had a sprained ankle. Another was being swept downstream in the Yuat gorge.

We continued, distraught and exhausted. After about a mile and a half, we were ready to turn back and admit defeat, but John was yet to be found, so we scrambled on. Then, around the next weave of the

river we saw the boat—upside-down and moored to a cliff, with John passed out in exhaustion next to it—just above a long, large rapid. (RB)

For the next day and a half nearly every rapid was portaged, hardly the "conquest" of the Yuat we had hoped for. Only as the walls of the canyon began to taper off did the river mellow into rapids of a manageable scale. Even those were wild rides, plunges into deep troughs and climbs up thick high waves, where only the weight of the paddlers in the bow, thrown against the rising wall of water, kept our momentum going. But at least we were combating the Yuat, not avoiding it by portages; beating our way downstream, not being bested.

The next day we saw them—the saltwater crocodiles of New Guinea, the *pukpuk* (*Crocodylus porosus*, the estuarine crocodile), which may be the largest crocodile in the world. The largest ever caught measured an incredible twenty-one feet; these were a more credible eight feet, but their toothy smiles flashed at us from a sandspit just above a serious rapid. For David Dworski, writing later in *Quest* magazine, it was the final threat of an adventure far from his southern California home.

We need a decision in a hurry; run the whitewater to get away from them—and risk attack if we overturn—or drift quietly past, stop just short of the rapid, unload, and portage around.

Yost thinks we can slosh through the rapids. Bangs does too. We look to Jim Slade for the last word. "There are old boatmen, and there are bold boatmen," he recites, watching the crocs, "but there are no old, bold boatmen. We are going to make a very quiet portage." We ship our paddles and drift.

Fifty yards past them, we pull in. Our eyes scanning the beach for fresh pukpuk *tracks or waterborne arrivals, we quickly portage over easy rocks, then line the boat through a steep-falling set of boiling rapids. No crocodiles come to investigate.*

At last, on the sixth day on the river, we began to glide through a tropical paradise, hardly believing we had been living a nightmare two days before. Thick hardwood trees with flange-buttressed trunks stood like giants above ferns twelve feet high; strangler figs sent down their writhing roots; blazing rhododendrons, hibiscus, and bromeliads were in full riot. Golden herons, sulphur-crested cockatoos, parrots,

122

and lorikeets watched us from their roosts or darted overhead; after one spirited rapid, the sky was suddenly blackened by a flock of hundreds of flying foxes, among the largest bats in the world, with a wingspan of nearly two feet. As if to affirm its forgiveness, the Yuat even returned our lost raft, which had somehow been carried downstream from the gorge by the current ahead of us until it washed up on a logjam.

Curiously, we had seen no people since we began the descent nearly a week earlier. At one point we had even stopped at a village and found it empty, though the pelts of *cus-cus* (a small possom), bird-of-paradise feathers, dried corncobs, and animal skulls were strewn throughout. Finally, on the last full day on the river, the seventh, we encountered a family tending their garden of mango and coconut trees. We shared the sweet meat and the clear, tasty milk of coconuts with them, then set up camp on an island nearby. At dusk a group of natives in dugouts, decorated with expressively carved crocodile prows, paddled across the river. The shimmering, silvery twilight silhouetted the four natives as they dipped their spear-shaped paddles in perfect unison.

Early the next afternoon, humbled by the Yuat, yet ready for more, we reached the Catholic mission at Bewat. The missionaries were about to go down to the Sepik for supplies, so we hitched a ride on their motorized boat for the remainder of the Yuat's slow-moving run. As we motored between the banks of *pitpit*, a tall wild sugarcane that can reach heights of eighteen feet, we saw an astonishing sight: an island about the size of a house lot, complete with *pitpit* cane, grasses, and a clutch of small coco palms, floating down the river. We learned that such floating islands were not uncommon: the frequent rising and falling of the river erodes away chunks of the bank, and the roots of the cane and grasses keep them afloat. Sometimes they bear an unfortunate pig downstream with them; sometimes they are big enough to tether to a riverside house and to cultivate.

At the confluence with the Sepik River, we entered one of New Guinea's most famous regions. It was first thoroughly explored by the administrator of German New Guinea, Admiral von Scheinitz, who in 1886 traveled some 250 miles upriver. In 1920 Charles Karius found the river was navigable for over 300 miles for a large trading vessel, and considerably farther for canoes. But the river's fame is owing to the distinct art forms of the tribes that line its banks: ceremonial shields, face masks with crocodile and bird motifs, intricately carved figurines and footstools. With the colonization of the region, much of the artistic detail has gone out of the carving; but even today, the dugout canoes of the natives feature a figurehead cutting into the current, usually the grinning face of a *pukpuk*.

After our frustration on the Yuat, we decided to explore another river, the Watut, which we thought might provide a more satisfying expedition. So we loaded our rafts and other gear onto a plane at Marienberg, near the mouth of the Sepik, and flew over the flat lowland forests of the north coast to Lae, at the mouth of the Markham River. The Watut is a major tributary of the Markham, which, despite its relatively small catchment, has the burden of draining some of the rainiest terrain on the island, the mountains of Morobe District.

Our attention was drawn to the Watut because it, like the Fly, had been the scene of an early foray into the interior. In 1913 Arthur Darling, one of the legion of gold seekers who came to New Guinea from Australia in the early years of the century, started up the Markham from the coast town of Lae, then turned up the Watut with a small party in two whaling boats. When they came to the rapids of the Watut gorge, Darling stashed his boats and led his party upriver on foot. They were ambushed by the natives of the mountains, the Kukukuku, and most were slain. Darling himself managed to return to his boats in spite of a multitude of spear wounds and escaped to a mission station downriver. Although he was able to write his account of the expedition, the wounds eventually proved fatal.

The episode did not discourage the prospectors, however; the 1927 discovery of gold on a tributary of the Watut, Edie Creek, led to a gold rush comparable to the Klondike strike in the Yukon. Persistent trouble from the Kukukuku led to efforts to avoid the long and dangerous overland trail, and history's first airplane-based gold rush resulted. Strips were built in Lae on the coast and at Wau in the upper Watut valley, and personnel, equipment, and supplies were flown in—and over $10 million worth of gold was

125

OPPOSITE The decoration of
dancers at a *sing-sing* rivals the
birdlife and flowers of the
tropics. CLOCKWISE FROM TOP
Watut dancer (David Judge).
Victoria crowned pigeon
(Mike Boyle). Ochre-daubed
man (Danny Lehman/
Globe). Black-capped
lorikeet (Liz Hymans).

There are forty-two different
species of bird of paradise,
thirty-eight of which are found
on New Guinea, and the rest
on surrounding islands. The
birds are rarely seen perched,
and for some time after their
discovery, observers believed
that they had no feet and were
forced to remain eternally in
flight. Their long, flowing,
colorful tailfeathers have
proven to be their greatest
liability: the natives of the
island, always eager to
decorate their ceremonial
dress with bright colors, have
probably hunted the birds for
thousands of years. One
ornithologist estimated that, at
a *sing-sing* of some 500 native
dancers, nearly 10,000 birds
would have been killed to
provide ornamentation. Since
the introduction of firearms to
New Guinea, five of the most
beautiful species have been
hunted almost to extinction;
and, today, hunting them by
other than the traditional
means of arrows, spears, and
snares is forbidden.

flown out during the twenty-year mining operation.

The Kukukuku have the reputation of being one of the fiercest of New Guinea's tribespeople, and the record of being one of the oldest. Archaeological records show that people came to New Guinea 60,000 years ago, over the now-submerged Melanesian land bridge that linked the island with the Australian mainland; linguistically and biologically, the Kukukuku are identified with those earliest immigrants.

Like most tribal people in New Guinea, the Kukukuku have elaborate decorative impulses, as if attempting to mimic the vivid coloration of the flowers and birds of the tropics. The unusual tribal name comes from their word for the cassowary, a large flightless bird native to New Guinea, because the warriors wore a battle dress of cassowary talons around their waists.

What we knew about the Watut was promising: cascading from the Kuper Mountains on a roundabout route to the Huon Gulf, the Watut dropped about 100 feet per mile—certainly a spirited, but probably a runnable, gradient. We also knew the Kukukuku had not made a major raid in twenty-five years, so we felt our risks would be with the river. There were just five along for this run; Dworski and Sadler had returned to their more responsible lives as screenwriter and truckdriver, respectively.

Our first stop was the Wau Ecology Institute, a field station of the Bishop Museum of Honolulu, the world's foremost Pacific studies institute. Dedicated to the research of flora, fauna, and ecosystems of New Guinea—first explored by D'Albertis in the Fly River region eighty years earlier—the Wau Institute provided the opportunity to familiarize ourselves with the plant and animal life along our route. From there a washboard road led to a bridge over the Bulolo, a tributary of the Watut where we would begin our 120-mile-long river trip. The nearest village was called Sunshine—a fanciful name in a region that soaks in over 100 inches of rain a year.

The Bulolo was a clear stream, bounding over polished rocks and punctuated by sparkling rapids. At the bridge it was small, carrying about 350 cubic feet per second, barely enough to float our raft and its five paddlers. Although oars and frames make for cleaner runs, on an unknown river there is always the

likelihood of portages, as we had found on the Yuat. The less weight there is to carry, the faster our voyage could progress—and the better our spirits would remain. We decided to leave oars and rowing frames behind and had them trucked back to Lae. Everyone would paddle.

Within a mile after we put in, the Bulolo joined with the Watut and we rode the current through a settled country where cattle grazed on the banks, kids played in the shallows, and trucks raised clouds of dust on the nearby roads. This was the gold country of the 1920s and 1930s, and the evidence was everywhere: dredges fallen into disrepair, abandoned sluices, rusted gearboxes cluttering the banks, and even a gnarled old native prospector panning for gold in the shallows. He looked up in shock as we approached and watched us silently as we floated down toward the Watut gorge.

Seven miles downstream the river left the highland valley and, joining with the Snake River from the Herzog Mountains to the northeast, cut sharply west into the 10,000-foot Kuper Range. We anticipated a progressively wilder ride as we cut through the range, since the windward side of the mountains had by far the more rainfall, which meant the easily eroded limestone would be cut into steeper terrain. Indeed, we were given a tantalizing glimpse of what was to come: rising compression waves, tricky eddies, and trickier holes that seemed to lurk in wait for the unwary. It was all manageable and fun and exotic, with the raucous cawing of the sulphur-crested cockatoos filling the air above the Watut River and the limestone walls of the mountains rising above us.

Early that first afternoon a cry from shore arrested the downstream progress, and a young native boy motioned us over to visit the village of Taiak. About 200 Papuans lived there in a tidy compound of huts, with sweet potato gardens for each family, and coconut trees and coffee fields managed by all. Pigs, dogs, and chickens wandered underfoot, and children were everywhere. There was no road to Taiak; all its business with the outside world—primarily the export of the coffee grown there—was carried out along a footpath leading through the dense rain forest. As the path came to the river, it crossed over by means of the narrow suspension bridges that span nearly every river on this heavily populated island.

Coffee was introduced in the early 1950s, and by 1977 it had become the most important cash crop of Papua New Guinea. Until 1961 nearly all of the coffee exported by the island was grown here in the Morobe District near Wau. The villagers of Taiak were in the midst of drying the bright red beans, which were spread out on the flat sunny ground throughout the village.

We were already set for coffee in the black bag that held our food; we longed instead for a cooling beverage. Beer was our preference in the hot and humid tropics, but because it was too heavy to portage around whatever falls we might find downstream, coconuts were more appealing. John Yost, who willingly serves as camp cook on the expeditions he joins, led the negotiation for the huge nuts and finally convinced a young boy to climb up the long curved trunk of a coco palm. Whack! The boy's machete sliced through the air above our heads, and the heavy balls of sweet meat and milk fell to the ground with a thud. We set off down the river with a bilge full of fresh coconuts.

Soon the rapids began again: first, one straightforward drop, which we ran, then a series of two somewhat technical drops before the Watut twisted out of sight. As it was late in the day, Jim Slade suggested we pitch camp there and tackle the rapids the next morning. It was the wrong place for a good idea: there were no beaches or banks that far into the gorge. It seemed the villagers of Taiak had gotten the last good spot. We scoured the canyon walls until we found a narrow, vegetation-draped ledge well above water level. After a dinner of creole casserole, cooked over coals in the cast-iron Dutch oven, we curled up to sleep, listening to the sounds of the jungle and the river.

The volume of rain-forest rivers can change radically in just a few hours, rising when storms strike far upstream and falling even as it rains nearby. The next morning, as clouds pawed at the level of the pandanus trees on the canyon's rim 3,000 feet above us, the river level had decreased several feet, rendering the rapid just downstream too rocky for comfort. So our second morning on the river began in an all-too-familiar way: with a portage.

Tom Cromer, who had been down the Omo in Ethiopia and a number of other rivers with the group,

chose the calm water below that first portage to test the fishing in the Watut. In so doing, he missed the opportunity to scout the second rapid before his own run. He told the story later for *River World* magazine.

As we approached the lip of the cataract, John turned to me and grinned, "This one's going to surprise you." A rock divided the river at the top of the falls. It was a waterfall, not a rapid. The rock was partially submerged, and we would have to ease around it with considerable finesse or risk tipping as we fell off the edge. Too far in either direction could be disastrous. We had to thread a tight needle.

All this was explained to me as we ripped through the initial waves of the rapid. I could see the river disappearing ahead. Randy Simpson, in the stern, was shouting commands with hopes of coordinating our paddling. We were not, as yet, a crack team, and we might have done better had we left the boat to its own devices and foregone paddling. We hit the rock broadside at the top. As we twisted around, I could see a fifteen-foot vertical drop in front of me. I grabbed a gulp of air and held tight, readying myself for a leap should the boat capsize. We dropped over the edge backward and crashed into the eddy below. I opened my eyes and took a breath. We were still right side up. We decided to call the run a success.

The drop was the first part of four Class V drops in a row, a sequence that became known as Four-Part Harmony. Tight pivots around sharp boulders, forty-five-degree drops down ten-foot falls, and the ever-present risk of riding up or wrapping on one of the boulders hidden by the caramel-colored water made Harmony an adrenaline-pumping rush. It was rendered all the more tense by the uncertainty of what lay downstream.

Two more days of rapids in the Watut gorge provided all the thrills, and a few to spare, that the expedition could handle. At one point John Yost made another last-minute rescue of a raft from the lip of a falls, just as he had done on the Yuat. This time he leapt off a rock in midrapid, where he had been stranded just moments before, swam down to the swamped raft, and aided Tom Cromer and Jim Slade as they struggled to beach the craft.

The flexibility of the expedition, its guerrilla-style approach of light loads and quick portages, made the

OPPOSITE, TOP Melanesian women dance at annual fertility rites, Trobriand Islands (Mike Boyle). BOTTOM A dancer caught by flash during night's revel (Michael Nichols/Magnum).

PRECEDING PAGES Where a generation ago disputes were settled at spear point, today the *sing-sing* evens the score without bloodshed (Richard Bangs).

worst of the Watut's rapids pass by without further mishap. And there was always the unusual scenery and wildlife to enjoy: kingfishers and swifts swooping over the water and the eerie nighttime call of the Raggiana bird of paradise, one of the beautiful birds most prized by the natives for their feather headdresses. Because of the desirability of their long luminous pink and crimson feathers they are endangered; and national law prohibits hunting them with firearms—only traditional bow and arrow are allowed.

One afternoon, when the worst of the gorge seemed to be behind us, we rounded a bend and glimpsed a group of naked women bathing in the river. They quickly scurried into the jungle, but we pulled in at the beach, knowing a village must be nearby. Sure enough, the whole population of the village turned out to greet us, including the women, now modestly clothed in ankle-length missionary dresses. The village was an odd mixture of timeless native and enforced modern: a collection of grass-walled huts with thatched roofs in a roughly circular arrangement around a hardened clay common area, with a basketball hoop nailed to the top of a tall pole. We had seen such hoops in other villages in New Guinea, and this one, like the others, stood unused and out of place: we had never seen a basketball.

Native villages do change over the course of centuries, in spite of our romantic notions about the stability of tribal life. The hunter-gatherer people who originally settled New Guinea, beginning 60,000 years ago, underwent a dramatic change when Austronesians from Southeast Asia started arriving about 4,000 years ago. The newcomers brought pigs. No animal is more central to the Papuan economy than the pig, and their raising, breeding, and slaughtering form the framework for much symbolic activity as well. In some cases pigs are even better fed than people, although this is usually preparatory to the large pigkills that provide highland Papuans with their most important festivals. (Today, with the use of modern genetic techniques, attempts are underway to improve the breeding of pigs on the island. European pigs, however, have proven impractical for use in New Guinea: they are poor rooters, and they are vulnerable to sunburn in the tropics.)

Another dramatic innovation on the island took place when Spanish and Portuguese arrived from South America in the sixteenth century. Although, as we have seen, contact with the natives was uncommon and rarely friendly, it was the Europeans who introduced the sweet potato. Within less than a century, the *kaukau* had spread throughout the highlands and had became the most imortant cultivated plant in Melanesia. In the Papuan village of today, where every married couple has its own potato garden (with an average yield of over 5,000 pounds per acre), the sweet potato forms one of the cornerstones of native life.

Still another influence on the modern life of the native has been the effect of European contact on the language. Some 700 different languages, of two widely divergent families (plus a few anomalous tongues that belong to neither), have been identified on the island, and most people still speak their native tongue in their home village. In recent years, as the old barriers between tribes have been perforated by missionaries, colonial settlement, trade, and other modern influences, language itself has undergone radical transformation in the life of the Papuan. Intertribal communication today is frequently based on Pidgin English, a jargon derived from the mixing of German, Dutch, and English words with Papuan terms. It is a language that, when spoken aloud, reveals its meaning far more clearly and colorfully than any translation can achieve.

At the village at the end of the Watut gorge, as at Taiak upriver, not only did we have the chance to try out our facility with Pidgin, but they—more used to communicating in their own Papuan language—seemed equally pleased to test their Pidgin on us. *"Nem bilong dispela ples?"* Jim asked, testing the waters. It seemed to work: *"Wowas dispela ples."* We checked the map and found that Wowas was below the steepest section of river we would have to run. The worst was behind us.

As we feasted on trays of ripe pawpaws, bananas, and coconuts, the villagers constantly chewed betel nuts, the mildly stimulating fruit of the areca palm so popular in the highlands. To counter its laxative effect and to neutralize the acid it produced in the stomach, natives carry gourds full of lime (made from ground seashells) and use a spatula of wood or bone to dip lime into their mouths as they chew. Recognizing who were the greatest users of betel was

132

easy: after prolonged use the gums turn dark and the teeth go black. Seeing our interest, they offered us betel for dessert. Whether it was the betel or plenty of fresh fruits, we wound up giving an impromptu concert with harmonicas and kazoos, and our feast turned into a *sing-sing*.

Sing-sings are the celebrations of the people of Papua New Guinea. The word is, of course, Pidgin and often refers to tribal holidays or festivals, such as the Eastern Highlands Show held in Goroka every two years to unite clan groups—and traditional tribal enemies—from throughout the five provinces of the highlands. There, thousands of natives dress in their feathered finery, paint their faces and bodies elaborately, make music, and dance with enthusiasm and abandon. But most *sing-sings* are more modest, if not less fun: marriage and engagement celebrations, pigkill feasts, or spur-of-the moment parties, such as on the occasion of unexpected guests.

Sipping coconut milk (though still longing for beer) we continued our conversation, telling them that we were traveling from Bulolo to Lae: *"Mipela go long Lae, na mipela kam long Bulolo."* They didn't hide their disbelief as they said, *"Plenti stone long tap,"* pointing upriver. Then, as though to corroborate what the map indicated, a villager said, *"Plenti stone long tap, na stone wara long Lae,"* which we translated to mean the river was pleasant the rest of the way. Our rafts, we learned, were called *gumi kanu*—rubbery canoes.

When it came time to leave, we waded through wide-eyed children and semiwild pigs to the boats. One ancient member of the clan wobbled up just as we were about to embark and asked *"Mi laik draivim bikpela kanu bilong yu?"* How could we refuse?

He clambered aboard, and we spun out into the current. He tittered and chattered, and the entire village followed their eccentric elder along the banks. Some kids began pounding drums. The cicadas started up a raucous chorus, like special effects in a jungle movie. Every time we got close to shore, the old fellow creased his brow and motioned us back to midstream. Finally, almost two miles downstream, with stern insistence we got him off. He rewarded us with a happy, hearty wave, and we floated on.

We had passed through the roughest part of the river, but we had only descended about half our route. Now, as the river flattened out, the absence of whitewater was more than compensated for by the wildlife. Here in the oxbow turns of the slower Watut, we saw more birds than in the previous fifty miles: Papuan hornbills (called *kokomo* locally) eyed our rafts from branches just a few feet above our heads; egrets and night herons kept their stately distance; bar-eyed crows swept over the river above us with curious caws; and the colorful eclectus parrot and riflebird were seen from afar, their bright feathers flashing through the upper canopy of the forest.

When on the final day we merged with the Markham River, we found ourselves on a major waterway with ten times the volume of the Watut. We were closing in on civilization: dugout canoes boasted crossed masts and sails, and as more and more villages pressed against the banks, their people were less and less surprised to see us. Finally we pulled in and deflated the raft, finding shelter from an afternoon tropical storm under a bridge. As the day turned to night, we hitched a ride in a pickup truck back to Lae, the second largest city in Papua New Guinea and home of the South Pacific Brewery.

There was still the Purari system of the south side of the island to run, the second largest river on the world's second largest island. Its headwaters reach into the populous Chimbu and Asaro valleys, 360 miles upstream from the broad, wandering delta of the Purari at the Papuan Gulf. The Waghi is the longest tributary of the Purari, joining with the Asaro to form the Tua, which continues gathering tributaries and volume for another 100 miles before it becomes known as the Purari. Its course, its history, its size are great as only a great river can be; and although it would be six years before the opportunity would come to run the river, it took a great expedition to do it. Not necessarily great in terms of quality or bravery or ambition, but certainly in terms of scale.

In August 1983 a combined team of seventeen rafters, journalists, cameramen, and other media talent met in the town of Kundiawa, near the Waghi River. The group of seven rafters that made up the core of the expedition was outnumbered by the media covering it: a writer and a photographer from *GEO*; a director, two cameramen, a soundman, and a troubleshooter from the BBC; another camera-

Clay pots of the western Sago districts near the Sepik River.

Coffea arabica, introduced to New Guinea within this century, is now one of its largest cash crops.

133

OPPOSITE, TOP A secret special place off the Watut River (William Boehm). BOTTOM Highland boys enjoy the luxury of modern travel on the Waghi (Liz Hymans).

man, a free-lancer from the United States; an eighteen-year-old novice rafting guide from California, picked as the subject of an article for a magazine aimed toward eighteen-year-olds; and on-camera "talent" for the BBC program, a young woman adventurer who claimed to have ridden a horse and walked barefoot across the spine of New Guinea. In addition, the expedition was supported by a full complement of commercial products, from lifejackets to athlete's-foot powder, which had been donated by companies willing to have their names seen in at least two magazines and on the BBC.

The river was to be run in three sections. The first leg was the mild Waghi near its source off the flanks of Mount Hagen, in the central highlands. Here, the Waghi flowed through New Guinea's largest natural reserve of birds of paradise in a region of limestone caves and cascading tributaries, a natural paradise perfect for the television cameras. Next was the heart of the adventure, the Tua, down its ninety miles of whitewater from its confluence with the Waghi to its narrow, deadly limestone gorge. Finally, if all went well, a stretch of the mighty Purari itself would be run, perhaps just for the fun of it, without cameras or journalists or on-screen "talent."

As we sailed downstream from our put-in near Kundiawa, the Waghi was at first kind, treating us to visual delights in generous servings. Crystal waterfalls weaved down bright limestone cliffs; klinkii pine trees clung to ridges and mixed with glossy fronds and succulents; sand beaches shimmered like gold; and a Raggiana bird of paradise—the national symbol of Papua New Guinea—wheeled between the walls. The first night we camped above a masterfully crafted vine bridge, which brought some of the curious villagers across to our cluster of tents.

A surprise was in store: the BBC crew, uncomfortable in the thick heat and impenetrable terrain of the river canyon, decided not to camp with the river crew, but to helicopter back and forth from their Kundiawa hotel every day. Earlier they had proven their unwillingness to trust their equipment to the boats on the river by electing to do all their shooting from shore. They hired an American cameraman, Roger Brown, to get the necessary on-river footage—as long as he used his own camera.

After a late put-in the next morning, while the BBC director set up shots to make the jungle look more like a jungle, we drifted peacefully down the lazy river for a couple of miles. By midmorning the pace quickened: rapids grew in size and intensity, spraying bullets of whitewater across our decks. In contrast, the jungle seemed to soften, and the birds invitingly displayed more color.

Two days and countless rapids later, the name of the river changed to the Tua as it entered a steep gorge, where we encountered an impasse: a mile-long section of choleric cataracts, foaming and spitting in defiance. As if to further mock our efforts to float the river, the rapid was encased in sheer cliff walls, polished battlements that stabbed into the current. These made it impossible to line the boats along the banks and difficult to consider a portage. We had two options: hack a trail into the vertical jungle and carry all the expedition gear around, an operation that could take three days, or call in the chopper to airlift it all downstream around the rapid. Three hours later we waved a hearty farewell to the helicopter and the BBC crew and set up camp for the night.

After the gorge, the Tua changed direction to an east-west corridor just north of the village of Karimui. There the current rang quick and sleek and passed numerous waterfalls, a few isolated fishing villages, and two clumsy-looking cassowaries. When the Tua joined with the Mongo River, its size suddenly leapt to over 50,000 cubic feet per second—a flow of force and scale that could only mean furious rapids below.

After an uncomfortable night, sleeping next to the constantly rising river, as a rainstorm buffeted the canyon, we waited until the weather cleared before starting out. The river pulled us into an awesome limestone gorge, where powder-white cliffs arched almost 2,000 feet above the muddy flow, and clouds wrapped the peaks. The scene was primordial: if a pterodactyl suddenly screamed up the canyon, it would not have been out of place.

It was here, as the river plummets southward through New Guinea's greatest gorge, that we met The Rapid. It was the biggest, angriest piece of water I'd ever seen; yet to the other guides there appeared to be a path through the maelstrom. I didn't see it, and as it was my birthday, I didn't relish the thought of drowning. I elected to walk around the rapid and set up safety

throw lines at its base, where I might be able to help someone in trouble. (RB)

Skip Horner rowed the first boat into the mess. It tossed like a cork in a typhoon but emerged upright. Then Mike Boyle's boat, with George Fuller (expedition doctor) and Renée Goddard (the young California rafting guide) made its entrance, five feet too far left. It flipped end over end. Almost simultaneously John Kramer's boat entered, found an eddy, and picked Boyle out of the water. Fuller, too, found safety by swimming to shore, but Renée Goddard was swept downstream after climbing on top of the flipped boat.

I hurled the throw line to Renée, but it fell short. I grabbed the second line and hurled again. It, too, missed its mark, and Renée, pale as whitewater, was being swept toward the next rapid.

"Jump!" I screamed, as the raft careened near an exposed rock at the lip of the rapid. She didn't move, frozen in fear. "Jump, goddamn it!" I tried again with all the menace I could muster. She reacted, jumped toward the rock, and clutched its slippery surface as the unmanned raft disappeared into a dark wave.

Everyone was all right, but the capsized raft—with food, equipment, and cameras—was a runaway, washing downstream toward a major waterfall we had seen from an aerial scout. The third boat, piloted by John Kramer, had completed the last rapid upright. Now Kramer pulled on his oars in a desperate attempt to catch the runaway raft.

I assisted Renée to shore, then felt helpless. But this was no ordinary expedition: out of nowhere the helicopter appeared, sped over to my vantage and hovered just above me. Park, the pilot, gave me a signal, and I saw that he knew the situation and had a plan. I leapt up on the runners and pulled myself into the back of the chopper, and we zoomed downstream.

Two miles later we caught up with the raft. The helicopter lowered until it was hovering ten feet above the raft, staying even with it by matching the current's speed. Park nodded, and I jumped from the helicopter, landing on the slick bottom of the raft.

I knew I had to act fast. The waterfall couldn't be far away. I reached under the bow, found the bowline, and dived into the water. I tried to tow the raft toward shore, but I was unable to make much progress against the head-long current. I could feel my strength sapping as I pulled and strained to move the bulky craft. I began to doubt that I could make it.

Then the cavalry arrived: John Kramer, still heaving on the oars, at last caught up with the runaway raft. With the combined efforts of him and his crew, we wrestled the runaway to shore. Kramer lay in the bottom of his raft, exhausted, struggling for every breath. (RB)

The raft was turned over and its supplies inventoried. Miraculously, nothing was lost. Cameraman Roger Brown had shot the rapid from the shore, so he missed the real action two miles downstream. The BBC crew had left the river expedition to film local color farther downstream, so they, too, missed the day's action.

By twilight we were all reunited on a broad beach just above still another major rapid. Here we set forth arguments and counterarguments, took a show of hands, and made the decision to end the expedition. The film was complete, as far as the BBC was concerned; the Waghi and much of the Tua had been successfully rafted. All that remained were the lower stretches of the river system, the Purari, which promised to be the most difficult, the most dangerous—and the most enticing.

But then, something should always be left for expeditions to come.

OPPOSITE Aspects of the Waghi River. CLOCKWISE FROM TOP Entering the Waghi gorge (Liz Hymans). Boatman taking a cooling soak at day's end (Michael Nichols/Magnum). Sheer walls and waterfalls (Liz Hymans). A soaked crew powers through the last rapid of the Waghi River (Michael Nichols/Magnums).

Colorado

CHAPTER EIGHT COLORADO *River of Time*

PRECEDING PAGE The calm between storms, in Marble Canyon (Bart Henderson).

OPPOSITE, TOP Looking down into the oldest region of the Grand Canyon (Stan Boor). BOTTOM Tapeats Creek leading upstream into the heart of the canyon at Mile 134 (Liz Hymans).

*I*T ALL BEGAN, *for me, at a meeting of the Canoe Cruisers Association, the 700-member Washington, D.C., chapter. In the midst of the button-down capital there was an underground of cutoffs and T-shirts that each weekend assembled by the banks of some Shenandoah or Appalachian river to rake the whitewater with paddles. A recent high school graduate searching for life's passion, I joined up at the urging of my old Scout leader and was immediately hooked. My summer weekends were consumed as I broached Grumman canoes and splintered white ash paddles on a cluster of Indian namesakes—Chattooga, Nantahala, Youghiogheny, Monongahela, Potomac.*

Then, at a monthly meeting of the CCA, the main event was a super-8 movie of members who had canoed the Colorado River through the Grand Canyon. As the screen flickered, a spell was cast over me. I was mesmerized: the waves seemed oceanic, ten times the size of anything I'd encountered on the Cheat or the Rappahannock, even in spring spate; the scale of everything was overwhelming—the canyon walls, the crests and troughs, the eddies, the wet grins. Some invisible, powerful hand reached from the screen and pulled me in like no $10 million movie ever had. I drove home with a monomaniacal craving: I had to run the Colorado, or die. (RB)

It was 1968. Although the Grand Canyon had begun to soar in popularity with the attention it had received in a recent environmental battle, the rafting "business" was still barely discernible. In 1965 the Bureau of Reclamation had unveiled its plans to erect dams at two points in the Grand Canyon, which led the Sierra Club to take out full-page newspaper ads across the country, asking, "Should We Also Flood the Sistine Chapel So Tourists Can Get Nearer the Ceiling?" The dam proposals went down to defeat. Then in 1967 Senator Robert Kennedy floated the Colorado, adding the luster of the still-magic Kennedy name to the sport of river rafting (even though Barry Goldwater had beaten the Kennedy clan down the Colorado by twenty-eight years). Suddenly, rafting the Colorado was in vogue.

The first commercial trip had been in 1938, when Norman Nevills and his Mexican Hat Expeditions took seven people down the river—including the first two women to make the trip. Now, after thirty years of barely enough interest to warrant a newspaper ad, the handful of adventurers who would take novice passengers along for the ride found themselves sitting on top of a powder keg of possibilities. Hatch River Expeditions, which had grown to maturity under Bus Hatch—who had first run the Colorado in 1934—was one of several companies more than willing to meet the growing demand. More passengers meant more crew members, and there were few prospects: the career of river guide just wasn't known beyond Page, Arizona, and Vernal, Utah; and sons Ted and Don Hatch had already hired the best from both towns.

With no guiding background whatsoever, I composed a letter to Ted Hatch, asking for a job, lying through my teeth. I had never rowed the Green; I had never even traveled west of the Blue Ridge Mountains. I just let the compass spin and point west. "Report to Lee's Ferry April 28 for trip departing April 29," he wrote back. "Welcome aboard."

The flight into Page six months later over the southern rim of the Colorado Plateau, across magnificently cross-bedded deposits of Navajo Sandstone that coat the escarpment, was stunning. I'd never seen such a vast expanse of uninhabited land, devoid of almost any sign of human presence. In the soft, coral flush of daybreak, I pressed my nose against the window in utter awe of the spectral beauty below. No landscape ever appeared so dramatic. Then, like a giant gash in the skin of the desert, the Grand Canyon of the Colorado appeared, a dark, crooked rip tearing across the landscape to the horizon. (RB)

Rafting the Grand Canyon has become such an accessible adventure in America's recreational world that it's hard to believe that twenty years ago it was still a novelty, and twenty years before that, a rarity. The first person to go down the Colorado through the Grand Canyon—purposefully, as we shall see—was geologist, ethnologist, Union Major John Wesley Powell, leading a party of ten in 1869, with support from the U.S. Congress and the Smithsonian Institution, on a voyage of discovery and research. The hundredth person took the trip eighty years later, in

141

OPPOSITE Still waters of the Colorado in Marble Canyon, near Mile 31 (Bart Henderson).

1949. Commercial rafting began on a regular basis in the fifties and had taken off by the time the sixties drew to a close. Perhaps it was the same combination of social and economic factors that led to Earth Day, jogging, health food, and backpacking that created the Grand Canyon boom. Or maybe it was that finally the expertise and equipment were available. Or possibly it was just demographics: the postwar baby boomers were looking for something special to do during their two-week summer vacations, and rafting the Grand Canyon seemed to promise something very special indeed.

There is something special about the canyon. The natives of the region feared it; the Navajos, for instance, believe the waters of the ancient flood drained away through a hole in its bottom and would have nothing to do with it. Lieutenant Joseph Ives, who led a war department foray up the Colorado in 1858 in search of a western river as useful as the Mississippi, noted in his official report that the "depth and gloom of the gaping chasms into which we were plunging, imparted an unearthly character to a way that might have resembled the portals of the infernal regions." His report concluded, in words that ring with irony across the intervening century, "Ours has been the first, and will doubtless be the last, party of whites to visit this profitless locality. It seems intended by nature that the Colorado River, along the greater portion of its lonely and majestic way, shall be forever unvisited and undisturbed."

Even today some visitors to the viewing areas at the South Rim are physically shaken by the immense scale of the place. It drops a full mile, and more, from rim to river at its deepest point; it is 277 miles long, with an ever-expanding breadth from Lee's Ferry to Grand Wash. A total of nearly 2,000 square miles of eroded slopes drop from the surface of the Kaibab Plateau down successively more ancient rock layers toward the ribbon of river far below. Then there's the overwhelming silence that seems to rise out of the canyon, the almost tangible weight of all that empty space between the terraced walls ten miles apart, which leads to the uncanny absence of sensations, of perception, of meaning.

While some 4 million people stand on the rim of the canyon every year—most of them lost in admiration, not terror—only 15,000 ride through the canyon on the river that has cut it. That number is set by the National Park Service and has remained constant since 1973, when the sudden increase in river trippers over the previous five years required setting a limit. Still, many visitors to Grand Canyon National Park feel they have seen the canyon once they have stood on the rim. It is one of the world's great vistas, without question; but the two weeks it takes to float from Lee's Ferry to Grand Wash make all the difference in the world.

For the rafter, kayaker, canoeist, or passenger, they are two weeks of rising walls of vermilion limestone; of side creeks spilling into the river from fern-lined gorges; of cactus fringed with red or yellow blooms, and of the white blossoms of the sacred datura calling like a trumpet from its dense green bush. Two weeks of rocks progressively deeper and rougher, and more aged, slowly sweeping past as the current carries you into the primordial ages, and of rapids—161, not counting riffles—that have become the world's standard, the towering waves and holes big enough to swallow a delivery van at Crystal and Lava falls. Every day of those two weeks is filled with enough beauty from sunrise to moonset that those 15,000 feel like the most privileged people in the world.

Those who journey down the Colorado make a float through history and geology; and it begins at Lee's Ferry, which has a bit of both. There the Echo Cliff monocline slices across the Colorado, and the walls of the Kaibab Plateau kneel to the level of small rolling hills between Glen Canyon and Grand Canyon. Exploration by Mormon scout Jacob Hamblin in the 1860s showed that only at Lee's Ferry, and at Grand Wash 277 miles downstream, could the Colorado be crossed. Even today, in this age of bridges, tunnels, and land "reclamation," this is one of only two road access sites for the entire length of the canyon. The crossing was named for another Mormon, John Doyle Lee, who, on the orders of Brigham Young, set up shop in this pan-fried valley. For three years Lee ferried travelers across the river, using one of Powell's discarded expedition boats, while building a ranch and trading post on the nearby Paria River.

Lee was among the first recorded non-Indians to find a new identity in the canyon. He was lord of the

142

river, master of his own fate and that of his clients, who paid him for safe passage across this rare point of forgiveness in the terrain. Or so he thought. In 1874 he was tracked down and arrested for his part in the Mountain Meadow Massacre of 1857, when 123 non-Mormon pioneers were murdered in southwest Utah. He was executed in 1877, apparently a scapegoat: it was the only justice delivered in the matter.

John D. Lee was the first of the white settlers who sought sanctuary and a new life in the rarefied environs of the Grand Canyon. It is, if nothing else, far away—from the past, from commitments, from society. In some ways he was the precursor of the river guides who would come nearly a century later, looking for the escape that could be found only in the nearest faraway place.

My first job was to drive a winch-truck down to Lee's Ferry from Page. It wasn't easy for one who had never used a clutch before, but despite a minor conflict of interest with the Page Boy Motel's hanging plastic sign, the trip was a success. I clutched and double-clutched the fifty-mile route, crossed the 467-foot-high Navajo Bridge over the river I saw as my destiny, and wheeled down the ramp at Lee's Ferry.

A line of thirty-three-foot-long World War II surplus pontoon bridges, refitted as passenger-carrying rafts, were being inflated by gasoline generators. Stepping out into the dry ninety-five-degree heat, I faced my colleagues to be, and for the first time encountered river guides. Ten of them. Bronzed beyond belief, muscles like a Rodin sculpture's, hair thick and bleached by the desert sun, Skoal stains on their chins. One guide sported a tattoo, a fly chasing a spider. Everyone seemed several inches taller than my six-foot frame, and at least thirty pounds heavier—all gristle and sinew. As I made the rounds of introductions, I felt as out of place as a white-tailed deer in a pen of Brahman bulls. What was I doing here? If I'm fired, I thought, I'll hitch to Las Vegas and find a job as a bellboy.

These people seemed larger than life. I'd never seen anything like them. Exuding lava flows of self-confidence, fitter than any lifeguard, they went about their tasks with pure competence and blithe indifference. Not a one spoke with the enforced sense of grammar and syntax that had filled my upbringing. All were

from the West, and a different value system prevailed. Here, style, smile, and tan made nobility. (RB)

Before anyone could be a rafting guide on the Colorado, then or now, a strict apprenticeship must be followed. Almost feudal, with several levels of initiation, the pathway to river guide begins with the "swamper."

I was assigned the cook boat, piloted by twenty-six-year-old Dave Bledsoe, a black-headed bear of a boy, son of a Lake Mead marina manager. Sharing the raft with me was veteran Rick Petrillo and trainee Jim Ernst. Our job was to precede the ten-raft armada to each camp and set up the commodes and the kitchen. Each morning, after our passengers from the Four Corners Geological Society departed, we would linger behind to clean camp and bury the mountain of trash and excrement that 110 geologists, 10 boatmen, 10 assistants, 4 trainees, and 1 swamper had left behind. It was almost as much of a revelation as were the Vermilion Cliffs. Nowadays all waste, fecal and otherwise, is carried out of the canyon; but I doubt that the swamper's job has changed much.

As we launched into the swirl of green that is today's Colorado—the silt that led Spanish explorers to name it "red colored" now settles out in the reservoir fifteen miles upstream behind Glen Canyon Dam—I was grabbed by a view as otherworldly to me as that of another planet. Mesas, side canyons, bosses, ramparts, benches, monoclines, and faults all shaped the eerie landscape. I went into high gear, playing vassal to river guide Dave, and saw the canyon in all its glory. In turn, Dave showed me the ropes, literally, from half hitches to the canyon history. His syllabus was the open textbook of 1.7 billion years of exposed geology that surrounded us, more than a third of the earth's 4.6 billion year age. His lectures were filled with tales of crusty hermits, of florid raconteurs, of the gold-miner's greed and the romantic's bitter comeuppance. (RB)

Riding the river through the canyon, one continually touches upon traces of explorers gone by—of Jacob Hamblin, who named Badger Creek after shooting his dinner there one night; of railroad baron Frank Brown, who allowed his obsession with a train route through the Grand Canyon from Colorado to California to carry him to his drowning at Soap Creek Rapids, just eleven miles downstream from Lee's

OPPOSITE, CLOCKWISE FROM TOP Passing the hole at Crystal, most awesome of the Colorado's on-river dangers (Liz Hymans). Jubilant passenger at Granite rapid (Stan Boor). Entering the realm of Supai Group sandstones near Mile 12 (Curt Smith). Water-smoothed stone at North Canyon, Mile 20 (Liz Hymans).

145

OPPOSITE, CLOCKWISE FROM TOP Beamer's Cabin on the banks of the Little Colorado, Mile 61 (Liz Hymans). Unidentified bones at South Canyon, Mile 31 (M.P. Ghiglieri). Cross-bedded sandstones of the Supai Group, formed from ancient desert dunes (John Kramer). Relics at Bass Camp, used by miner and trailbuilder William Bass between 1883 and 1923 (John Kramer).

Ferry; of Bert Loper, who began running the Colorado in 1907 and died on the river forty-two years later of a heart attack at age eighty, in the middle of the rapid at Mile 24½. The human history of the canyon spins off like side canyons into the rosy rocks, echoing the amazement of discovery and the anguish of loss with every bend in the river. But few tales are as incredible and unlikely and somehow just barely possible as the legend of James White.

Horse thieves do not make the best witnesses, and James White was a horse thief. In the summer of 1867, according to his own testimony, he and three partners stole some mounts (from Indians, he claimed) and set up prospecting on the San Juan River in western Colorado. Trouble started when White and one of his partners got into a gunfight; trouble continued when Indians attacked the small party and killed another partner. Trouble multiplied when White and George Strole, his remaining companion, put onto the San Juan River on a makeshift raft to flee their attackers; and trouble reached logarithmic proportions when Strole was drowned in a rapid—either on the San Juan or after it joined the Colorado in southern Utah.

Then the real travail: according to White's best recollections (which, in light of the following, must be taken with a grain of salt), the raft was reduced to driftwood by rapids, and he spent fourteen days clinging to a floating log, during which time he was swept through the canyons of the Southwest—first Glen Canyon, then Marble Canyon, and finally the Grand Canyon. By the time three men pulled the starving, sunbaked, barely sensible White from the river, he was near Calville, Nevada, over 400 miles from the San Juan River. If false, it's quite a shaggy-dog story, even for a horse thief; if true, James White beat John Wesley Powell down the Colorado by two years, and he did it in considerably less time. And cheaper too.

River stories have a way of growing to grand proportions, even in canyons less than grand. On the Colorado the tales rival those of Paul Bunyan and Davy Crockett. John Hance, the canyon's first permanent settler, once claimed to have trekked by snowshoe halfway across the Grand Canyon on top of its dense cloud cover—until the fog began to break up, when he had to leap to a nearby pinnacle for safety. Another time Hance told of being chased by Indians while out riding on his pony. To escape, he cajoled his horse, Old Dusty, to try to jump across the gulf. Of course they couldn't make it, so they turned around in midflight, returned to the rim, and fought off the Indians. For some reason, the detail of his horse's name makes it all sound much more likely.

Of the many true stories, tall tales, and low jokes that punctuate every river trip down the Colorado, none is more mysterious than those of the Anasazi. The name itself means "ancient ones," in the language of the Navajos—recent arrivals themselves to the American Southwest. People were hunting in the canyon as long ago as 4,000 years, according to radiocarbon dating of the small willow-twig figurines of game animals found in Grand Canyon caves by Bus Hatch and others. These original visitors were of the Desert Culture, a widespread social configuration of hunters and gatherers who left behind arrowheads, stone spear points, baskets, and sandals. The Desert Culture evaporated, probably diffusing its influence over the region until a single culture was no longer recognizable.

The Anasazi appeared in the canyon about 1,500 years ago as a group of hunter-gatherer immigrants who brought with them the cultivation of corn and squash, probably from Mexico. Although they may have been in the Southwest for several centuries, it was only after they learned to till the earth, grind grain with handstones, make ceramic pottery, and bury their dead that they began to inhabit the canyon. These were the people whose signature "apartment house" cliff dwellings and ceremonial pithouses, or *kivas*, are in evidence throughout the Southwest—at Mesa Verde and Chaco Canyon most impressively.

From A.D. 900 to 1150 the Anasazi develped villages on the canyon floor, aided by the relatively wet weather of the period and their own cultural florescence. They cultivated the riverside fields at the Unkar Delta (Mile 73 downstream from Lee's Ferry), at Nankoweap Canyon (Mile 52), and at some 1,500 other sites within the canyon where today their petroglyphs, pot shards, granaries, cliff-clinging apartments, and even a few sacred smoke-stained *kivas* can be found.

The ancient ones inhabited one of the wonders of

146

the world for almost three centuries, then all sign of humanity in the canyon ceases. For a long time the mystery of what happened to the Anasazi was one of the puzzles of American archaeology: did they just disappear, leaving behind their elaborate cliff dwellings at Mesa Verde, at Cañon de Chelley, at Nankoweap? Were they wiped out by some plague or drought or by an aggressive invader from the south who found their peaceful lifestyle the very stuff of conquest? Some even found in their petroglyphs and pot styles evidence that the Anasazi were, like the Mayas and the Eskimos, colonialists from the region of Sirius, the Dog Star . . . and speculate that to the stars they did return.

It is more likely that the ever-drier conditions of the Southwest caused the Anasazi to retreat to more dependable sources of water. Even the Colorado River might have dried up at the end of the twelfth century. The Anasazi themselves, from the evidence, probably moved to the east and founded the village of Oraibi by 1200, where they are now known as the Hopi. Perhaps more than any other tribe of Native Americans, the Hopi preserve the continent's ancient culture in their remote mesa homeland in Arizona, surrounded by the Navajo reservation and the white man's world.

The Hopi still believe that the origin of their people is a travertine spring in the desiccated, saline Little Colorado Canyon. Where the Little Colorado flows into the Colorado—at Mile 61½—John Wesley Powell and his party rested for three days in 1869 to dry their supplies after nearly three months on the river from their start at Green River Station, Wyoming. Powell found a ruin of the long-departed Ana-

sazi at the mouth of the Little Colorado, which in light of the Hopi beliefs as we now know them may well have been a religious site of great importance. We will never be able to explore this theory: a hopeful miner, Ben Beamer, built his cabin on the spot in 1890, using the stones of the ancient ruin.

All of the Indians of the Southwest—whether ancient ones like the Hopis or the more recent arrivals such as the Paiutes and Navajos—have myths about the Grand Canyon. The scale of the place makes myth making as natural as breathing, and a religious reaction is as common to white man as to red. Clarence Dutton of the U.S. Geological Survey, who in 1882, under Powell's guidance (Powell was by then the second director of the U.S.G.S.), wrote the first geological report of the canyon, had an interest in Eastern religions. To him fell the honor of naming many of the landmarks in the Grand Canyon, and he took full advantage of it: Shiva Temple, Brahma Temple, and the Hindu Amphitheater are but three of his christenings. Other cartographers have followed suit, and we now find Wotan's Throne, Apollo Temple, Isis and Osiris, the towers of Ra and Set—all rising alongside such native christenings as Indian Dick and the Maiden's Breast.

■ ■ ■

To enter the Grand Canyon is to enter a time antecedent to human history, Indian or otherwise. As one passes deeper into Marble Canyon—Powell's name for the section of the gorge between Lee's Ferry and the Little Colorado tributary sixty-one miles downstream—the red-stained walls rise higher in glorious tiers of rock ever more ancient. River guides tick them off one by one as the boats drift onward and the

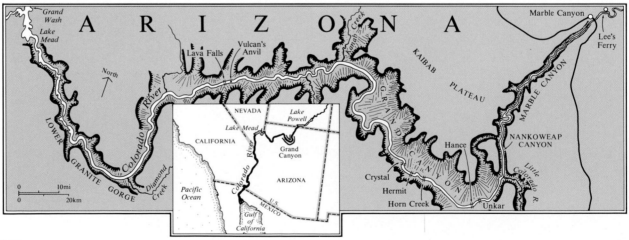

texture of the walls changes: Hermit Shale, the Supai Group, Redwall Limestone, Bright Angel Shale, Tapeats Sandstone, and, finally, the Great Unconformity—250 million years of no geological record whatsoever. These first few days spent descending into Marble Canyon are like the unfolding of a blossom, the discovery of an ancient mystery of the planet's creation. The revelations that follow are as much personal as geological: as the passenger sheds his watch and, with it, the rhythms of the forty-hour workweek, time stretches into new configurations, measured in millennia, not hours.

The deepest strata of the inner canyon, which the river runner comes to some seventy-five miles down from Lee's Ferry, often oppress these expanded senses as they close off the sky with their dark pre-Cambrian antiquity. This is Zoroaster Granite and its still more ancient underlayer, Vishnu Schist. These are rugged, homogenized rock layers whose secrets have been forever transformed by pressure and heat and the ages. They are among the oldest exposed rock on earth, nearly 2 billion years old, older than the first stirrings of multicellular life on the planet. With the entrance to the Upper Granite Gorge at Mile 77, the journals of the early explorers, including Powell's, turn from a sense of wonder to dread.

From this point on, what had been a scenic float trip along a 300-foot-wide, gentle river flowing through a geological museum changes in character: the rapids grow in size and frequency, with the first big one, Hance, coming at Mile 77, followed by Sockdolager at Mile 79. For those whose idea of a vacation does not include life-threatening rapids and claustophobia-inducing scenery, the Bright Angel Trail from Phantom Ranch up to the South Rim offers escape at Mile 88. For those who stay on, the experience, though sometimes difficult, can be exalting; in these somber and even bitter moods, the greatness of the gorge is slowly and painfully revealed.

The big rapids come closer together as the walls of the canyon press inward. Between Mile 90 and Mile 98 four major rapids stand like guard dogs to the secrets of the interior: Horn Creek, Granite, Hermit, and finally Crystal. All of them may warrant a scout from shore before running, and flips or accidental swims are possible in any of them. But Crystal, at Mile 98, is in a class of its own: a narrow approach down a rapidly accelerating current into a boulder-choked chute, culminating in one of the largest hydraulic holes on any river in the world. In 1983 the Bureau of Reclamation misjudged the runoff from winter snows and was suddenly forced to release almost 100,000 cubic feet of water per second from Glen Canyon Dam, in early July, in the midst of the commercial rafting season. The inevitable happened: one of the so-called unflippable thirty-three-foot-long J-rig passenger rafts (five pontoons lashed together, carrying up to twenty people) flipped in Crystal Hole, spilling its passengers into the powerful current. Fortunately no one was hurt, but Crystal's reputation was amplified. (Said the captain of the J-rig flip: "I ran it last week, and it was a puppy!")

■ ■ ■

In many ways the miles between Crystal and Lava falls are the heart of the canyon. By this point of any river trip, the passengers have grown to know one another and to enjoy each other's company in a way their acquaintance on the "outside" might never allow. Warm nights are spent swapping stories and, sometimes, secrets. It doesn't matter if you wash cars for a living or if you are a bank executive: on the river there are no titles, no rank, no last names.

The charms of the Grand Canyon reveal themselves, and the claim that the Grand Canyon is one of the "wonders of the world" is justified. Breaks in the near walls of Vishnu Schist reveal the retreating magnificence of layer upon layer of strata rising to a distant canyon rim, slopes and tables of a wilderness of cactus, juniper, and an occasional bighorn sheep or feral burro. The many small tributaries of the Colorado are accessible and often reveal a rare and unique character. A clear stream spills into the river down seventy-foot Deer Creek Falls. A side hike up the small Matkatamiba Creek follows an ever-narrowing gorge until one must chimney-climb between sheer walls to reach an open chamber of pools, ferns, and huge stone altars set in cathedral-like serenity.

Most impressive of all is Havasu Creek at Mile 157. Its calcium-rich waters are aquamarine, marbling the waters of the Colorado at its inflow with the luminous color of turquoise; upstream it spills over wide, shallow shelves of travertine, the mineral accretion on the rocks and trees that have fallen into the river.

By A.D. 1000 the Anasazi in the Grand Canyon region—known as the Kayenta Anasazi—had developed their skills in finely decorated ceramic pottery, using, among others, the motifs shown here. They traded their pottery over a wide area, and it is found in the cliff dwellings of Chaco Canyon, Mesa Verde, and elsewhere in the Southwest.

149

More than five miles upstream, Mooney Falls drops 200 feet from a fern-fringed grotto into a deep sky-blue pool. The falls derive their name from an Irish mineral hunter who in 1880, thinking his 150-foot rope would reach to the bottom of the falls, lowered himself over the lip. Some say he held on for two days before letting go of the rope; he is buried nearby. Still farther up Havasu Creek, nine miles from the Colorado River, is the village of Supai, where the Havasupai live—the "people of the blue-green waters."

The Havasupai are the only Native Americans who presently make their homes in the Grand Canyon. About 300 live in Havasu Canyon, though their reservation was expanded in 1975 from 518 acres to 185,000, including tablelands above the canyon where they grow corn, beans, squash, and melons. They hunt for deer or antelope on their traditional hunting grounds (but only during the Arizona-approved hunting season) and enjoy an ancillary income from the hikers and rafters who pay their remote village a visit.

■ ■ ■

Within these gorges, as the rapids come one after another and the space between the walls narrows to seventy-six feet at Mile 135, the modern river runner, too, may be moved to create a myth or two during the long nights beneath the narrow band of stars, around the small Indian-style campfires, in the depths of this holy gash. And one of the biggest is the Myth of the River Guide.

I witnessed and was part of an odd transmutation that took place during those years on the Colorado. Ordinary people—many of them college dropouts, ski bums, and ranchers' sons from the hard patches of Utah, New Mexico, and Arizona—became extraordinarily capable on the river. They turned into men who faced danger with chests and chins thrust forward, with a smug curl of a smile under any circumstance or crisis. People who were a bit soft or insecure around the house turned gneiss-hard on the Colorado, resolute souls who held together when lawyers, doctors, and corporate presidents panicked. They were men who lured wives away, if only for a fortnight, with the arch of an eyebrow, men who lived by wits and wile and animal resourcefulness in a Spartan way: with a pair of sun-faded shorts, a Buck knife, a sleeping bag, a bottle of Jim Beam, and a pair of pliers. (RB)

The subject of these myths—and their perpetuator too—is the river guide himself. (There are a handful of women guiding boats down the Grand Canyon, and since they tend to be smaller and lighter than the men working the same job, they sometimes must rely on better timing and judgment than their male counterparts. Most of them accept the term *boatman* as their job title without so much as a shrug of the shoulders.) Most river guides are quick to capitalize on their position at center stage: they sing off-key before appreciative audiences, they tell bad jokes that send laughter reverberating between the Supai sandstone walls, they play rudimentary recorder as passengers sway revival style. Most of all, though, every guide takes advantage of the rapids—all 161 of them. Those white knots in the river's long, emerald ribbon are chances to shine, to polish the legend of the dauntless river guide.

As big and visually impressive as the Colorado rapids appear, they are, by all measures, quite safe. If a raft flips, wraps, broaches, jackknifes, tube-stands, noses under, or all of the above, the entire crew could swim the rapid from tongue to tailwaves, yet everyone would be relatively certain to emerge intact in the quiet water below. Of the more than 200,000 people who have floated through the Grand Canyon, only a handful have drowned, and all under freakish circumstances: an elderly woman trapped under a capsized raft, a man caught in a monstrous recirculating hole in the 1983 record high water, an intoxicated woman taking a midnight swim off the back of the raft. But the boatman seldom admits to the rapids' general forgiveness. That's a secret.

The script calls for high drama at each rapid, especially the majors such as Hance, Crystal, Horn Creek and Hermit, and the boatman knows how to milk the scene dry. "Hold on tight. This next one's a killer."

"House Rock rapid coming up. It flipped five boats last trip."

"Grapevine. That's where Sanderson hit the wall and rolled his baloney boat."

"Bedrock. Hatch once put a twenty-seven-foot rip in the floor of his raft here."

"Upset Rapid next. That's where Shorty Burton, a Hatch boatman, drowned in 1967. What happened? Well, his raft capsized, and his lifejacket clipped onto

OPPOSITE, TOP Darkness falls over the lower canyon (Liz Hymans). BOTTOM Detail of Vishnu Schist at river level, oldest rock in the Grand Canyon—1.7 billion years of age (Liz Hymans).

Four species of rattlesnakes are found in the Grand Canyon, including the endemic *Crotalus viridis abysses*, a docile pink rattler found throughout the river corridor.

151

OPPOSITE The canyon is grand not only in its scale, but in its detail (Mark Jensen).

a gas can. Don't worry, though, we don't use life-jackets with clips anymore."

All this theater reaches its climax at Mile 179—Lava Falls. Formed of flows from eruptions within the last million years, it was named by Powell upon his arrival at its chapped lip on August 25, 1869. He was the first boatman to wax theatric about the volcanic intrusion. "What a conflict of water and fire there must have been here! Just imagine a river of molten rock running down into a river of melting snow. What a seething and boiling of the waters; what clouds of steam rolled into the heavens!"

Rimmed with black burnished rock, chopped into a mess of crosscurrents and nasty sharp holes, the rapid drops thirty-seven feet in 100 yards. It has been clocked at thirty-five miles per hour, claiming the title of fastest navigable waters in America. Statistics notwithstanding, Lava Falls strikes terror in the hearts of first-timers—swampers and boatmen included. It appears so angry, confused, and huge, with no evident passage, that the initial urge is to look for a hidden staircase out of the canyon or a bush to crouch behind. It is all quite deceptive, nonetheless. Wherever a boat enters this thundering, fuming, spitting monument to chaos, the chances are better than even it will issue upright at the bottom. If a boat flips—and many have—the passengers have the swim of their lives. But they bob out of it okay, unscathed, every time.

For the boatman, however, the performance begins days upstream with a casual campfire mention of the upcoming confrontation. The anecdotes build over guacamole salad, with tales of near-disasters, party to or witnessed. Then one day it dominates the conversation over breakfast, building to a crescendo as the boats float downstream to Vulcan's Anvil. This basaltic neck, the core of an ancient volcano, now sits midriver one mile above Lava Falls—looking, some boatmen say, like a forty-foot tombstone. From this point on a respectful silence descends, and the boats drift closer to the low, guttural groan of Lava.

The boatman's *danse macabre* begins at Lava's lip. The boats are beached, and the guides climb to the sacred vantage, a basalt boulder some fifty feet above the cataract. Once there, weight shifts from heel to heel, fingers point, heads shake, and faces fall. This is high drama, serious stuff—and passengers eat it up. This is the reason people spend good money to sleep on hard ground, eat stew mixed with sand, and go where they find no hot running water and no flush toilets: quite simply, they get scared in a safe, spectacular setting. Lava gives everyone his money's worth, and then some.

After the scout, which can take half a day, the boatmen, somber as pallbearers, return to their rafts to check riggings, remind passengers of emergency flip procedures, then launch, one by one, into the maelstrom. Lining up is the key to a "clean" run, one that loses no passengers or gear and doesn't flip. Once in the fist of Lava, there is no control—just the hanging on as it shakes its intruders like hot dice.

Then, of course, after crashing through hell itself, staring defiantly into the pits of bottomless holes, and purling into the eddy below, the passengers erupt into applause and praise, as though a divine hand had just delivered them from an eternity on the river Styx. At that dizzy instant a boatman can't help but beam.

On my third canyon traverse I was allowed to man the oars at Lava, though I could barely lift them. Dave Bledsoe sat behind me on the captain's bridge and bellowed commands over the pandemonium: "Right oar. No, left. Now both. Harder!" In the eye of this typhoon, I tried to follow orders, but it seemed to me I had barely executed a few inches of a right-oar pull when Bledsoe would be clamoring for the other. Nevertheless, when we made the landing, amidst the applause and backslapping from our passengers, I turned to Dave and asked the all-important question: "How'd I do?"

Dave pulled a bottle of champagne from his ammo box, shook it violently, and popped the cork so it shot across the river and into the white spinning skein of Lava's last wave. "You did great," he winked. It was several more trips before I learned the meaning of that wink. It was all show, pomp and ceremony, for the benefit of the clients, Big Top performance material. And I learned to play it with three-ring stagecraft. (RB)

Below Lava Falls, the boatman is bathed in a powerful limelight, washed in post-navigation euphoria. That night the guides are treated as though they'd hit the winning run, bottom of the ninth, at the World Series. After days of boating through the canyon, with no contact with the outside, the universe has been reduced to the party at hand, and this universe claims these boatmen as superstars charged

152

OPPOSITE, CLOCKWISE FROM TOP
The whistling call of the
canyon wren is a common
sound in the Grand Canyon
(Liz Hymans). A flash flood
pours its silt-laden waters into
the Colorado (Liz Hymans).
A mule deer watches
intruders near Deer Creek
(Stan Boor). Hedgehog cactus
spreads its spines and flowers
on the talus slopes of the
upper canyon (Christian
Kallen).

with extraordinary courage and skill. Heady stuff for any soul.

This can do strange things to a young man's psyche, some good, some not so good. On the positive side, it can instill self-confidence, and latent talents might surface. The first generation of Colorado boatman after the river's explosion of popularity from 1968 to 1972 spawned photographers, writers, businessmen who went on to achieve inspired works and recognition. One can't help but wonder if those achievements were not at least in part the result of having spent a series of summers on the river.

For others, though, the river seems to induce a kind of egocentric state that is not easy to cope with or resolve. In the closed universe of the canyon, there is nearly constant adulation, but reality always returns with summer's end.

Returning to college, I found it difficult to adjust. While I had recently been in a whirlpool of activity in one of the most sublime settings on the planet, I was now cloistered in pale library walls, lost among the thousands of milling students, buried in books and papers. The Colorado never left me, not for a waking instant. At every opportunity I launched into long-winded descriptions of how I had spent my summer vacation. As one who has thoroughly learned a new language, I now thought in Grand Canyonese. I fancied myself a river man . . . that was my first and foremost identity.

I couldn't understand why the world outside the canyon didn't appreciate my talents. Just weeks before I was being praised by kings, America's royalty sought my council, and all heralded my accomplishments with loud cheer. At school nobody noticed. My tan faded quickly, my stomach bulged a bit, and I sank into anonymity. When a professor handed back a paper with a low mark, I wanted to stand and yell, "Hey, you can't do that. I'm a Grand Canyon boatman!" (RB)

For some, the only way to cope with this game of ego basketball was to play a series of little games and tricks, using the passenger's expectations of the guide's infallibility as the subtext of the humor. Curiously, however, though this gambit may have originated to reflect the boatman's pretensions as much as the passenger gullibility, it only served to amplify the myth of river guide as rivergod.

There was, for instance, the pumice routine. A passenger awakes and stumbles over to the campfire where a black pot of coffee steams. "Coffee ready?" he asks.

The boatman strolls to the pot, bends over the brew, and drops into it a stone, which promptly sinks from sight. "Nope. Too thin," the guide declares and goes back to his kitchen chores. A few minutes later the passenger inquires again, and the routine is repeated, with the same results. "Nope." The third time the boatman palms a piece of pumic and drops it into the coffee. Naturally it floats. "Yup. Coffee's ready."

Another gambit is the scorpion shield. Making certain he is being watched (and they almost always are), the boatman punches a small hole in a paper plate, then slides it up the bowline so it stands like a shield between the beach mooring and the raft, where the guide sleeps.

"What's that for?" some comely miss inevitably asks.

"Scorpion shield. Keeps them off the boat. Hundreds of them on the beach, ya know. They come out at night. By the way, where're you sleeping tonight?"

One of the more elaborate "pimps," as these pranks came to be called, was devised by Dave Bledsoe. In a Flagstaff surplus store he picked up a pair of glasses, the type with Coke-bottle-thick lenses, even though his vision was 20-20. At Lee's Ferry, as the passengers boarded, he donned the glasses and went through the orientation as though the eyewear were normal attire. Then just as his raft was about to drop into Badger, the first rapid, Dave let out a mighty sneeze, and, at the brink of the first wave, his glasses sailed into the bilge. "Oh my God, I can't see," Dave cried, and he fumbled with the tiller as the passengers looked back in horror.

■ ■ ■

All good things must end, and too soon the river's last rapid tosses a parting wave of water into the boat. The walls of the canyon open up to reveal horizons on either side, and Diamond Creek enters the Colorado near Mile 226.

Another Native American group lives here, on the southwest outskirts of Grand Canyon National Park —the 1,000 members of the Hualapai tribe ("people of the pine trees," after the ponderosas on the Colo-

154

rado Plateau). While much of their economy today is based on lumbering, mining, and livestock, a substantial portion is derived from their ownership of the Diamond Creek Road. The trucks and buses that use the washboard dirt road for access to the river must pay a toll to the Hualapai.

For many runners of the Colorado, this is where the side canyons, the big rapids, the towering walls of vermilion fade into the stuff of fond remembrance, behind the rising veil of dust created by the bus that rumbles up Diamond Creek Road, away from the Colorado, into the flat dry heat of Arizona's summer.

For others, the river journey may continue another fifty-five miles to Pierce Ferry, the terminus of the early Grand Canyon expeditions, now a comfortable landing on the shores of Lake Mead. Like many other rivers in America, even the mighty Colorado flows between dams: its flow is controlled by the release at Glen Canyon Dam fifteen miles upstream from Lee's Ferry, and its waters are stilled by the reservoir behind Hoover Dam. The passage between Diamond Creek and the waters of Lake Mead encounters Travertine and Gneiss canyons, the forbidding walls of Lava Cliff, and even a handful of small rapids. The biggest of the rapids in this lower canyon is drowned now in Lake Mead, which reaches upstream to Mile 238. This lost rapid was the scene of one of the saddest dramas of Colorado River exploration.

On August 28, 1869, after twenty-four days in the Grand Canyon, down from the Paria River (at today's Lee's Ferry), John Wesley Powell's first expedition reached the biggest rapid it had yet encountered. The walls of the canyon were closing in again; spirits were low, and provisions even lower. All three boats were in need of repair, and although none of the party of ten had lost his life, three members felt it was only a matter of time. Oramel and Seneca Howland and William Dunn voted to walk out of the canyon at that point, rather than face the largest rapid; Powell and the other six reluctantly agreed to let them go.

The remaining flour was cooked up into biscuits, which were divided between the two parties; weapons and ammunition were also divided. At first light the three men walked up what is now called Separation Canyon toward the North Rim. Powell abandoned one of the boats—the Emma Dean, his flagship—and the remaining party continued to brave the unknown river. Separation Rapid was run without incident; on the following day the Grand Canyon abruptly ended at Grand Wash, and Powell and his party made their way to a Mormon settlement on the Virgin River. The Howland brothers and William Dunne were never seen again, probably killed by raiding Paiute Indians in the wilderness to the north of the Grand Canyon.

■ ■ ■

The Colorado no longer surges with the force of its flood stage roaring out of the Rockies on its crust-cutting way to the Gulf of California; there is no need to blaze trails down from the comfortable hotels at the South Rim nor to pick routes through the uncertainty of unrun rapids; Separation Rapid's turmoil and heartbreak are silent beneath placid waters. Gone are the days when John Hance had to spur Old Dusty to a magnificent leap to flee his spectral attackers, or when Bus Hatch and Russ Frazier could come upon a cache of ancient willow-twig figurines, twisted by a hunter's hands into magic dolls of desired game. But for those who run today's Colorado, no journey is complete, or even possible, without a sense of the Grand Canyon's history and those who make that history come to life: the ancient ones who have moved to other desert homelands, the pioneers of the past, and the river guides of today.

One common current runs through all those who have drifted into the life of a guide on the Colorado River—the indelible memory of those life-asserting moments when all the universe was reduced to a cool, wrapping white wave, when with the pull of an oar or the twist of a tiller, the wave was crested, the top of the world was reached, and when, for a magical instant, all was good and great.

No river guide, in fact no river runner, can escape that memory, and like a narcotic it beckons, cries to be repeated again and again. Every guide, no matter how far his pursuits have carried him, comes back to the river, back to the Colorado. (RB)

OPPOSITE A wonderland of rock and water. CLOCKWISE FROM TOP Redwall Cavern at Mile 33, deep enough for a soccer game (Mark Jensen). The flood-carved pools at Elves Chasm, Mile 116 (M.P. Ghiglieri). Bridge climbing in narrow Matkatamiba Canyon, Mile 148 (Liz Hymans).

Now the danger is over, now the toil has ceased, now the gloom has disappeared, now the firmament is bounded only by the horizon, and what a vast expanse of constellations can be seen! The river rolls by us in silent majesty; the quiet of the camp is sweet; our joy is ecstasy. We sit till long after midnight talking of the Grand Canyon, talking of home.
John Wesley Powell, 1869

Tatshenshini

ONE OF THE WORLD'S greatest river systems—that of the Alsek River and its main tributary, the Tatshenshini—is all but unknown in its own homeland. The two rivers forge their channels by slicing through the massive coastal mountains of the inside arc of the Gulf of Alaska. The St. Elias and Fairweather ranges build to summits between 16,000 and 19,850 feet, including Mount Logan, Canada's highest. They also rise above the world's largest non-polar glacier system: there is more ice in this region of southeastern Alaska than in the much drier Brooks Range, a thousand miles to the north, inside the Arctic Circle.

On the map the Alsek and Tatshenshini can be found at British Columbia's border with the Yukon Territory, just to the east of the southern tail of Alaska. The rivers appear to provide viable routes into the Yukon, the rich interior of Canada, from the waters of the Inside Passage. Perhaps they did in the periods when the glaciers were gone from these mountains. But in recorded history there has been no easy way through the St. Elias and Fairweather ranges. Not that some haven't tried to find one.

Long before the National Geographic Society was founded to give credibility to exploration for exploration's sake, publishers discovered reader interest in little-known parts of the world. Sir Henry Stanley tracked down Dr. David Livingstone in Africa in 1871 on assignment for the New York *Herald*; and by 1890 *Leslie's Illustrated Newspaper*, a New York weekly, was capitalizing on the public thirst for similar exploits. Among the stories of that year was one about the first descent of the Tatshenshini River, by reporter Edward James Glave.

Glave led his party of six men up the Chilkat River at the head of Lynn Canal from Haines and overland to Kusawa Lake. Four of them continued to the upper reaches of the Yukon, with its newly discovered gold fields, while Glave and Jack Dalton, his packer and guide, headed down the Tatshenshini on foot. The two men reached the Tlingit Indian riverside village of Neska Ta Heen in the early summer;

there they borrowed a dugout canoe twenty feet long and three feet wide and the guide services of a medicine man referred to as Shank and his companion, Koona Ack Sai. Glave's hair-raising account of the expedition appeared later that year in *Leslie's*:

We embarked and shot into the stream and were whirled along the raging torrent. The stream, rushing through several channels cut in the rock-strewn valley, at times is hemmed in narrower limits by the approach of the rocky mountain walls which form its banks. Its forces then combine in one deep torrent which tears along at a bewildering rate, roaring as if enraged at its restricted bounds. Our little dugout, dextrously handled, plunged along the disordered surface, her sharp bow dashing through the waves, drenching us all with spray but shipping little water.

The Indian Shank, a forerunner of modern river guides, proved his knowledge of the river and its canyons by merrily recounting to Glave all previous accidents and drownings. Glave photographed and described the settlements of Neska Ta Heen and Klukshu, which were inhabited by the Gunean, Stick, and Nua Quas tribes. All have long since vanished from the river valley, victims of the diseases of white men and the tribal relocation programs. Five years later, at the age of thirty-three, Glave himself died in Africa on an assignment concerning the abolition of the slave trade with his colleague Henry Stanley.

Jack Dalton lasted a bit longer and made a greater mark in history. Born in Kansas in 1859, Dalton traveled to Oregon before he was twenty in search of the vanishing American frontier. Arrogant and quick-tempered, he had trouble keeping his gun in his holster. A shooting scrape resulted in his being run out of Oregon in 1883, so he went north; he was then charged with killing a man in Juneau but was acquitted. In the late 1880s, when the Klondike gold strike brought a swarm of miners to the North, Dalton rediscovered an old Tlingit trail from Haines, Alaska, to the Yukon River at Whitehorse. He personally guided parties over this trail, which soon took on his own name; and, not missing a trick, Dalton

PRECEDING PAGE Face of a glacier in the Tatshenshini-Alsek river corridor (Kebos).

OPPOSITE Summer's fireweed and Indian paintbrush stretch to the St. Elias Range, bordering British Columbia and Alaska (Mark Jensen).

OPPOSITE The glaciers along the Alsek, downstream from its confluence with the Tatshenshini (top right, Bart Henderson; others, Mark Jensen).

planned the route so the parties would overnight at his humble hotel on the banks of the Tatshenshini. (Continuing on by boat, the miners could reach the gold fields of the Klondike. The Dalton Trail was one of the two major routes into the Yukon Territory during the rush for riches; the other was the more rugged but shorter Chilkoot Trail from Skagway to the headwaters of the Yukon.)

By 1900 the Klondike gold rush diminished, and Dalton, who had had yet another scrape with Chilkat Indians near Haines, fled south to Mexico. He later turned up at diamond diggings in British Guiana, and it was reported that he killed more than once there too. Dalton continued fast and lucky. Improbably, he died in his bed in San Francisco in 1944. The cause: varicose veins.

The prospectors headed for the Klondike during the 1898 gold rush who read Glave's series of articles published in *Leslie's* must have discounted the stories as newspaper sensationalism. The Alsek-Tatshenshini route still looked to them like a way inland that avoided Jack Dalton's more circuitous trail, and one party of over 300 attempted a march up the Tatshenshini valley from the coast in search of an easier route to the Yukon. After a year of struggling over the ice and up the canyons of the Tatshenshini and Alsek, twelve survivors staggered into Dalton Post.

Though some of the gold rush prospectors did "impossible" things they didn't bother to recount, the first recorded descent of the Alsek from Haines Junction to the Gulf of Alaska may have been made in 1961 by kayakers Clem Rawert of Fairbanks and John Dawson, a student at the University of Alaska. It wasn't exactly smooth sailing, or kayaking: only a ten-mile portage around Turn-Back Canyon enabled them to reach Dry Bay, the inappropriately named outlet of the Alsek-Tatshenshini flow.

D. B. Crouch, who went down the Alsek in March 1970, called his expedition "the second descent" when his account appeared in the March 1971 issue of *Alaska* magazine. Because of surges in the Tweedsmuir Glacier, which impelled the giant river up against the walls of Turn-Back Canyon, a nine-mile stretch of pure whitewater hell stopped Crouch and his party of three halfway down the river. Crouch concluded, "The canyon is unrunnable as far as I am

Following the discovery of gold on Bonanza Creek in 1896, the Klondike gold rush inspired an immigration of over 30,000 fortune hunters into the isolated Yukon Territory, most of them following the Yukon River north from the region of Skagway, Alaska. In 1900 some $22 million worth of gold was mined in the Klondike; thereafter production diminished, though mining continued into the latter half of the twentieth century.

concerned. We had the brutal experience of walking out seventy-five miles cross-country to the highway."

In 1971 Idaho surgeon Walt Blackadar decided to make a solo attempt on the Alsek. Blackadar, almost fifty years old, had learned to kayak only five years earlier, but he had already begun to make a name for himself by making high-risk runs that hotdoggers thirty years his junior wouldn't even consider. As he recounted in his *Sports Illustrated* article ("Caught up in a Hell of Whitewater," August 8, 1972), Blackadar took out a two-week $50,000 accident policy, authorized his pilot to spend $6,000 to prove him dead or alive if he didn't show, and headed down the Alsek.

All went well until he came to the now infamous Turn-Back Canyon, where the Tweedsmuir Glacier shouldered the river into a demonic frenzy: "One huge, horrendous stretch of hair, thirty feet wide with a twenty-degree downgrade." The Alsek here is too fast for salmon, which makes it the only large river known where the speed of the river, rather than dams or falls, stops fish from spawning upstream. Blackadar looked at the run, and even he said no. It was certain death—Niagara Falls proffered better odds. So Blackadar decided he would have to portage. While trying to paddle as close as he could to the gates of this hell, so he could cut down on his portage distance, Blackadar was swept into the maw of the Tweedsmuir rapids and flushed like flotsam through the infernal gorge.

"At Turn-Back Canyon," Blackadar reported, "I rolled six times and the last time had my kayak torn apart. I want any other kayaker or would-be expert to read my words well—the Alsek Gorge is unpaddlable!" He walked out after his accident and was found unharmed by his pilot.

The Tatshenshini, though, looked to be a different matter. Its course bypasses the deepest canyons in the St. Elias Range, and its flow is less awesome than the larger Alsek's. Several times during the early 1970s, parties of kayakers had made the descent down the Tatshenshini, including one trip by Walt Blackadar. Each of these groups described the Tatshenshini as an exceptionally beautiful whitewater wilderness trip. And that was enough to fire the imagination of Bart Henderson, another of the Grand Canyon guides whose experience and enthusiasm had led him to pursue the far and unrun rivers of the world. Hender-

The hind foot of the grizzly measures up to 10 inches in length and 5½ inches in breadth; the front foot—which appears *behind* the hind foot in tracks—is a little over half as long.

son, a blond, boyish-looking crewman on the second Omo River trip of 1973, put together a small group of river rats in August 1976 to make an exploratory run down the "Tat," as it came to be known. It would be the first raft navigation of the river, perhaps not a world-shaking distinction, but still something to be proud of. Even so, it was the prospect of running a big, free-floating stream from close to its source to its mouth, through country as wild as any in the world, that was the irresistible incentive.

■ ■ ■

With three vehicles loaded like a Dust Bowl convoy, the party of eleven trundled north 2,000 miles from Salt Lake City to the pile of logs that marked the ruin of the old hotel called Dalton Post. The site was marked with a sign: The public is warned that grizzly bears are abundant in this area and must be considered dangerous.

Even the usually circumspect scholars of Linnean classification awarded this beast a distinctly descriptive name: *Ursus horribilis*. As fast as a racehorse, stronger than a dozen men, the grizzly is one of the few animals in the world that unprovoked will attack a human. "I would give the grizzly first place in the animal world for brain power," says Enos Mills in his classic field study of that dominant mammal. "He is superior in mentality to the horse, the dog, and even the grey wolf. Instinct the grizzly has, but also the ability to reason." And, like people, the ability to act irrationally.

The river was milky and fast, dashing by at about five miles an hour. Its temperature was forty-seven degrees Fahrenheit, surprisingly warm for a flow that started just fifty miles upstream, at the foot of a glacier. A diamond-clear tributary, the Klukshu, entered just downstream and was choked with Chinook and sockeye salmon returning to their birth places to spawn. Swarming in the turbid Tat itself were dolly varden and rainbow trout, coho salmon, and grayling.

We planned to raft from Dalton Post nearly 120 miles down to a fish cannery in Dry Bay, a route that would take us through the St. Elias Mountains and from the Yukon Territory to southeast Alaska, with a brief dip into British Columbia. Our put-in was at an elevation of 2,000 feet on a chalky beach across which hoary marmots darted. Surrounding us was a

primeval world of bristly sitka spruce, stately western hemlock, and shimmering poplar and alder. On a nearby branch a whisky jay (north-country nickname for the gray jay) eyed us, rare intruders in his Yukon wilderness. In the background to the west loomed the saw-toothed, snow-salted beginnings of the St. Elias Range, a nearly unbroken chain of 8,000-foot and higher summits—many of them unnamed, most unclaimed by climbers and explorers.

Our reverie was broken by a yelp from Doug, our cook. "Oh my God, look at this!" We scrambed over to find Doug standing with both boots within the footprint of a grizzly. The tracks crossed the beach and disappeared into the river. We leapt into protective action: Bart built a platform in a poplar to store the food for the night, and the rest of us started drinking water. One way to keep grizzlies away from a camp at night, according to the oldtimers of the Yukon, is to surround the area with bodily wastes. That's how they stake out their own territory, goes the reasoning; and it's a border they supposedly respect. We spent the rest of the afternoon and evening creating our boundaries.

The sighting recalled a passage from Glave, when he stood in the same area eighty-six years earlier: "There were quite recent tracks of large bears around our camp; and a few eagles, angry at our unusual intrusion, hovered and screamed overhead. A flock of gulls who penetrated to these wild regions for their nesting, add a mournful din to the senses around. There is such an incessant display of scenic wild grandeur that it becomes tiresome; we can no longer appreciate it; its awe-inspiring influence no longer appeals to our hardened senses."

Unfamiliar voices calling outside the tent awoke us the following morning. Two rangers with the Canadian Fish and Game Department were working their way up the Klukshu River counting salmon. They matter-of-factly told us that earlier that summer two kayakers had twice tried to make it down the Tatshenshini, but both times they had been thwarted when their boats were destroyed in a gorge an hour downstream, and they had to hike out. This was disturbing news: a kayak is more navigable in wild water than an inflatable raft, and our expedition included three rubber boats and a single kayak.

Most of the day was spent rigging the rafts and

packing duffel. Finally, at 4:00 P.M., we poured a christening bottle of tonic water on a thwart, shoved off, and were swirled downstream. The banks zipped by almost too fast to register; a brisk refreshing wind whipped upstream, and whoops and hollers from the crew sailed over the water. A few hundred yards downriver we all caught an eddy behind a boulder and celebrated with a slug of Yukon Jack.

That evening we camped only two miles from our launching point, at the mouth of Village Creek, which once flowed through a tiny Chinook Indian village. The beach was covered with grizzly tracks, so once again we cordoned the area with bodily wastes —a ritual repeated at each campsite throughout the trip. A few of us rifled through our dunnage and pulled out army surplus mosquito-net hats in anticipation of an onslaught from the so-called Alaska dwarf hummingbird—the giant mosquito of lore. The expected swarm never came, not that night nor any on the trip. The evening was almost balmy. A bowl of chili, a cup of coffee, and a peaceful night on the Tat.

An hour after we left camp the next day, we came to the dreaded gorge. The water level was in our favor, however, and, instead of a seething cauldron of potential disaster, we found a sporting section of whitewater. Or, rather, graywater: the Tat flows milky from the slow, grinding action of the glaciers sliding over the mountains. So much granitic silt turns the river the color of liquid pewter, which often hides barely submerged rocks and gravel bars and makes navigation difficult.

The second day Stan Boor was at the oars of the lead boat, steering cautiously into the first rapid, his oars digging into the chalky waters. Suddenly the raft was sucked sideways into a hidden hydraulic, a trough of recirculating water, and his only passenger was thrown out.

The boat stopped dead, shimmied violently, then pitched and canted to one side, dumping me into the frothy mess. My head seemed to explode in shock. I knew from years of listening to river-running stories that a person can function for only a matter of minutes in ice-cold water, then hypothermia sets in. I had to get to the boat fast. My arms desperately dug into the crashing water, and my legs pumped like pistons. Suddenly, I found myself next to the heaving raft. I reached up, grabbed the bowline, and tried to pull myself in. But I couldn't—my strength was already seeping away, and I was losing my grip. Stan appeared above me over the bow, grabbed the back of my lifejacket, and hauled me into the bilge.

The incident took all of six seconds. In another three the boat was out of the hydraulic, and I was frantically bailing. Stan rowed the boat to shore so I could change clothes, and as I caught my breath, I felt as if I had undergone a sacrament, as if I had been immersed and baptised by the Cold River. (RB)

The gorge continued for four exciting and exhausting miles before opening up slightly to a steep valley. Overhead two bald eagles wheeled in flight, at home in this area where one of the world's greatest concentrations of their kind is found. Camp that second night was at the mouth of Silver Creek, a tributary running beneath the low-slung sun, whose glimmering sheet of light played over the dancing waves, broken only by the shadows cast by aspen and spruce.

With almost eighteen hours of light here at over 60

The Tlingit Indians of the southern coast of Alaska— northernmost of the northwest-coast Indians, which include the Haida, Kwakiutl, and Bella Coola— have been described as wealthy, artistic and fierce. Their wealth came not only from the naturally rich environment of the region's salmon, crustaceans, berries and land game, but from their occasional forays to plunder their southern neighbors. The lasting elegance of their woven blankets, carved and painted long houses, and totem poles has made their name familiar to art collectors around the world.

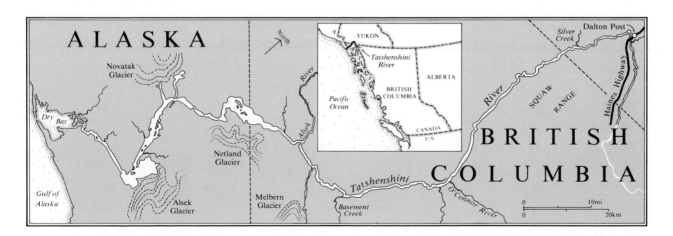

degrees north, there was always time to explore; the question was not what to see, but how to see it safely. It was not prudent to tramp through this bear country without a bell or noisemaker to warn away grizzlies. We had searched Haines for such and had come up with only a single dinner bell, with no clapper. So when a contingent led by veteran backwoodsman Skip Jones decided to wade up Silver Creek in pursuit of a salmon dinner, they jerry-rigged noisemakers out of Sierra Club cups and Swiss Army knives dangling from their belts. As they disappeared into the evening fog, they clanked like the approach of bad news.

Those who stayed behind got a fire started and marked off the camp's perimeter in the now-familiar manner. As we paced our border, stopping every few feet to give the earth our scent, four sets of moose antlers were discovered lying in the grass. The Alaska, or Kenai, moose, largest species of the deer family in the world, tips the scales at up to 1,800 pounds. The antlers can weigh up to 85 pounds per set and measure over six feet across. As we hefted the racks on top of our heads for photographs, the whole universe reverbertated with two shortly spaced booms. It was Skip Jones's Winchester .32, the rounds fired off too close for target practice. Either he was firing at a moose or some other game animal, or a grizzly had confronted him, and it was too late to retreat.

We huddled around the fire, speculating as the sun lost its strength and the air grew slowly colder. If Skip and company didn't show in half an hour, we planned to form a search team and head up the creek. Twenty-five minutes later, the biggest grin we'd ever seen appeared out of the thicket. Behind it was Skip, shouldering a twenty-pound salmon on a stick.

Before making their freshwater spawning run, salmon gorge themselves so they needn't stop to feed during their final race upriver. As a consequence, it's nearly impossible to catch a running salmon with live bait. It takes special spinners, a net, or the nefarious "short rod," which was Skip's technique. The catch was a fey female, having already spawned, yellowed with fungus, but certainly still edible. No time was wasted in cleaning the fish and cutting fat steaks, and in less than half an hour we were enjoying the silky smooth taste of fresh Alaska salmon.

According to our backwoods calculations, we floated across the border from the Yukon into British Columbia the next morning. Somewhere around the unmarked provincial frontier we saw him: "Old Ephraim," "Grizz," "King of American Wilderness," the fiercest *ferae naturae* in the Northwest, the toughest quadruped in North America. The grizzly bear. He was poised on the right bank, presenting an elegant sight. Once the word was passed of his presence, hypnotic silence descended over the rafts. As we drifted closer, he looked up in dispassionate curiosity. Then, without a hint of fear, he lumbered off into the thicket, looking for a less-crowded milieu. Before he vanished, however, someone pointed to the opposite shore. There, directly across the river, was another grizzly. Thoughts flashed: Was this a den? Were we surrounded? How can we camp?

If grizzlies are frightful creatures, humans are curious ones—or foolish. As we pulled our cameras quietly from ammo boxes, one of the kayakers in our party paddled over to the second grizzly. There were some muffled objections, since grizzlies are reportedly good swimmers. They can also run about thirty-five miles an hour, so the only way to escape a charging grizzly is to climb a tree, assuming you get there before he gets to you. Unlike his smaller and less ferocious cousin, the black bear, a grizzly cannot climb trees. Because of his tough skin and thick skull and forehead plate, it is difficult to kill a grizzly with one shot of almost any gun, of any caliber. And often there's time for just one shot.

While all three of our guns were held cocked and ready, Dick cautiously stroked over to the majestic beast. Even in the untainted breezes of the Tat, it seemed unlikely the animal had ever smelled humans before. Dick braced and held about twenty feet from shore where the grizzly was positioned, his head tilted in wonder, nose sniffing. He appeared to weigh less than 500 pounds; full-grown adults can reach 1400 pounds. But he didn't look small, and he certainly didn't seem to be afraid.

Dick spoke to the bear as if coaxing a dog to let him near the mailbox. The grizzly responded with wide eyes and flared nostrils. A fifteen-minute pantomime ensued, during which the bear followed on shore, seemingly inquisitive about this unusual floating creature, as Dick was carried downstream. It didn't

167

OPPOSITE, TOP Rolling hills on plateau above the Tatshenshini canyon (George Wendt). BOTTOM Taking a hike on Walker Glacier among seracs and crevasses (Jim Slade).

Fishhooks of the Tlingit were useful in catching river fish, primarily the five species of salmon that migrated up coastal rivers to spawn. The Tlingit believed that the souls of the dead followed the salmon upriver to the ice country of the mountains, where the living dared not venture and from where the dead never returned.

appear to be a malicious pursuit, but one of curiosity. It ended only when a cliff prevented downshore travel for the bear. With a glance of what might have been regret, he turned and ambled off.

Since we knew that this youngster wasn't the only bear in the neighborhood, we decided to camp that evening on an island, to have some warning in case a bear tried to splash across the strong current in the middle of the night. The next morning the island beach was crisscrossed with fresh tracks the size of deflated soccer balls. Nobody had heard a sound all night long.

The Tatshenshini turned south and entered the Alsek Range, the 8,000-foot-high arm of the St. Elias, which separated us by fifty miles from the Alsek River basin. At first the river ran adjacent to the mountains for fifty miles; in another couple of days, it would cut directly into them, the blue ribbon on the map that enticed the Klondike gold diggers eighty years earlier. Here, however, we saw for the first time the glaciers and ice fields that made traversing the range forbidding. Blue rivers of ice poured out of the range, bisecting the spires and summits of the mountains.

We drifted downstream through a natural aviary of riverine birds: semipalmated plovers, spotted sandpipers, northern phalaropes, and water pipits, with pine siskins, tree swallows, and clumsy willow ptarmigans in the riverside brush, a variety of hawks and falcons overhead, and a passing wedge of honking Canadian geese in the high blue distance.

Camp that night was in a bed of white wildflowers near a sediment-filled creek, surrounded on all sides by a score of cascading waterfalls, some of them several hundred feet high. In the American Southwest, any one of those falls would be a major tourist attraction, good for several thousand visitors a year. But along that section of the Tat they are so numerous that the eye finally dismisses the fortieth Bridal Veil as if it were a leaky faucet.

On the fourth morning a delicate frost was sprinkled across the flowers. The mountains were reaching out to us with their colder air. It was still chilly when we put on the river, but after the sun warmed the air to a toasty seventy-five degrees, Dick yielded his kayak to another trip member, Kal, a tenderfoot kayaker anxious to try out his new double-bladed paddle. He climbed into the kayak and paddled stiffly downstream, trying out his braces and strokes against the eddies.

Rounding a bend, Kal met a dam of warped, webbed spruce trunks. The river was twisting back on itself in an oxbow, crammed with logs and snags. He tried to backpaddle, but the current was too strong; then he tried to turn around but didn't have command of his strokes. The boat was swept sideways into the tangle. Kal leapt from the kayak like a frightened doe, not a second too soon, as the kayak rolled upside-down and jammed, half submerged, into the log pile. Struggling through a slalom of sticks and logs across the fast water, Kal sought and finally reached the shore, suitably frightened.

More drownings occur when kayaks and canoes get pinned under fallen branches and forest debris than in any other type of boating accident; in fact Dr. Blackadar was to lose his life in such a manner on an Idaho river less than two years later. Bart and Dick freed the wedged boat, and after an hour of licking wounds, patching the kayak, and counting our blessings, we were off again.

Late in the morning, along a granite face high above us in the steepening mountains, two flossy-white, woolly mountain goats appeared. Although they are not actually goats and are related to an Asian antelope believed to have migrated across a frozen Bering Strait millennia ago, they still make a good photograph, and we scrambled for our cameras. Before we could get our ammo boxes open, though, we were swept around the corner and were careening down an accelerating flume. The river was suddenly rolling along at ten miles an hour or better; velocity waves formed, and a strong wind bit through our lifejackets. But as we eyed the river sharply from the boats, we saw no dangerous rocks or hydraulics interrupting the smooth rush of the current. It was a joy to run, a boatman's dream, a safe yet speedy shot between the ever-rising mountains of the coast ranges of the Northwest. By evening, with no effort, we had covered thirty miles and were at the confluence with the McConnell River, the largest tributary to the Tatshenshini.

We had yet to get closer than fifteen miles to a real glacier, but all around was evidence of their activity. Much of the river bank was made up of glacial mo-

raine, an accumulation of boulders, stones, pebbles, and sand carried and deposited by glaciers past. All the tributary canyons and valleys, and the sharp granitic pinnacles and bizarre rock formations, owed their existence to the sculpturing force of glaciers.

Dinner simmered as an eight-hour sunset completed its low horseshoe-shaped crescent around the horizon. Before dipping behind a distant peak, it bathed the glaciers and mountains surrounding our camp with alpenglow, a diffusion of soft light more passionate than daylight's cold blues. As we enjoyed the spectacle, we reflected about the fact that we were the first group ever to raft the Tatshenshini—a dubious distinction, since a number of kayakers had preceded us, but one that gave us a certain degree of pride nonetheless. "It will probably be some time before another rafting party gets down here," was somebody's spoken thought. Suddenly our cozy postprandial campfire conversation was interrupted by a cry from Bart Henderson, "Hey, there's a raft coming down the river!"

"Impossible. He's joking," Skip Jones said. But stroking through the descending darkness was a black raft, slowly coming toward us like a visitation from the dream world. Who else could possibly want to raft this little known river? Only when we saw the words Blackadar Support emblazoned in white across the side did we understand the situation.

The raft beached, and out jumped two young couples, including the effervescent Bobby Blackadar, son of the kayaking physician. We hustled Bobby and his crew up to the fire for some coffee and baited them for their story. "Dad and I just finished running Devil's Gorge of the Susitna," Bobby said. Bart's jaw dropped: he had researched many rivers in Alaska before deciding on the Tatshenshini, and he knew that the Susitna—the largest river draining Mount McKinley—was considered unrunnable. And he said so.

Bobby just nodded. It seemed that Dr. Blackadar's antics had caught the attention of ABC television, and he was approached about filming a segment for the "American Sportsman" series. The producer had asked if Blackadar could provide a first descent down a river no one else had been foolish enough to run. Blackadar bit and chose Devil's Gorge of the Susitna, with its nine-mile cauldron of whitewater.

Bobby had rowed the support raft down the gorge during the shoot a week earlier and had almost lost his life in a nasty capsize. After the excitement and pandemonium of the ABC project, Bobby decided to float a gentler river, and his father had recommended the Tatshenshini, adding that he could claim first raft descent. It was only after Bobby arrived at the put-in that he heard we were one day ahead of him, so he had spent the last five days trying to catch us.

We talked deep into the night, exchanging information, sharing river stories, swapping lies. Finally sated with talk, we all slipped into our tents and went to sleep. The next morning Bobby rowed out ahead of us toward Dry Bay. He would beat us down the Tatshenshini, but we swallowed our pride. There was enough river, and scenery, for everyone.

With the addition of the McConnell River, the Tat had a sizable flow, about 12,000 cubic feet per second. That morning we scudded down the river at the usual freeway speed, but the adrenaline wasn't pumping quite so fast. We were getting used to the velocity, as well as the incredible scenery. Fresh snow frosted the surrounding peaks; a golden eagle sawed through the air above us, and three gulls loitered in airborne helixes.

Without warning the river whipped around a sharp bend and washed up onto a peninsula rock. Before we could react, we were in it—a fifty-yard stretch of monstrous boils, whirlpools, hydraulics, and souse holes, a virtual glossary of river dynamics. It was all too fast and abrupt, rendering the oars useless; body English was the only effective tool we could employ to keep from flipping. When the boat bucked and keeled one way, the three of us threw our weight the other. We spun and lurched and filled with water; and as suddenly as we were in it, we were out, bobbing in the eddy below.

We had to catch our breath after the scare, so we pulled in below, built a quick fire, put on some coffee, and buzzed about the unexpected rapid. Then somebody looked up. Downstream the Melbern Glacier, which flows continuously over the ridge to the heart of Glacier Bay some thirty miles to the south, was bathed in sunlight. From deep within its blue core, a magical, prismatic glow welled up, opening like an icy conflagration. It was too stunning a view to by-

OPPOSITE, TOP Fluted sculptures of ice, afloat in Dry Bay, at the end of the Tatshenshini River trip (Stan Boor). BOTTOM The calving of a glacier, as a glacial wall gives birth to icebergs (Hayden Kaden).

Woodcarving knives of the northwest-coast Indians.

171

OPPOSITE, TOP Rushes grow to cover an abandoned beaver pond—ideal moose habitat (George Wendt). BOTTOM Birch and nettles, Tatshenshini region (George Wendt).

pass, so we pitched camp right there to enjoy watching the effect of a full day's sunlight on the glacier. That evening, to embellish the menu, Bart went hunting for natural edibles and found sour grass, wild cucumbers (the size of peanuts), wild celery, and lowbrush cranberries.

The following day the river started first to meander, then to braid. The bends that the Tatshenshini cut through the mountains created a series of gravel bars, false channels, and broad but shallow sweeps across the floodplain, built on the floor of the long-gone glacier. In some cases it was impossible to tell which of several channels to take. Because we were still traveling along at a sprinter's pace, we had to make split-second decisions; more than once our choices proved wrong. What appeared to be the main channel would divide, then divide again, and again; we would find ourselves stranded on a shoal, at which point there was nothing to do but pull on our wet-suit booties, get out, and push.

The scenery was fuel enough to keep us going. On the right was the Noisy Range, its stark gray granite shoulders skirted by a lush forest of evergreens. In striking contrast the St. Elias Range loomed to the left, its glacial glory almost blinding in the sunlight.

Sometime in the afternoon of the seventh day the Tatshenshini merged with the Alsek River, and we were abruptly floating atop 60,000 cubic feet of water per second—a level that would be termed *floodstage* on most other rivers. The silt the river carried off the flanks of the granite ranges surrounding us was so thick it made an almost deafening noise as it scratched the bottom of our boats, sounding like sand being poured down a tin slide. The banks of the river were a mile apart. Instead of sailing down the river's center, we hugged the left shore in order to keep swimming distance at a minimum in case someone fell out of the boat.

We hadn't gone far, however, when a field of purple and red wildflowers erupted into sight next to us, framed by a series of glaciers that looked to be only one or two miles away. Since the spirited flow of the river had put us far ahead of schedule, we all made the unspoken decision to choose our camps based on purely scenic criteria. We pulled over and spread out on the wildflower carpet.

Up to that point none of us had ever actually walked on a glacier. Since our river-running experience had been limited to West Virginia, California, Arizona, and Ethiopia, the opportunity had simply not been there. After setting up camp, several of us tried to hike to the base of the closest glacier, but after hiking a good six miles and finding ourselves not appreciably nearer the glacier, we realized the deception. The scale of the terrain was staggering; nowhere in North America could one see so much topographic relief from a major river, yet the clear air of the remote North made everything seem intimately close. Defeated, we turned to head back to camp.

I took a step, and the ground began to shake and grumble. I remembered reading that this area was the most active seismic zone in North America, and I heard myself yell "Earthquake" as I hit the dirt. But no, looking back I saw a sheet of ice boulders hurtling from the flanks of the glacier, the vestiges of a much larger fall. A piece of the universe—hundreds of feet thick and miles long—was breaking loose. All night the earth growled as glaciers moved and house-size chunks of ice calved off. Geology in action. (RB)

Since ice is just solid water, a glacier is only a river in frozen form, flowing over the flanks of mountain ranges. Some crawl forward a few inches a year, although most are receding during this current epoch of relative heat. The Lowell Glacier on the upper Alsek is galloping ahead at forty feet per year; the Steele Glacier once was recorded as moving two feet an hour, its speed a result of heavy snowfalls and earthquake-born avalanches. Coupled with the mutability of water, which switches between liquid and solid states more quickly and frequently than any other matter on the planet, the erosive power of glaciers is enormous. All around us was the evidence.

The next day we crossed into the forty-ninth state and into the Tongass National Forest. Again we didn't get far. After an hour's floating, we came to a glacier that actually flowed right into the river: no deceptive distances there. In 1879, on his epic trip through southeastern Alaska, which resulted in his discovery of Glacier Bay—then the very foot of a glacier, resting atop a hidden inlet—John Muir came upon a similar sight and put it to pen:

We rowed up its fiord and landed to make a slight examination of its grand frontal wall. The berg-producing portion, a mile and a half wide, was broken

172

OPPOSITE Wildlife of the Tatshenshini-Alsek region. CLOCKWISE FROM TOP Mountain goat (Stan Boor). Bull moose (Rollie Ostermick). Northern fur seals at river mouth (Jim Slade). Grizzly cubs fishing for salmon (Mac's Photo).

into an imposing array of jagged spires and pyramids, and flat-topped towers and battlements, of many shades of blue, from pale, shimmering, limpid tones in the crevasses and hollows, to the most startling, chilling, almost shrieking vitriol blue on the plain mural spaces from which bergs had just been discharged. Back from the front for a few miles the glacier rises in a series of wider steps. Beyond, it extends indefinitely in a gentle rising prairie-like expanse, and branches along the slopes and canyons of the Fairweather Range. . . . It seemed inconceivable that nature could have anything finer. (From *Travels in Alaska*, 1915)

This was the opportunity we had been waiting for: a glacier walk. We secured the boats, scrambled up the sides of the frozen mountain, and set foot on top of its rugged surface.

It was eerie. We walked over an electric-blue expanse; beneath our boots we could hear the sound of melted ice rushing through honeycombed chasms. We had to step slowly, gingerly, over crevasses and around sinkholes. Making our way over the billowing, serrated expanses of frozen crystal, listening to the sound of rivers tumbling under us like rolling empty oil drums, we explored the glacier, ducked into ice caves, and tiptoed across the edge of deep crevasses. We treaded carefully to the edge of a stream of water disappearing into a blue grotto, what glaciologists call a *moulin*. One slip and a body could disappear into that fifty-foot gash, which might then close abruptly with the shifting ice. The snout of ice had no name on our map, so at the conclusion of our five-hour walk we christened it Walker Glacier.

The next day, for the first time, bad weather cuffed us. The wind blew icy out of the mountains, and cold rain poured down. After only six miles on the Alsek, we decided to set up camp across from the Novatak Glacier to wait out the brooding weather. The day was spent playing chess, reading, writing in logs, and every now and then glancing up at the glacier that beckoned us from across the Alsek. By dusk the clouds were dissipating, and the sunset gave us a panorama that seemed otherworldly: colors and tones seemed exaggerated, the blues iridescent, the rosy hues of the sun's last light preternaturally sanguine. And the Novatak Glacier, ten miles wide, appeared to sweep through the high mountains as an enormous eraser wiping a blackboard clean.

Mounts Hubbard and Kennedy, at the respectable heights of 14,960 and 13,900 feet, sat at the end of that sixty-mile-long swath of erosion, looking no larger than two tiny white pyramids. The latter mountain was named in 1965, when Robert Kennedy was the first to stand atop its peak, in honor of his slain brother. Mountaineering purists, no matter what their political affiliation, are quick to point out that Kennedy was helicoptered to the 11,500-foot level, thus qualifying his first ascent.

Our international journey continued with a new twist as, with the weather once again smiling the next day, we skirted the Barbazon Range, named when the Russians had possession of Alaska. We were swept into a broad basin where, simply by pivoting the raft, we could count twenty-one different glaciers, twisting and pouring out of the granite from every cleft in the ranges. The Ice Age wasn't over there, at least not yet. Finally, as we washed around a promontory—we had long since ceased to regard ourselves as "rafting" that huge river, for we were completely in its grip and under its spell—we were bedazzled by the presentation of the Alsek Glacier.

Its seven-mile-wide face poured right into a bay annexed to the river. Chunks of ice the size of ships were almost continually cracking off the face and crashing into the water. This "calving" of glaciers is an incredible display of nature, but no sane person wants to be too close to such exhibitions. About 500 yards away from the edge of the bay we made camp—far enough to be out of danger, but close enough to witness the dramatic show. Each time a major piece fell, about once an hour, the sky seemed to rumble as though its foundations had been shaken, and the ground trembled in sympathy. The sounds were shocking, impossible, the clangor at the end of the world. And they made it difficult to sleep.

The morning sunlight slowdanced across the peaks, bringing a suffused glow to our tents; the clouds were on the lam. It was a perfect summer day; we were camped at one of the most beautiful places on earth, and we took advantage of it.

First we wandered over to the edge of the molten-lead-colored lagoon at the foot of the Alsek Glacier, scaring a black bear from his fishing spot along the way. We sat down on a driftwood pile and gazed across at a berg just thirty yards offshore, directly in

174

front of our perch. Its resemblance to a submarine, both in shape and size, was uncanny, and no sooner had we christened it the Nautilus than it was torpedoed, or so it seemed. Without warning, a several-ton piece broke off the stern bridge and plopped into the water, leaving the main body rocking and reeling until it actually rolled over and sank. The fantastic seemed be the norm on this trip. (RB)

That evening, as the last rays of twilight silhouetted the encompassing peaks, a sudden murmur ran through those still hovering around the fire. A faint, green glow appeared in the northeast, upriver over the Novatak Glacier, in the direction of the North Pole. Then, very quickly, shafts of aquamarine light stabbed the sky. Shouts rose from different parts of camp, and those tucked into tents darted out. The streaks split into bands and danced and fanned across the firmament. We were sitting in front-row seats for nature's greatest show, the aurora borealis.

The lights built to a pulsating green, then grew into an electric fury of ten or more different colors flashing across the horizon in syncopated rhythm. Each change in intensity, each new display, brought hoots and hollers from us, and the lights seemed to answer in visual chorus. The whole sky gradually filled with the hues and harmonies of the northern lights. Some of us had to sit down to avoid vertigo.

For almost an hour the show shimmered, exploding in purples and reds, transforming greens to yellows, while we sat openmouthed. Around 2:00 A.M. some began to drift off to bed, despite little decrease in the show's intensity. A few kept a faithful vigil, waiting for the grand finale. We weren't disappointed. The sky darkened, making the silhouette of the mountain masses separate substance from the ethereal. I had the feeling of being inside some great fishbowl, a captive on the inside, peering out to a larger universe. A thin, nebulous cloud of green appeared directly overhead and hovered, changing form every few seconds. Suddenly, the fishbowl was alive as flickering tongues of green licked at the "glass" of the bowl and dancing flames encircled us, spreading up toward some unknown height.

By the time the sky had faded enough to permit us to stumble wearily to the tents, it was 4:00 A.M., just two hours before the sun would again begin its long, circuitous journey across the Alaskan horizon. (RB)

The morning was bell clear, and it was with both regret and enthusiasm that we put on the river again. Almost at once we were rewarded by a spectacular view that had long eluded us: to the southeast, Mount Fairweather presented its 15,300-foot crown, just thirty miles away. Most of the peaks around us capped off at 7,000 to 9,000 feet, so seeing a mountain twice as high as its neighbors from such a short distance was impressive.

Finally we met up with the bergs that had calved off the Alsek Glacier, joining hundreds of ice floes of every conceivable shape and size. The river became an obstacle course, but a strange and beautiful one. We wove and glissaded through the maze of shimmering ice flotsam, mammoth pointed polygons turning slowly in the current, sparkling like windowcase jewels.

On the final bend we saw our last grizzly, scooping up, perhaps, a fifth of the 100 pounds of salmon he eats in a day. Then, too soon, we were at the Dry Bay Fishing Company, an isolated five-man netting and cleaning operation that's the only outpost of civilization for hundreds of miles in any direction, reachable only by small plane—and now, for those who choose the route less traveled, by river.

OPPOSITE Evening light reflects clouds in the Tatshenshini's currents (Skip Horner).

Tuolumne

ON THE DRIVE EAST into the Sierra Nevada from the populated western part of California, gentle foothills follow foothills, and even the entrance to Yosemite National Park up Highway 120 is deceptively mild. Then, suddenly, the 7,000-foot level is reached, and the forests open to views of nearby mountains 3,000 feet higher, broad meadows of wildflowers and alpine lakes and distant snowfields that linger long into summer. Beyond the blue bowl of Lake Tenaya at the foot of Tresidder Peak, the road rises to 9,000 feet and the broad green expanse known as Tuolumne Meadows.

Though far less dramatic than the sculpted monuments of Yosemite Valley, Tuolumne Meadows is as central to the value of Yosemite National Park as is the emblematic Half Dome. There are no sheer walls of granite, no cascading streams plummeting off the cliffs; yet because of its quiet distinction, the meadow is all the more appreciated. Beauty is found in the details of nature, not just in the grand spectacle; and for many tourists who visit Yosemite National Park, Tuolumne Meadows is a quiet revelation.

Wildflowers no bigger than bottlecaps hide in the thickets; tiny trickling creeks meander across the meadow in a subtle network; grasses undulate in the breezes, changing their hue with every wave of wind. As one climbs the vast gray bulk of Pothole Rock at the base of the meadow, the granite underfoot glistens in the sunlight, its surface polished by glaciers long since melted. Up high one can see the Sierra peaks that shoot into the sky—the sharp twist of the Unicorn, the ancient red cones of Mounts Dana and Gibbs, and the faraway bulge of Half Dome. It is the granite heart of the Sierra Nevada, a range 430 miles long, 80 miles wide, and 200 million years old.

The waters of almost a dozen tributaries—among them the Lyell and Dana forks, Delaney and Rafferty creeks, and others, draining the broad canyons at the Sierra crest—coalesce at the base of Pothole Rock, uniting their waters into a single channel. The resulting river is immediately compressed between the walls of a narrow U-shaped canyon, down which the longest glacier in the Sierra once forced its way. From the top of Pothole you can hear two conflicting rushes of sound, each very different yet, from there, high above both, oddly similar: the petroleum-powered rumble and hiss of automobiles along Tioga Pass to the south and the hydraulic roar of the Tuolumne River to the north.

On September 12, 1984, the U.S. House of Representatives passed the California Omnibus Wilderness Bill, mandating the addition of 1.8 million acres of California land to the federal wilderness and parks systems. It was the culmination of years of effort and decades of controversy, and not a little compromise on both sides, over many of the state's conservation issues. The omnibus bill included the designation of eighty-three miles of the Tuolumne River as a part of the National Wild and Scenic Rivers System, the first addition to the system in five years. For supporters of river recreation and preservation, it was the final victory of a long fight.

Created in 1968, the Wild and Scenic Rivers System was designed to provide the same kind of federal protection for the rivers of the nation as its parklands had long been assured. The Rogue River in Oregon, the Middle Fork of the Salmon in Idaho, and the upper section of the Rio Grande in Colorado were among the first eight rivers named to the system; some fifty more have since been added. Criteria for inclusion focus on a river's "scenic, recreational, geologic, fish and wildlife, historic, and cultural" values —a wide range of qualities that has created a national river system of variety and depth. A river receiving federal Wild and Scenic designation is protected from dams, diversion projects, and riverside developments that would alter its character. For river runners, those who find their pleasure in riding the currents on inflatable rafts, kayaks, or canoes, Wild and Scenic status is seen as the government's guaran-

PRECEDING PAGE Sunrise bathes Rock Garden Rapid in golden light (Bett Lonergan).

OPPOSITE, TOP The confluence of Clavey Creek, left, with the main fork of the Tuolumne, at Mile 6 of the river run (Don Briggs). BOTTOM Digger pines and blue oaks on Jawbone Ridge above the Tuolumne (Liz Hymans).

181

tee of permanence. And the inclusion of the Tuolumne, long regarded as one of the country's premier whitewater runs, renewed faith in the legislative process—a faith that had been sorely tested.

The Tuolumne River flows wild between the boundary of Yosemite National Park and the reservoir behind the New Don Pedro Dam thirty-six miles downstream. (The other fifty-one miles designated as Wild and Scenic include the unhindered flow above Hetch Hetchy Reservoir in Yosemite and below the Don Pedro Dam.) First explored by kayakers in 1965 and by rafts from 1968 on, the Tuolumne's main run is the eighteen miles between the Lumsden Campground northeast of the small town of Groveland on Highway 120 and the stilled waters of Don Pedro Reservoir. It has become an extremely popular recreational run, and currently some 6,000 people enjoy its isolated canyon and wild rapids every year. There is an even wilder stretch of whitewater above Lumsden, perhaps the wildest in the country: the fabled Jawbone Canyon run, from Cherry Creek down nine hair-raising miles, with an elevation drop of 105 feet per mile. Commercial trips have been offered there—to experienced paddleboat passengers only—since 1981, giving the Tuolumne River the distinction of providing two of the country's best whitewater vacations. Wild and Scenic status for the Tuolumne was a natural, and its protection was hailed as essential.

■ ■ ■

Somehow, though, the whole issue of federal protection for a river is odd. It is an intersection of two widely different fields, the world of granite and silt, grasses and trees, fish and birds, currents and eddies on the one hand, and a realm of paperwork, contracts, easements, and blueprints on the other. The world of God versus the world of Man, some might say. The Tuolumne's story is older than a political conflict and more broad than an act's decree. Its headwaters reach deep into Yosemite to the Sierra crest; they also reach far into the past, to a time before either white men or Indians, over the epochs of geologic history to the very birth of the mountains themselves.

Just what caused the mountains to form had been the subject of confusion and controversy for decades, until the belated acceptance of the theory of plate tectonics in the late 1960s. The crux of this theory is, simply put, that continents float: their peaks and ranges are but the lightest matter of the earth's crust, and the broad expanses of ocean floor are heavier deposits of basalt flowing slowly from the mantle through long narrow splits in the crust. Huge and slow but powerful currents in the fluid molten material of the mantle help drive the continental masses (plates) apart, leading to the phenomenon of *continental drift*. But just as they are driven apart so they are thrust together at the other end of the circular subcrustal currents: that is where mountains are born.

Where two plates collide, a process called *subduction* occurs as one plate slides beneath the other, encouraged by the downward flow of the mantle's convection currents. At the outset of the Mesozoic era, 225 million years ago, the Pacific Plate pressed into the North American Plate and caused such geologic stress that ancient land masses melted and, solidifying once more as they rose toward the surface, restructured themselves into huge wells of granite. Lying beneath the Paleozoic (the oldest era of earth history) layers of sedimentary and metamorphic rock, these slowly rising bubbles of granite—called *plutons*, after the Roman god of the underworld—helped create the structure of the Sierra Nevada.

The process of building the Sierra had hardly begun. Millennia passed, during which the land was uplifted and eroded away again; volcanoes erupted and covered millions of acres with ash and magma. Days of fire were followed by days of ice; with the onset of the Pleistocene epoch 3 million years ago, the Ice Age cooled the hemispheres to such an extent that huge glaciers covered nearly half of North America—as well as large parts of Asia, Europe, and South America. Simultaneously the Sierra continued to build, this time tilting upward toward the east along a long fault zone. The ice came and went and came again; the tilting continued, and the Sierra became a rugged, rocky spine laced with glaciers, towering above the warming continent.

While glaciers are now rare in the Sierra, as recently as 10,000 years ago they carved their distinctive signatures in the landscape of today's high Sierra: polished granite, headwalls plucked sheer by retreating ice, long lines of rubble at the edges and ends of the long-gone fields of ice, the hanging valleys of tributary glaciers that today are marked by high waterfalls, and small, isolated cirque lakes orphaned by the glaciers' melting.

The glaciers' final retreat created the string of rivers that run out of the Sierra, like fingers reaching out toward the broad, flat Central Valley. For tens of thousands of years they brought with them organic materials and silt from the mountains and filled the valley with incredibly rich soil. At the north end of the mountains, the Feather River flows off the southern slopes of the Mount Lassen volcano; it earned its name in 1817 when Luis Arguello saw "feathers" on the water. (Some naturalists think he saw willow pollen; river runners think he saw whitewater.) Its tributary, the Yuba, became a major salmon run and source of plenty for the Maidu Indians when the Sierra became inhabited, at about the same time the glaciers retreated a hundred centuries ago. The American River, the next major drainage to the south, was the scene of the start of the gold rush—curiously coincident with California's statehood. These rivers all flow into the Sacramento River, which drains the northern Sierra and much of the Siskiyou Range on the California-Oregon border.

The rivers of the southern Sierra flow into the San Joaquin; its tributaries include the Stanislaus, named after an Indian renegade who was given the name of a Polish saint by a Spanish priest; the Tuolumne and Merced, which drain the high country of Yosemite National Park; and the Kings, drainage of the granitic wonderland of Kings Canyon National Park. Together, the Sacramento and San Joaquin join in a great delta and flow into San Francisco Bay.

This network of rivers, from the Feather to the Kings, was the lifeblood of the Indians who lived in the Sierra. The Maidu to the north of Donner Pass and the Miwok over the central and southern Sierra down to the edge of Death Valley elaborated a simple yet stable economy based on the available resources, trade with their neighbors, and seasonal migration. Where today we see "wilderness" suitable only for backpacking or logging, those hunter-gatherers saw plenty: staples such as roasted pine nuts and ground acorn flour, and delicacies such as deer and bear, rabbit and gray squirrel, and the salmon of the rivers. Some tribes had totemic animals, a creature after which they named themselves. For the Miwok in the narrow valley of the Merced River, their totem was the grizzly bear—*uzumiete*, Yosemite. (When the white man came, all Indians in the West were called "diggers." And the grizzly was hunted to extinction.)

■ ■ ■

Even after the glaciers retreated and the rivers and valleys became inhabitable, the tectonic movements that uplifted the Sierra through a series of earthquakes continued. Though earthquakes there are not as frequent today as in the geologically more precarious Coast Range (where the San Andreas Fault marks the interfacing of two plates), they have occurred with surprising vigor and strength even in historic times. In fact, one of the strongest earthquakes in history occurred in the Sierra just over 100 years ago, in March of 1872. It would probably rate around 8 on the Richter Scale (the devastating Alaska quake of 1964 was about 8.4 on that scale); it leveled all the stone buildings near its center in the Owens Valley, caused damage over a circular area

Both coho and Chinook, or king salmon, found their way into the waters of Sierra rivers to spawn in centuries past, where the Maidu, Miwok and other Native Americans caught them in willow weirs or speared them. The Maidu have a legend of a great flood in the Central Valley, during which the frogs and salmon ate drowning humans.

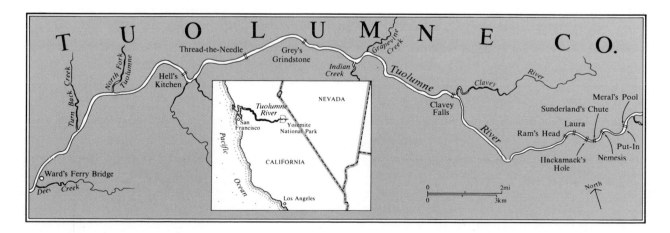

OPPOSITE, CLOCKWISE FROM TOP Glacier-polished Lembert Dome reflected in meadow stream; snowy banks of the upper Tuolumne; waterfall buttercups in Tuolumne Meadows; rime-rimmed ferns and grasses (all by Liz Hymans).

some 200 miles in diameter, and was felt as far away as Salt Lake City. In the Yosemite Valley a young naturalist who was hatching some earth-shaking ideas of his own was a witness to the force of the quake, a full 125 miles from its epicenter:

The shocks were so violent and varied, and succeeded one another so closely, that I had to balance myself carefully in walking, as if on the deck of a ship among waves, and it seemed impossible that the high cliffs of the Valley would escape being shattered. In particular, I feared that the sheer-fronted Sentinel Rock, towering above my cabin, would be shaken down, and I took shelter back of a large yellow pine, hoping that it might protect me from at least the smaller outbounding boulders. For a minute or two the shocks became more and more violent—flashing horizontal thrusts mixed with a few twists and battering, explosive, upheaving jolts—as if Nature were wrecking her Yosemite temple, and getting ready to build a still better one. (From John of the Mountains: The Unpublished Journals of John Muir, 1938).

It is in the last phrase that we see the soaring optimism and faith of John Muir. His own preservationist ideas were derived from that optimism: that nature has reasons of its own, reasons which give each plant and animal and rock and river its justification *apart* from the schemes, purposes, or concepts of humankind. Such a world view is difficult to grasp, in a culture as materialistic and anthropocentric as ours. But for Muir, it was a fundamental perspective.

Born in Scotland in 1838, Muir was raised in a religious family strict even by Scottish standards and indoctrinated with the virtues of hard work and privation throughout his early years. His father led the family to the United States in 1849, settling in Wisconsin where more hard work was in store. The eldest son, who bore the brunt of his father's demands, displayed mechanical aptitude and creativity that led to a more independent path. Although he had little formal education, the young John Muir invented a multitude of labor-saving devices, including self-feeding lathes and saws, and alarm clocks that tossed a sleeper out of bed. Working for factories and mills as a machinist, he followed his curiosities around the country in the years following the Civil War. Finally, while working as a sheepherder in the California foothills, at the age of thirty John Muir

first set foot in Yosemite Valley. It was an encounter that resonates still in the history of conservation.

I rode to the very end of the valley gazing from side to side, thrilled almost to pain with the glorious feast of snowy diamond loveliness. The walls of our temple were decorated with exact reference to each other. The eye mounted step by step upon the dazzling tablets and flowering shrubs which ruled the mountain walls like a sheet of paper, and published the measure of their sublime height. . . . A filmy veiling, wondrous fine in texture, hid the massive front of Capitan. Only in little spots with melted edges did the solemn gray of the rock appear. . . .

From end to end of the temple, from the shrubs and half-buried ferns of the floor to the topmost ranks of jeweled pine spires, it is all one finished unit of divine beauty, weighed in the celestial balances and found perfect. (From John of the Mountains: The Unpublished Journals of John Muir, 1938).

Muir found in the isolation and beauty of this wild and veering land a magnificence that showed absolutely nothing of humanity, and owed nothing to it. Using primarily his acute observations and common sense, Muir was the first to recognize the glacial origin of Yosemite's most dramatic features. As his career evolved from those Yosemite insights, his achievements included many first ascents of peaks in the Sierra, the discovery of Glacier Bay in Alaska, the founding of the Sierra Club, the personal enlistment of two presidents (Theodore Roosevelt and William Howard Taft) in the fight to create and save Yosemite National Park, and leadership in establishing a number of national parks and monuments in addition to Yosemite.

Muir's deeds fell short of his dreams. The biggest defeat he suffered was the loss of one of his favorite retreats, the Hetch Hetchy Valley of the Tuolumne River. Situated at the same elevation as Yosemite Valley, with similar meadows, flora, and waterfalls, surrounded by glacier-carved rock walls, and within the boundaries of Yosemite National Park, Hetch Hetchy ("grassy meadows," to the Miwok Indians) had the misfortune to be less accessible than Yosemite and, hence, less well known. A bill that allowed water conduits through national parks was hurriedly passed through Congress in 1901, and San Francisco used the legislation to solicit and finally

184

gain the right to dam the Tuolumne at the base of Hetch Hetchy to provide drinking water for its fast-growing population.

Despite Muir's most earnest efforts, and some of his most memorable writing ("These temple destroyers, devotees of ravaging commercialism, seem to have a perfect contempt for Nature, and instead of lifting their eyes to the God of the mountains, lift them to the Almighty Dollar. Dam Hetch Hetchy! As well dam for water-tanks the people's cathedrals and churches, for no holier temple has ever been consecrated by the heart of man."), in 1913 the city of San Francisco won its legal right to dam the Tuolumne River, and the O'Shaughnessy Dam was begun. A disappointed and weary Muir died a year later at the age of 76. The valley became a lake of drowned trees and steep, slimy banks with the dam's completion in 1924; and the Tuolumne was stilled, just as it reached its maturity in Hetch Hetchy.

■ ■ ■

"History doesn't repeat itself," that old gold rush reporter Mark Twain once noted, "but it does rhyme." Fifty years later another Mother Lode river was subjected to the same skirmishes, maneuvering, and, eventually, fate the Tuolumne had suffered. This time, however, another element was involved: instead of the small group of hikers and botanists who lost a treasured sanctuary (no less a treasure for their small numbers, let it be noted), the fight over the Stanislaus River affected hundreds of thousands of people who had enjoyed the pleasures of a new sport along its currents: river running.

I had gone rafting a couple of times in the Northwest, but when I went to California to raft the Stanislaus in 1977, it was my first overnight river trip. The rapids of the upper five miles were as wild as any I'd yet experienced, and with names like Widow Maker, Devil's Staircase, and Death Rock, I was sure I was at the very farthest reaches of river excitement. Yet it was at camp that the special magic of the Stanislaus took over. Regina, our head guide, told us we should try to find some time to be by ourselves. (Only later, when I started working river trips myself, did I realize that this was in part a ploy to get the passengers out of the kitchen while dinner was being prepared.)

I did what she suggested and wandered down the *dusk in the warm glow of sunset to an isolated beach. There I did the first part of the t'ai chi form I was learning in Seattle. Our class was in a wide meeting room in the university's student union, with fluorescent lighting and a hard linoleum floor. Here, it was different: the soft sand took the abstract patterns of my feet's simple movements, the oaks arched over my waving arms, mergansers swept by upstream as I bowed to the sunset. Lao Tzu compared the tao to a river; now I saw that this was not a metaphor but just plain description. (CK)*

The Stanislaus is the major drainage north of Yosemite National Park, drawing its waters from the same type of glacier-scarred granite high country as the Tuolumne. Its course, however, takes it down into the Paleozoic level of limestone, the ancient seabed deposits that predated the rising Sierran wedge. Between Camp Nine, an old mining access to the river from the nearby towns of Calaveras County, and the small wood-frame town of Melones, numerous caves were formed in the limestone by the percolating effect of drainage. Miwok Indians found that the caves provided perfect shelter during their summer camps along the river; gold rush bandits such as Joaquín Murrieta may have hidden from justice in them; and it was recreational cavers (spelunkers) who discovered the Stanislaus canyon in the 1960s. At the same time the river itself was being rediscovered by kayakers and rafters who found a steep-walled canyon of rare beauty, thrilling Class III and IV rapids, and the foundations of the dam that would eventually drown the Stanislaus.

The New Melones Dam, to take the place of a much smaller flood-control dam at the same site, was first authorized by the federal government in 1944 as one element in an ambitious Bureau of Reclamation Central Valley Project, with an initial price tag of $6.1 million. Ten years later the estimated cost had jumped to $47.8 million, and the proposal was shelved, according to Tim Palmer's study *Stanislaus: The Struggle for a River* (University of California Press, 1982). In 1957 Congressman John McFall of Manteca (on the banks of the lower Stanislaus) began to take an active interest in the dam, and new economic feasibility studies magically doubled its potential water yield without an increase in the dam's size—the kind of legerdemain that can only be done on paper. In 1962 the dam received final authorization as a 2.4-million-acre-foot reservoir, more than five times the size of the original proposal. It was to be built just west of Highway 49, a few miles from Angels Camp—the town made famous as the site for Mark Twain's "Jumping Frog of Calaveras County" yarn. The town would soon be hopping again.

Opposition to the dam was present from the beginning, from groups as diverse as the foothill irrigation districts, who opposed such massive federalism in their backyard, to local residents who protested the waste of CVP funds on such a huge project with little direct justification. The project stalled until Christmas 1964, when torrential rains caused the Stanislaus to flood its banks in the Central Valley—as indeed the river had been doing for hundreds of thousands of years. Now, however, it was flooding "valuable farmlands," and farmers along the river began to push in unison for the dam. No other flood-control options were considered, and no smaller dam was discussed. In the spring of 1966 construction began on the New Melones Dam, the country's sixth highest (second highest earthfill dam, behind the Oroville Dam on the Feather River), an enormous plug 625 feet high and 1,560 feet across at the gate of Iron Canyon.

While the on-again, off-again New Melones Dam proposal moved slowly toward construction, something was beginning to happen in the canyon above the dam site. Tim Palmer recounts the situation in *Stanislaus*.

The environmental movement had not yet arrived; the wilderness canyon was a secret. Like the Colorado's fabled Glen Canyon, dammed in the 1960s, the upper Stanislaus was a place that few people knew about. The first known paddlers were a group of Sierra Club members in 1960; the first commercial outfitter appeared in 1962.

During the early New Melones debate, the United States had no Environmental Policy Act requiring environmental impact statements. The nation had no wild and scenic river system, no wilderness system, no coherent water policy. When plans were completed for the demise of the canyon, the green-and-white dynamo of a river, and the marble-cobbled beaches below 800-foot walls of white limestone, almost no one cared about the place, and nobody questioned the logic and validity of the corps's calculations. In all this debate

over New Melones Dam, no one mentioned the place to be flooded, the land to be buried beneath hundreds of feet of slackwater. Nobody, that is, until Gerald Meral.

A canoeist who learned on the waters of the Michigan and Pennsylvania, Meral came to California to attend graduate school at Berkeley, and to run the rivers of the West. His first run was on the Stanislaus in 1967, a year after construction on the dam began. Although the local rafters and kayakers had watched from a distance, albeit with distaste, the peregrinations of the dam's authorization, they fatalistically accepted the eventual demise of the Stanislaus canyon. Not Jerry Meral: he began a one-man study program on the facts and assumptions of the project and came up with a series of challenging counterarguments to the bland figures and assumptions that the Bureau of Reclamation and the Corps of Engineers had been presenting.

His charges resulted in a long battle with a revolutionary goal: since the dam was already under construction, build it, but don't fill it. At least not all the way, just enough to satisfy the flood-control needs the dam was ostensibly being built for. The notion was anathema to the world view of construction workers, farmers, water resource people, hydroelectric experts, and certainly the Corps of Engineers and the Bureau of Reclamation. But once stated, it was embraced by river runners who knew the Stanislaus canyon was a resource that could not be measured in dollars or kilowatts.

Out of the struggle grew Friends of the River, a populist lobbying organization created to unite efforts against the New Melones project. In 1974 the organization sponsored a statewide initiative—Proposition 17—that called for preserving the wild state of the Stanislaus canyon. When the votes were counted, after a bitter anti-17 campaign, Proposition 17 was narrowed defeated. Many voters later polled admitted that they had been misled by the campaigns; 60 percent actually favored the initiative. But the election was over, and the dam builders had won it.

Members of Friends of the River (FOR) were not ready to give up so easily. If the voters had been misled, they believed it was their duty to continue to contest the filling of the dam. They filed appeals under the National Environmental Policy Act and

California's entrance to the Union in 1846 was characterized by the most remarkable social movement of the time—the gold rush. Although it had been rumored for 300 years that there was gold in California (and it had existed for 150 million years, the result of mineralized solutions shooting up through fault zones in the granite), John Marshall's discovery at Sutter's Mill on the American River in 1848 deeply affected the social character of the state. In 1849 over 80,000 reached the state; in 1850 only 8 percent of the population were women, and in the mining communities of the Mother Lode the number dropped to 2 percent.

the Historic Preservation Act, calling attention to the large number of Miwok archaeological sites and historic gold rush ruins in the canyon. Their aim was the partial filling of the dam, just to the level of the Parrott's Ferry Bridge; that would preserve most of the historical sites, as well as the limestone caves, Miwok petroglyphs and grinding stones, and nine miles of whitewater, without sacrificing the flood-control or hydroelectric purposes of the dam.

Out of the continued battle emerged another FOR leader, Mark Dubois. The six-foot eight-inch caver and rafter seemed to have endless energy to combat the Corps of Engineers, and something else besides: a sense of symbolic importance—not only of the Stanislaus, but of the rôle of FOR. In 1979, when the gates of New Melones Dam slammed shut and the Stanislaus began to flood, the lanky advocate became a lightning rod.

For a week in May 1979, Dubois chained himself to a rock somewhere in the Stanislaus canyon, at the partial-fill level FOR had been arguing for. The reservoir was rising at the time, and the Corps had stated that they might not be able to control its eventual fill level. The initial reaction from the dam advocates was that Dubois was nuts—like all the other conservationists who wanted to stand in the way of progress. But for Dubois, it was an act of conscience, not grandstanding: only one person knew where Dubois was, in a remote location far from any easy access. Dubois could be drowned at any time, and he knew it.

The next day two more rafters chained themselves to a tree at the partial-fill level, in solidarity with Dubois, but at a more accessible place so direct media access could be guaranteed. They were joined over the next few days by several more men and women. Suddenly Angels Camp was flooded not only by rafters and friends of the river, but by reporters, TV crews, stringers from every major newspaper in the state, and CBS-TV. The action attracted nationwide attention, forcing the Corps of Engineers to agree to maintain the partial-fill level, and resulting in the belated nomination of the Stanislaus as a member of the National Wild and Scenic Rivers System.

For a while it seemed as if the river had won the war; then nature proved a fickle friend. Several years of heavy rain and snowfall in the Sierra gave the Bureau of Reclamation the excuse it needed to call

Maidu pots, made of woven rushes, and bone flutes.

for the filling of New Melones Reservoir, to prevent flooding. The floodplains of the Central Valley were not flooded as they had been in 1964 and for millennia into the past; but the Stanislaus canyon was. The reservoir was filled to capacity during the winter of 1982. Total price tag: $341 million, fifty-eight times the original budgeted cost.

. . .

I moved to Angels Camp in the spring of 1982, just after the reservoir had filled up over the previous winter. For the first time in almost twenty years, there was no spring influx of rafters. Businesses were closing up and down Main Street, which was only a block to begin with; there were shell-shocked river guides locked inside their houses all day long, watching television game shows and drinking beer, unable to think of finding any other job; a palpable sense of loss was in the air, an invisible black crepe curtain draped over the foothills. Nobody even said the word Stanislaus: *the hurt was too great, the wound still fresh.*

I drove up Parrott's Ferry Road, winding between the oaks and grassy meadows still green from the spring rains. At the bridge I pulled over and looked down on the thick, slow arm of water thrust unkindly into the canyon. Somewhere down there was Bailey Falls, Mother Rapid, the beach where I had camped five years earlier. I could feel the loss, perhaps only because, for me, it was slight: my one trip down the river was nothing, compared to the intimacy so many had developed with the canyon.

A pair of turkey vultures swept close to the canyon wall, their eyes alert for displaced gophers, rabbits, rattlesnakes. A large American car drove up, and two middle-aged women got out to stretch their legs. "What lake is this?" one of them asked me, perplexed, "It's not on the map."

"It's new, this year," was all I could answer. Her face relaxed in relief. "Oh, that's nice," she said.

A host of arguments welled up in me, a battery of angry comebacks and denials; then they faded away, like dying wind. There really wasn't anything I could say, and I got into my van and drove slowly back to town. (CK)

If there was a beneficial side to the loss of the Stanislaus, it was that California and, to a certain extent, the whole country were made aware not only of the battle over the Stanislaus, but of the diminishing recreational and spiritual resource that rivers hold. Suddenly a new dimension was perceived about rivers: they were good for something other than hydroelectric projects and flood control. As important as power and safety are, these ends can be met by conservation, smaller projects, and alternative energy sources. When you dam a river, it's gone: 200 million years of geology, 60 million years of erosive sculpturing, 3 million years of botanical evolution and biological adaptation, perhaps a million generations of salmon, and, finally, thousands of years of human reliance, tradition, and pleasure.

Dam builders frequently point to the large reservoirs created behind their projects as "recreational windfalls" that make the river available for such summer pleasures as waterskiing, speed-boating, and sailing. Such arguments bring rafters to a boil, frequently an incoherent one. Rivers are a recreational resource too: just as many people can go floating down a river as can go motorboating on a reservoir; probably more, on a river as popular as the Stanislaus. If there is a difference, it is not in quantity, but in quality: riding an oar-powered raft or a paddle-powered canoe or kayak over the currents, waves, and hydraulics is a *river* experience. It is taking pleasure from a natural situation, one connecting the individual with the rhythms and situations of the real world, the world of creation.

The people of California—which became the most populous state during the years of the Stanislaus controversy—took another look at their diminishing rivers. The Feather's main fork has two major dams, including the country's largest earthfill dam at Oroville; its north fork lost a world-class kayak run to hydroelectric projects in the 1930s. The Yuba was severely affected by hydraulic mining during the 1860s, a practice that led to the siltation of millions of acres of the Central Valley and the nation's first environmental legislation, in 1887; now the Yuba supports one of the world's most elaborate hydroelectric systems, and few of its salmon survive. The American has long since been dammed at Folsom, though prime runnable stretches still remain on its three main forks; but a still larger dam project has been in the planning stages at Auburn since the 1950s. It threatens over fifty miles of wild river; and, like the New Melones project, its costs have been rising and its benefits decreasing with every passing year. Of California's thirty-seven major river systems, only one is entirely without dams: the Smith, tucked into the remote northwest corner of the state. California has a full 10 percent of the world's large dams—those over 150 meters, or 490 feet, high.

With the loss of the Stanislaus, where 40,000 people a year enjoyed a release from the pressures of a heavily populated state and found a return to the rhythms, sights, and smells of nature, the public eye cast its gaze on the Tuolumne and found there the same kinds of threats that had drowned the Stanislaus: dams and diversion projects in the works.

The major threat to the twenty-seven mile stretch of the Tuolumne where recreational river running takes place was a project by the combined Turlock and Modesto Water Districts, long smarting over having to buy power and water from San Francisco (which purchased the Tuolumne's resources at the turn of the century). The plan was to create a diversion dam, penstock, and power-generating station network running fifty miles overland from Cherry Creek just ten miles outside of Yosemite down to Clavey Creek. It was, as river projects go, a modest one—no huge plug would fill the canyon beneath Jawbone Ridge with an immense backfill. It would drain the Tuolumne of most of its water, leaving only 10 percent of its annual flow, and make a mockery of the river's attributes as a recreational resource.

Since the Tuolumne was already dammed both upstream of and downstream from this stretch, some development advocates argued that it was far from being "wild and scenic" any longer. Perhaps true, countered the now-seasoned (and battle-scarred) veterans of the Stanislaus fight; but surely the same criteria of exclusion would then apply to the Colorado through the Grand Canyon, a river that 15,000 people a year know lacks nothing in wilderness or scenery. The Tuolumne already does its share, they argued, providing a considerable amount of California's total energy supply, supplying San Francisco and its suburbs with drinking water, and irrigating hundreds of thousands of acres of farmland in the Central Valley. It is, they insisted, a "hard-working river" already; to take its last remaining miles of wilderness—with their proven recreational use—was unnecessary.

189

Friends of the River, by now an influential organization with lobbying contacts in Washington and offices in San Francisco and Sacramento, took an active role in pushing for Tuolumne protection, as did the Tuolumne River Preservation Trust, an alliance of FOR, commercial and private rafters, and other groups. They were quick to enlist the support of the city of Berkeley, which had long operated a family camp on the Tuolumne River above the Lumsden Campground (where most commercial trips begin). Fishermen, too, enthused about the Tuolumne's bounty: according to the California State Department of Fish and Game, the main fork's waters support 1,000 pounds of fish per acre, primarily brown and rainbow trout.

In hearings in the House of Representatives over the inclusion of the Tuolumne in the 1984 California wilderness bill, Don Moyer, a middle-aged Republican fishing enthusiast, took issue with the Turlock and Modesto figures that showed improved "fishability" of the Tuolumne should the power project go through.

Well, fishability is different that fishing. Fishability means, for example, if the water is chest deep and I can't get 'way out there in the middle of the river to fish it, it's not very fishable. And so when you drop 90 percent of the water out of the river, you can get out there and fish it, even though there may not be any fish there. So the fishability *may be better, but the* fishing *isn't worth a hang.*

Part of FOR's strategy for the Tuolumne was to enlist a broad base of support, not just the ragged, though healthy, river-rafting contingent. The message was clearly that the Tuolumne was a national resource with a range of uses—the kind of criteria decision makers in Washington demand for inclusion in the Wild and Scenic Rivers System. FOR made it a point to utilize its most effective tool for selling the river to influential people: take them down the river.

■ ■ ■

Back in Angels Camp, one of the guides still left in town urged me to raft down the Tuolumne as often as I could, while it was still there. "You watch," he said. "Once they get started, they're going to dam that thing so fast you won't know what hit you."

In the next breath he was telling me stories of impossible wraps on sharp rocks; of narrow chutes and channels *that had to be run backward or the oars would jam against the walls on either side and splinter; of a series of rapids at the start of the run, one right after the other, so demanding of a boatman's skill, timing, and strength that more than once he had found himself throwing up over the side of the raft five minutes after putting on the river, suffering from adrenaline shock. It sounded interesting.* (CK)

Put-in on the Tuolumne is at the end of the steep, narrow Lumsden Road. Your first trip in the back of the equipment truck, going down into the canyon, dodging sweepers of poison oak, instinctively leaning away from the vertical walls that slide by the right side of the truck, convinces you that the road must be more dangerous than the river. Then you look down and see the rapids, white chutes of turmoil funneled between boulders and steep walls.

There's a tension in the air where the boats are rigged up, at Meral's Pool, named for the same Jerry Meral who kicked off the Save the Stanislaus movement and who was the first canoeist on the river. The jokes are a bit too loud, the tubes are checked for air pressure far too often. If the passengers are late coming down the road, boatmen invariably cast off and power upstream to the base of the small rapid above Meral's Pool, warming up or just burning off nervous energy.

Finally there comes the time when everybody's there, everything's ready, and there's no place to go but down the river. The rapids come fast in those first four miles; the water drops about eighty feet per mile, over ten times the drop in the Grand Canyon. The first rapid is Rock Garden, a maze of boulders that gets trickier at lower water; after mid-July, getting stuck in Rock Garden is as much a part of the river experience as the warm summer sun and the clear unpolluted water. After Rock Garden, Nemesis rears its head in the next quarter mile, with its "helicopter turn" between two staggered rocks that makes the hair on the back of a boatman's neck bristle. Then Sunderland's Chute, a steep drop between three boat-eating holes that must have been dropped there in retribution by the Corps of Engineers. Then Hackamack's Hole and Laura; finally the accelerating current reaches Ram's Head.

There the river quickens its pace and careens around a blind corner, with an irregular chaos of

OPPOSITE The "hungry" hole at Clavey Falls—apex of the Tuolumne's whitewater (clockwise from top: Curt Smith, Curth Smith, Brian Fessenden, Liz Hymans).

RIVER CLASSIFICATION SYSTEM
Class I Easy rapids with small waves, clear passages.
Class II Rapids of moderate difficulty, clear passages; maneuvering necessary.
Class III Numerous waves, some rocks and eddies; passages narrow but clear.
Class IV Long rapids with powerful, irregular waves and dangerous rocks. Scouting mandatory on first passage.
Class V Extremely difficult, long and violent rapids with little room for recovery. Obstructed passages, powerful current, steep gradient; close study required before each run. Requires considerable experience and skill. All possible precautions must be taken.
Class VI Unrunnable.
Based on American Whitewater Association river-classification system.

OPPOSITE, TOP Logjam—one of the unspoken costs of dam building on wild rivers—at the end of the Tuolumne River run, as it feeds into Don Pedro Dam (Curt Smith). BOTTOM Boatman relaxing after a hard day at the oars (Bruce Helin).

rocks along the right bank. The main current heads directly for a nasty pour-over, the Ram's Head.

Remembering a too-close-for-comfort approach to the pour-over on my last trip, I hauled hard to the right and tried to slide between two rocks with a ribbon of water splitting them. It looked just barely possible, but it just barely wasn't. I jammed in solid, caught like a fat man in a thin door.

We got out the safety ropes and throwlines, trying to hoist the boat over the rocks and into the current below; it was hard and discouraging work, made all the worse by my keen awareness that I could have missed these rocks entirely if I hadn't been trying to act cute. (Her name was Becka, and she was younger than I.) Nothing seemed to do any good: I was jammed in between those two uncaring, unmoved rocks.

Just then another group came down the river, barreling through Ram's Head. Looking at the boats, I knew it was the FOR group we'd seen at put-in, no doubt taking down some influential so-and-so to witness my embarrassment. I glared at the paddleboat as it went by and was shocked to recognize Charlton Heston, star of biblical epics and friend of Senator Pete Wilson, digging his blade into the current with a wide grin on his face.

I recovered myself in time to shout, "Hey, Chuck, how about parting these rocks?" *He must not have heard, for it was another half hour before we continued downstream.* (CK)

Every great river has its Waterloo: the Colorado has Lava, the Zambezi has Number Five. On the Tuolumne it's Clavey Falls. After eight nerve-wrenching rapids in the first three miles, the Tuolumne eases up a bit and shows off its steep canyon of digger pine, blue oak, and grasses, with the bright pastels of pink redbud and green buckeye glowing in the springtime. The respite is short-lived. At Mile 6, the sixty-mile-long Clavey River tributary comes spilling around a corner of polished and folded chert, bringing with it in flood stage a cargo of boulders.

These stones have been washed into the Tuolumne over the centuries, building up a rocky rim over which the river leaps fifteen feet down a forty-degree chute into a pool. The current, fast and furious after the drop, exercises its vengeance by propelling any craft arrogant enough to get this far directly toward a

barely submerged boulder lying eight feet from the sheer left wall. This is Clavey Hole, a hungry monster with catholic tastes that seems to reach out and sample every boat that goes by. To ride the falls is relatively straightforward; missing the hole is another matter. Naturally, boulders big enough to be gift-wrapped with neoprene are everywhere, just to make the rapid a challenge.

It's a seething well of risk, and boatmen know it. An hour can easily be spent scouting the rapid, though there's really not much choice of routes. You weave through the rock maze above the falls, ship your oars, and take a deep breath. Capsizing in the falls is rare, but being able to anticipate which direction you will be facing when you emerge is even rarer. There are reasons, though, for the long scouts: formalizing plans and fallbacks, options and alternatives. And this is where experience counts. Novice boatmen lose precious seconds immediately after the falls trying to evaluate the available options, by which time there are no options. The Hole gets dinner.

Past Clavey Falls, a veil seems to lift. The most dangerous rapid on the river is behind now, and there are still eleven miles of the eighteen-mile run to the take-out at Ward's Ferry, a mile in to the flatwater backed up behind the New Don Pedro Dam. There are rapids aplenty on this stretch, and many of them risky: Grey's Grindstone, a half-mile-long labyrinth of split currents, blind approaches, and midstream boulders; Thread-the-Needle, a choice between narrow chutes and narrower chutes; Cabin and Hell's Kitchen, a twin set of fast approaches to oppressively tight boulder drops.

There is time to relax; and there are wide sandy beaches on which to camp beneath the clear summer skies, abandoned mines, even a decommissioned powerhouse from the turn of the century, and broad walls of polished chert and limestone. Those rocks are the Paleozoic underpinnings of the Sierra, and they have been twisted and fluted by time and the river into elaborate shapes. A golden eagle may soar overhead; dippers chirp and swoop over the river, finding a rock in midrapid from which to watch the passing boats. A group of kayakers might slice past and be met in the next rapid as they play in the waves and reversals of the current, making impossible maneuvers with effortless strokes and shifts of weight.

For veterans of the fight to save the Stanislaus, running the Tuolumne was a painful reminder of the loss they had endured and a reminder of the loss they might soon suffer again. Now, thanks to the 1984 legislation, the Tuolumne will remain wild and scenic, for a few years at least—for man's laws are written only to be rewritten. No river runner ever believes the fight is over. A river cannot speak for itself; it needs envoys and ambassadors—poets, painters, photographers, and politicians—to represent its case. Dollars talk; rivers just burble. And progress seems to speak the language of money.

The agricultural businessmen who demand more and cheaper water to grow their crops too frequently see a river as just another pipe, too far away to do any good unless it's dammed, penstocked, and gravity-fed to their lower 400 acres. The fact is that nearly half of all water used in California is for livestock, either directly (grazing) or indirectly (growing feed). If the same acreage and water were directed toward protein-rich legumes and grains, fewer resources would be needed to produce the same food value.

Of course, the effect of dams on river sports is two-sided: many rivers, including the Tuolumne, have a more regular and often heavier summer flow, thanks to dams upstream that hold back spring's flush and release it more evenly over the following months. Rafters on the South Fork of the American, one of the most popular whitewater stretches in the West, enjoy moderate release from the dam at Chile Bar through October, which extends the runnable season four months beyond that of the neighboring North Fork. Still, relying on controlled release has its drawback: the South Fork's flow is runnable only six days of the week; woe to the rafter who chooses a Sunday morning to begin the seventeen-mile run. Ultimately, the question comes down to diminishing resources. To fill a river canyon with the backflow from a dam is to lose that river forever; we have already lost dozens, if not hundreds, of stretches of river with historical, biological, geological, and scenic value, to say nothing of recreational potential. This loss is not just in California, either, the most dammed of the fifty states; increasingly, it is a loss felt around the world.

For the wild rivers of the world, refuges of water nymphs and rivergods, there is plenty of bad news

and not much good: on the Zambezi, on the Euphrates, on the Bío-Bío, and elsewhere, dams are being planned, built, or completed that will drown these vigorous rivers. The justification for such projects is that they will provide farmland, employment, and power for the local population—the same arguments used in the United States. All too often, it is not the local population that benefits, but the engineers who build the dams and large agricultural corporations and industries that are rarely owned by locals. The irrigation potential is used to grow cash crops such as coffee and cotton for export, not sustenance; hydropower is sold at inexpensive rates to corporations that have located in Third World countries because of the cheap labor. The salinization of farmlands, resulting from unneeded flood control; the loss of native fish resources; and the displacement of populations in the regions innundated by reservoirs make modern dams less beneficial to the indigenous populations than to the First World financiers. Finally, the lack of coordinated water planning results in absurdity: if the water projects in Turkey, Syria, and Iraq proposed for the Euphrates River are all effected, 140 percent of the river's flow will be diverted.

We may be reluctant to impose our own restrictions on others after we have dammed so many of our own rivers and used their resources to support one of the world's highest standards of living. But rivers are one of the most important elements in world ecology, and to tamper with them frequently results in environmental disaster. The much-touted Aswan Dam on the Nile in Egypt resulted in severe disruptions in the Nile estuary far downstream, the salinization of farmland, a reduction of commercial fisheries, and an increase in bilharzia owing to stagnant water in canals, to say nothing of the drowning of ancient dynastic temples. Furthermore, dams have a limited lifespan: siltation eventually fills the reservoirs, sometimes so rapidly—as at the Laoying Reservoir in China—that the dam itself can never be completed. Rivers are in more ways than one the bloodstream of the planet; to dam and divert the natural flows is to tamper with the most precious fluid of life. Dams are blockage; concrete, the cholesterol of rivers.

It's easy to enjoy most any river, pleasant to float

beneath overhanging willows on a gentle current during a long summer's day; but you can love only a river that demands the best of you, that tests and challenges and dares you, for her rewards are special, savory with the spice of life. Ten miles downstream from Clavey Falls, the North Fork of the Tuolumne enters the main stem from the right. Following the creek along its rocky course, fording from one side to another, ducking under the low branches of streamside trees, you finally come to the trail's end: a pile of shoes and shirts next to a pool beneath a sheer wall.

You have to wade into the pool and swim around the wall to discover the real treasure of the North Fork. Ten feet from the end of the trail, a new world opens up: a jumble of granite boulders, polished by ancient floods, through which percolates a crystal-clear stream. The cliffs on either side rise to forty feet, from which the brave leap joyously into a swimming hole. At the far end of the diving pool, the stream drops down a five-foot falls, perfect for sliding or just enjoying the serenade of rushing water.

I had forgotten the roundabout route beneath the falls to the left side of the creek, where you can climb out and sun yourself on the smooth, warm rocks. Instead I try to power my way along the right wall in front of the falls, combating the current and exhausting myself as I search desperately for a handhold on the slippery rock. Finally I pull myself up and lie panting in the sun, trying to get my strength back, looking across the canyon at the digger pines swerving up through the broad canopy of blue oak crowns.

Another group of hikers arrives, kayakers we had seen at several points along the river. They dive into the pool and swim toward the current from the falls, and, like I did, they struggle to pull themselves up. All but one: a broad-shouldered young woman, her pale hair cropped close, who is at first visibly surprised by the hidden strength of the current. Then, with a wordless and featureless animal urge, she plows into the heart of the rush, swimming as hard as she can into its fullest force, wallowing in the combat. Her arms pump rhythmically, powerfully, holding their own against the water. At last she tucks into somersault, spinning with a flip, first forward into the current, then back as she lets the force of the water take over. Slowly she revolves, arching her bare face, neck, breasts, stomach into the bright watchful warm sun above the churning waters. I am reminded of otters, of dolphins, of orcas, of playful natural creatures at home with their strengths. And all seems right. (CK)

Other Great Rivers

AFRICA

RUFIJI (Tanzania): Flowing through Tanzania's Selous Game Reserve, the Rufiji is the main access into the world's largest uninhabited game areas where Peter Matthiessen researched *Sand Rivers*, his 1981 book on Africa's diminishing wildlife. Here elephants, rhinos, hippos, and crocodiles are found in numbers unmatched in Africa, or anywhere else on earth. The Rufiji headwaters are in eastern Tanzania, its principal tributary is the Great Ruaha—one of the most lyrically named flows in Africa. Although the Rufiji is only 175 miles long, its delta at the Indian Ocean south of Dar es Salaam is nearly 30 miles wide, owing to its broad area of drainage in Tanzania's central mountains. Along its course there is even a stirring dose of whitewater in Stiegler's Gorge, a 17-mile-long section named for one of the first "white hunters" in this game-rich region. He was trampled to death by an elephant near the gorge's entrance, and a stone monument marks the site.

NIGER (Mali/Nigeria) Africa's third longest river starts its 2,590-mile course in the Fouta Djallon Mountains of Guinea, less than 150 miles from the Atlantic; then it heads north toward the Sahara to Timbuktu, Mali. There its enthusiasm for the increasingly arid north is dampened, and it turns east and south to return to the Gulf of Guinea. One of its many names over the centuries has been the Black Nile. A more popular nickname, the strong brown god, which is the title of a historical study by Sanche de Gramont, is derived from T.S. Eliot's *Four Quartets:* "I do not know much about gods; but I think that the river/Is a strong brown god—sullen, untamed and intractable. . . ." From the time of Herodotus until modern times, the exact course of the Niger remained a compelling mystery. Some visitors to Timbuktu—a trading center in the Middle Ages—said the river ran west; others said it ran east. The fact that it runs north, east, and south in its long arc led to speculation that if it wasn't a tributary of the Nile, it must be a tributary of the Congo (as the Zaire was then known). Its first great explorer was Mungo Park, an intrepid Scot who descended nearly half of its length before drowning in a rapid in 1796. (The fact that the rapid which claimed Park is now itself drowned by the waters behind Nigeria's Kanjii Dam is his only revenge.) The mouth of the Niger was finally confirmed in 1830 by Englishmen John and Richard Landers, but large portions of the river—where rapids roil and native tribes of Tuareg, Malinke, Hausa, and other ethnic groups continue their ancient traditions—remain but imperfectly explored in modern times.

BLUE NILE (Ethiopia): One of the two main tributaries of the world's longest river, the Blue Nile, originates in the same mountains as the Omo, the Ethiopian plateau, where it is called the Great Abbai. Traveling up its length, James Bruce sought the fabled source of the Nile in 1770—"rediscovering" its source, according to generous historians; rafting down its length, the Great Abbai Expedition led by Captain John Blashford-Snell attempted "The Last Great First" in 1968. The burden of its history should not obscure its tangible magnificence: rising from Lake Tana, the Blue Nile falls 6,000 feet out of the plateau region through an Ethiopian canyon as grand as any in the United States; along the way it plummets over Africa's second greatest cataract, Tississat Falls. At the end of its 950-mile course, the Blue joins with the White Nile at Khartoum, forming the main stem of the river of the Pharaohs. During the summer months, in fact, the Blue Nile provides 68 percent of the Nile's flow, the White only 10 percent (and the other main tributary, the Atbarah, 22 percent), which led the explorers of the past up the larger fork in search of the river's source.

ZAIRE (Zaire): The largest river in Africa is not the 4,000-mile-plus flow of the Nile, but the much shorter Zaire. Formerly known as the Congo, the archetypical river into the unknown (see Joseph Conrad's *Heart of Darkness*), the Zaire's 2,716-mile course takes it from the Mountains of the Moon at 4,560 feet in the Katanga province of the African nation of Zaire to a natural whirlpool—the Devil's Cauldron—near its mouth on the Atlantic. Along the way the entire encyclopedia of hydraulic effects, from spectacular waterfalls to long peaceful navigable sections

OPPOSITE, CLOCKWISE FROM TOP Copper River in Alaska at entrance of Woods Canyon (Kebos). The crowded Yangtze (Richard Bangs). The Alas River, flowing through Gunung Leuser National Park, Sumatra (Kebos). The sandstone terrain of the American Southwest, and the San Juan River (Liz Hymans).

199

OPPOSITE, CLOCKWISE FROM TOP
The Snake River, in lower
Hells Canyon along Oregon/
Idaho border (Curt Smith).
The Chattooga River, setting
for the film *Deliverance* (Slim
Ray). The Motu in New Zea-
land, not listed in text. (Bart
Henderson). Costa Rica's Río
Chirripó (Curt Smith).

and back to cataracts again, has long made the Zaire one of the most difficult of African rivers to explore. Among its highlights are the entrance to 75 miles of rapids known as Portes d'Enfer; the seven cataracts of Stanley Falls and the thirty-two cataracts of Livingstone Falls; and a submarine canyon extending far into the Atlantic from its mouth. Also, the Zaire is the only major river system in the world that flows in both the Northern and Southern hemispheres. Exploration began in 1482 when the Portuguese navigator Diego Cao discovered its huge outflow, but substantial approaches up the forbidding current were delayed for almost four centuries, until the 1871 expedition when David Livingstone, in pursuit of the source of the Nile, explored the Zaire's Chambezi tributary. Henry Stanley followed Livingstone's footsteps three years later with the first major survey of the river, starting with 350 men at the confluence of the Lualaba and Lufira tributaries, and ending with only 115 men 999 days later at the Atlantic. More recently, in 1974, Captain John Blashford-Snell led a British expedition of 170 explorers (in the style of his Great Abbai endeavor) down almost the entire length of the Zaire.

ASIA

TONS (India): One of the headwaters of the Yamuna—the river of Delhi and a chief tributary of the Ganges—the Tons flows between the steep gorges of the Kumaon Himalaya between the states of Uttar Pradesh and Himachal Pradesh toward the Indian plains. Its course links the practitioners of three of the world's major religions—the mountain Buddhists, the intermediate Hindus, and the Moslems of the flatlands. A river runner's dream comes true at an elevation of about one mile, as the Tons percolates through an evergreen forest toward a series of Class IV and V rapids that equal any in the world. From the villages of polyandrous Garwhali Buddhists to the nomadic Moslems near the take-out point nine days later, the Tons unfolds a panorama of native cultures, fantastic Himalayan scenery, and whitewater without peer.

SUN KHOSI (Nepal): From its headwaters in the high Himalayas on Gosainthan Peak in eastern Nepal to the broad tropical valleys of the Terai, where it joins with the Arun and Tamur on its way to the Ganges, the Sun Khosi is only 160 miles long—little more than a capillary in the Himalayas' circulatory system. In these miles, however, the Sun Khosi slices through a cross section of Nepal: gorges tortured by geology into dramatic anticlines and synclines of strata, isolated meditation retreats of rishis, and Newari villages with suspension bridges over raging rapids.

ALAS (Indonesia): The island of Sumatra harbors one of the world's richest and most diverse wildlife populations, and the Alas slices through its rain forests on a wild ride of discovery. Rhinoceroses, leopards, tigers, and the colorful birds of the tropics take a back seat to the most unusual of the great apes, the orangutan or "wild man of Borneo." These big red apes have their largest free-ranging population near the Ketambe Primate Research Centre, through which the Alas runs. Gibbons, siamangs (black apes), macaques, and leaf monkeys are also found at Ketambe, making it a paradise for primatologists. The river itself begins on the northern face of Gunung Leuser, Sumatra's second highest mountain (12,300 feet). From there it plunges 200 miles through the largest national park in southeast Asia, primary rain forest, cathedralesque gorges, and Class III and IV rapids to the Indian Ocean. It was our first run in 1984.

BRAHMAPUTRA (China/India): One of the four rivers that originate near the holy mountain of Tibetan Buddhists, Mount Kailas, the Brahmaputra first runs nearly due east through Tibet north of the towering Himalayas, then doubles back through the deep canyons between 23,000-foot mountains to head through India's Assam Valley. At 1,800 miles long, it is longer than the Ganges; and it contributes more alluvium to their joint delta at the head of the Bay of Bengal than does its sister river. Its name means "son of Brahma," after one of the three main gods of Hinduism; but in Tibet it is called the Tsangpo, "the Purifier." Statistics and etymology aside, the Brahmaputra has earned its greatness as the world's highest navigable river of any length. For some 400 miles at an altitude of 12,000 feet, small boats made of hides and bamboo, called *caracles*, trade between the major cities of Tibet, including Lhasa and Lhatse Dzong. Rafters

have long been eyeing the 80 miles between Pe in Tibet and the Indian border, where the river compresses through the Himalayan gorges and drops from 6,600 feet to 1,665 feet, averaging a bracing 62 feet per mile. Until the Chinese government is as cooperative in issuing rafting permits as they are mountaineering permits, the hidden scenic spectacles, high-altitude rapids, and cultural treasures of the Brahmaputra will remain a "what if," not a "remember when."

YANGTZE (China): Asia's longest river rises in the Tanglha Range near Tibet and sweeps 3,434 miles across China to the East China Sea. In its first 600 miles it drops an average of 120 feet per mile—making at least portions of its headwaters ideal for whitewater rafting. As yet, however, permission to navigate those upper reaches has not been forthcoming from the Chinese government. Still 1,000 miles from the sea, a regular trade in tea, silk, and tobacco is carried on with the rest of China and the world via ocean-going vessels that can navigate the Yangtze as far upriver as Wuhan. Between Wuhan and Wanhsien, however, the Yangtze is penetrable to shallow-bottomed riverboats that have ascended through the famous gorges of the Yangtze for thousands of years. Boatmen on frequently run American rivers have christened many rapids and a few of the larger hydraulic features; in the Yangtze gorges, every *rock* has a name, with generations of lore attached to it.

OCEANIA

FRANKLIN (Australia): The wooded isle of Tasmania off Australia's southeast coast has many natural treasures, not least of which is the Franklin River, recently awarded international protection as one of the few United Nations World Heritage Sites. From icy headwaters in the Cheyne Range through narrow gorges and serene pools beneath eucalyptus groves, the Franklin offers boulder-strewn drops that challenge the best rafters and kayakers. It proves its excellence in the Great Ravine, where rapids called Churn, Corruscades, Thunderrush, and the Cauldron push boatmen to their limit—and boats to the wall. However, the region earned its protected status because of its wildlife. As an isolated extension of the Australian continent, Tasmania has unique marsupial species found nowhere else in the world. The most famous are the Tasmanian devil, a small, voracious creature with a black coat marked with white, and the Tasmanian wolf, or thylacine, a dog-like marsupial with a long tail and a wolflike head. Both species are rare and endangered, unlikely visitors to any river expedition on the Franklin.

SNOWY (Australia): Although only 270 miles long, the Snowy River is one of Australia's most well known, a beautiful stream that begins on the flanks of Mount Kosciusko (7,316 feet) in the state of New South Wales. Its fame comes not from the plentiful wildlife nor from the serene white beaches of Tullock Ard Gorge, nor from the eight major rapids and many smaller ones along its most commonly run stretch through the Great Dividing Range, but from Banjo Paterson, a down-under backwoods minstrel. Paterson's "Waltzing Matilda" is sung around the world, and his verses and tales of the Snowy River region make him the Woody Guthrie/Will Rogers of his country. The Snowy is well utilized, however: nine hydroelectric dams and a dozen power stations are built or planned for its relatively short length.

NORTH AMERICA

NOATAK (Alaska): With its headwaters reaching into the gates of Arctic National Park, the Noatak stretches leisurely 400 miles across some of the wildest of North American wilderness. Caribou migrate across its watershed, wildflowers erupt in rainbows across its vast tundra basin, grayling and char erupt from the icy waters, and the long days north of the Arctic Circle give way at night to the aurora borealis. Its isolation gives the explorer down the Noatak's mild current unbelievable visibility: it seems possible almost to see all the way from Walker Lake in the heart of the Brooks Range to the end of the river at the Eskimo village of Noatak on the Chukchi Sea.

COPPER (Alaska): The 300-mile-long Copper is named for the mining industry that brought it to the world's attention. Copper was discovered on Indian lands in 1885, and four years later the Indians sold the mineral rights for a cache of food. Yet during the first half of the twentieth century so much copper was mined from its lode that a $40-million railway was built 164 miles into the Alaskan wilderness, from the port town of Cordova. From the Kennicott Reserve in the Wrangell Mountains, the Copper pours north, then flows south through the Chugach Mountains to its outflow near Cordova on the Gulf of Alaska, where harbor seals frolic among the icebergs. Along the way thick forests of spruce and fir press in upon the milky, glacier-fed current; moose and grizzlies stalk the banks; and the mile-wide face of Child Glacier spills into the river. The enormous force of the river—with volumes up to half a million cubic feet per second—makes running the Copper an experience in true wilderness.

SALMON (Idaho): "The river of no return" was among the first eight rivers to be named to the National Wild and Scenic Rivers System in 1968, and with good reason. From the rafter's put-in at the confluence of the Middle Fork and Indian Creek, one nail-biting rapid follows another, such as Velvet Falls, Porcupine, and the famous Redside. But it takes more than whitewater to make a river great, and the Salmon has more: Indian petroglyphs, wildlife—from black bear to bobcat to porcupine—and the soaring scenery of the Sawtooth Range. The entire length of the Salmon is 420 miles. From its source between Lone Pine Peak and Bald Mountain at the 10,000-foot level in the Salmon River Mountains, it runs to its desert confluence with the Snake on the Idaho/Oregon border, bisecting the Idaho Primitive Area, the largest wilderness area in the contiguous United States.

SNAKE (Idaho/Oregon): In terms of pairs of wet tennis shoes per day, the upper stretch of the Snake near Jackson Hole, Wyoming, is the most popular whitewater river in the West, with its sprightly rapids percolating between narrow banks within sight of the Tetons. Over a thousand miles downstream, the Snake becomes one of the country's largest rivers, and the major tributary of the 1,234-mile-long Columbia. The Snake's heyday comes when it forms the border between Idaho and Oregon, having gathered the waters from five states (Wyoming, Idaho, Oregon, Nevada, and northern Utah) and carrying them through the continent's deepest gorge, Hell's Canyon. Here the big drops include Granite Falls,

Waterspout, and Wild Sheep, but the biggest drop is down from the summits of the Seven Devils Mountains to water level: 7,700 feet, over a thousand feet deeper than the Grand Canyon of the Colorado. In western Idaho the river flows through the recently designated Birds of Prey Natural Area, where fifteen different species of raptors come to nest in a ruggedly beautiful canyon. Eagles bald and golden, six species of owl and four of hawk, and both prairie falcon and the endangered peregrine falcon are among those that slice through the skies above the Snake River, celebrating the mating season. However, the government giveth, and the government taketh away: the Snake's biggest rapids—Kinney Creek, Squaw Creek, Buck Creek, and Sawpit—exist now only as legends, drowned in 1967 beneath the reservoir of Hell's Canyon Dam.

SAN JUAN (Utah): In the sculpted sandstone country of the American Southwest, the San Juan has plenty of competiton for greatness—the Dolores, the Green, the Yampa, to name a few. But the course of the San Juan takes it not only through the geologic wonderland of the mesas, buttes, and pinnacles so characteristic of the Southwest, but past several famous Anasazi sites as well, including the misnamed Aztec Ruins National Monument and a spectacular petroglyph wall displaying *kachinas* (spirits), bighorn sheep, and an array of mysterious symbols. The headwaters are in southwestern Colorado's San Juan Mountains. The San Juan then dives into New Mexico, reenters Colorado briefly, and finally arcs across southeastern Utah to its confluence with the Colorado at Lake Powell. Along with occasional rapids and the desert scenery and wildlife, one of the highlights is Goosenecks Canyon, nearly 2,000 feet deep, where the river twists for twenty-five miles through a series of bends and advances just five miles west as the raven flies.

NAHANNI (Northwest Territories): A tributary of the Mackenzie River—which flows into the Arctic Ocean from Canada's broad northern wilderness—the Nahanni is situated in an environment that earned recognition from the United Nations as one of its first World Heritage Sites. As "an exceptional natural site forming part of the heritage of mankind," the Nahan-

ni was cited for a wealth of reasons, foremost its wildlife and scenery. It purls unpolluted through virtually untouched wilderness of Dall sheep, caribou, brown bear, wolf, moose, and one of the last remaining herds of wood buffalo. It runs through a spectacular canyon 4,000 feet deep that is lined by natural hot springs and cascading waterfalls, including Virginia Falls—at 318 feet it is twice the height of Niagara. Rafters, canoeists, fishermen, and kayakers have found that a journey down the Nahanni is a week spent in wilderness unlike any other.

FRASER (British Columbia): The Fraser rises on Mount Robson (12,972 feet) in the Canadian Rockies and swoops through British Columbia's dense forests over 850 miles into the Georgia Strait at Vancouver, gathering a constellation of tributaries along the way. Since its catchment includes some of the rainiest country in the rainy Northwest, the Fraser grows by huge volumes in its relatively short length, and by the time it reaches the rapid at Hell's Gate in Fraser Canyon, the waves tower over even the largest inflatable rafts. Among the Fraser's many tributaries, several are worthy of mention. The Chilko rises in the Coast Range and drops over 100 feet per mile, including Lava Canyon, a rapid two miles long, during its 62 miles of navigable whitewater. Its first cousin, the Taseko, has only recently been rafted over its 84 miles amid the wilderness scenery of British Columbia's mountains. The Chilko and Taseko combine to join the Chilcotin, a no less stimulating glide of another 80 miles through winding canyons to the Fraser. Other Fraser tributaries include the Quesnel and Cariboo, both of which offer whitewater and scenic wilderness gloriously typical of the Canadian Northwest.

RIO GRANDE (Texas/Mexico): From its birth in the snowfields of the San Juan Mountains of Colorado, the Rio Grande flows not toward the Colorado (like the San Juan) nor toward the Mississippi (like the Arkansas, which begins not far to the east), but on its own course south 1,885 miles to the Gulf of Mexico. Midst the fir and aspen forests of Colorado and the humid coastal plain between Laredo and Brownsville, the Rio Grande cuts three deep canyons in the region known as El Despoblado, "the unin-

habited land," now Big Bend National Park, over 700,000 acres of mountains, grasslands, arid badlands, and canyons. One popular stretch of the river is through the vertiginous Santa Elena Canyon, where 1,500-foot walls seem to lean in over the narrow turbid waters. Rock spires, arches, and bridges line the river's route; hawks and falcons soar overhead; and burros scamper away from pumas in the rugged wilderness. Challenging rapids and soothing hot springs combine with the splendid scenery to make the Rio Grande one of the country's least known, and best, river trips.

CHATTOOGA (South Carolina/Georgia): Were it not for the novel and film *Deliverance* in the early 1970s, some say river running would never have caught on to the extent it has. Maybe, maybe not. But James Dickey's adventure epic on the Chattooga certainly brought out the amateurs along with the experts, and the number of drownings that occurred on the Chattooga for several years after the film's release made it the deadliest river in the United States. From the put-in at Earl's Ford down twenty-two miles to Lake Tugaloo, the Chattooga hurtles at freight-train speed through dozens of rapids, dropping 275 feet in the last six miles, forty-six feet per mile. The surrounding country is remote and historic, and hikers can reach several beautiful mountain areas, including Chauga Gorge and the Bartram Trail.

GAULEY (West Virginia): The Gauley's 104-mile length lies entirely within West Virginia, from its origin in the Alleghenies to its confluence with the New River, where it forms the Kanawha (a tributary of the Ohio). Both the Gauley and the New are outstanding whitewater rivers, pouring down Class IV to V rapids in steep ancient gorges in a surprisingly beautiful near-wilderness that's only a couple of hours' drive from the nation's capital. The New, in fact, may be the continent's oldest river, having run an unchanged course through its canyon for over 200 million years—an irony in nomenclature that is compounded by its original Indian name, River of Death. The Gauley's claim to greatness lies in its scale: with over sixty major rapids (Class III or greater) in just twenty-four river miles and hefty waterflows of up to 10,000 cubic feet per second in the spring, it is si-

OPPOSITE, CLOCKWISE FROM TOP The Noatak flows through the tundra of the Arctic, north of the Brooks Range, Alaska (Jim Slade). Terraced fields along the Tons River in northern India (Stan Boor). Fishermen on the Zaire (Mark Smith). The Río Tambopata spans Peru's lifezones from the Andes to the Amazon on its way to the Río Madre de Dios (John Tichenor).

OPPOSITE Shinumo Wash
on the Colorado River
(Liz Hymans).

multaneously intimidating and intoxicating. Pillow Rock, Lost Paddle, and Iron Ring are just a sampling of the Gauley's long list of challenging and exhilarating rapids, set deep within one of the East's most scenic river canyons.

PENOBSCOT (Maine): The state of Maine's largest river flows 350 miles off the flanks of Mount Katahdin (5,267 feet) in the Grand Lakes region, heading south to Penobscot Bay, collecting tributaries along the way. In the 1620s the Pilgrims established a permanent settlement on the river, naming it after the Penobscot Indians who lived there; and during the French-British conflicts over the border region, the river saw many bitter battles. Today the action is with the rapids, a series of pitched drops through the white-pine landscape at the foot of Katahdin. Moose graze on aquatic plants on the shore, beavers slap their tails at dusk, and the call of loons awakens campers at dawn. Meanwhile, the rapids bear the usual colorful names: Cribwork, Exterminator, and others. Although the river was formerly known for its plentiful runs of Atlantic salmon, lumber and pulp mills situated downstream from the rapid-rich headwaters have eliminated that resource. A nearby river has brought Maine distinction in the Northeast as a river runner's mecca: the Kennebec, begins at Moosehead Lake and roars through a steep-walled canyon known as The Forks.

SOUTH AMERICA

TAMBOPATA (Peru): Between the cloud forests of the Andes and the jungle basin of the Amazon, the Río Tambopata cuts a 120-mile course of wildlife and whitewater without peer. First explored in 1982 by John Tichenor, the Tambopata's 800 species of birdlife have already attracted the attention of famed ornithologist Roger Tory Peterson and the National Geographic Society: several species each of parakeets, macaws, toucans, kites, kingfishers, and countless other winged rarities have been catalogued. The rest of the region's wildlife is no less exceptional, with reported sightings of otter, ocelot, spider and howler monkeys, coati, and jaguar. Meanwhile, the technical, sometimes capricious, but always exciting, rapids swell from rock gardens to roller-coasters as the river descends to the gold-min-

ing boom town of Puerto Maldonado and the main artery of the Río Madre de Dios, one of the many stems of the distant Amazon.

CHIRRIPÓ (Costa Rica): Tumbling off the flanks of Mount Chirripó (12,532 feet) in the heart of Central America's cordillera, the Río Chirripó's race to the Caribbean is accelerated by a gradient of 50 feet per mile and flows of up to 8,000 cubic feet per second. The result is a series of nearly 100 rapids in forty miles, gushing between six waterfalls that cascade into the river from the densely forested side canyons. Meanwhile, iguanas sun themselves on the rocks, otters splash happily in the eddies, and tropical birds flit overhead, their long colorful tails marking their flight like rainbow contrails. The Río Pacuare, running down a parallel canyon, has an even steeper gradient, but a railroad that follows the river to the coast makes it less pristine than the Chirripó. Nonetheless, both rivers are runnable all year round—a bonus to two already exceptional rivers.

USUMACINTA (Mexico/Guatemala): The name means "sacred monkey" in the Mayan language, and the eerie, almost ghastly roar of the howler monkey echoes over this jungled river's most isolated beaches. Toucans and macaws shout it out for second-loudest creature, while iguanas and a few crocodiles silently watch. But the main attraction of the Usumacinta is its past: along its course some of the largest and most artistic complexes of the classic Mayan civilization arose, and it is their presence that gives the Usumacinta its fame as the "river of ruins." Bonampak, with its well-known array of murals; the towering facades of the temples at Yaxchilán; and the shattered ruins of Piedras Negras, reclaimed by the insatiable rain forest, all testify to the grandeur of the lost empire of the Mayas. Unfortunately all these valuable sites may be lost, for the Mexican government is building a dam just downstream from Piedras Negras. For 187 of its 270 miles, the Usumacinta forms the border between Mexico and Guatemala; some of its ruins are in the one country, some in the other. In times of political turmoil in Guatemala (sadly frequent in recent years), river runners are advised to camp on river left, the Mexican side.

206

INDEX OF PEOPLE AND PLACES